ADVANCE PRAISE

"Renard's narrative voice is lighthearted and witty ... a thoughtful work that delves into the intricacies of marriage and longing."
KIRKUS

"*Swing* is the sexiest, funniest, most deeply felt memoir you will read this year. If Shonda Rhimes were a homeschooler and skating coach instead of a television exec, if Cheryl Strayed visited exclusive sex clubs instead of canoodling on the trail, if Elizabeth Gilbert stayed married after all her soul-searching, then one of them might have written this book. And then again, maybe not, because Ashleigh Renard is one in a million."
ANDROMEDA ROMANO-LAX, author of *Annie of the Wolves* and *Behave*

"In *Swing* Ashleigh Renard has created an entirely new genre: the hot self-help book. With its wit and grace and wisdom—and some steamy interludes—this book belongs on your shelf next to Glennon Doyle and Brene Brown and Luvvie Ajayi."
DR. DEBORAH WILLIAMS, Professor, NYU

"By turns charming, funny, sad and surprising, *Swing* shows how having the courage to blow up the love you have makes room for the love you deserve. Turning the pages is like being at an all-night slumber party with your favorite sister, best friend, and coolest aunt all rolled into one hilarious, honestly flawed spiritual guide and marriage counselor."
ALLISON K WILLIAMS, author of *Seven Drafts: Self-Edit Like a Pro from Blank Page to Book*

"*Swing* is fearless and funny, the perfect book for women who want marriage and motherhood to feel like a breathtaking adventure."
ALIA VOLZ, author of *Home Baked: My Mom, Marijuana, and the Stoning of San Francisco*

"*Swing* takes an unflinching, unapologetic look at what happens when women try to martyrize themselves. Ashleigh puts it all on the table, challenging the reader to the same. This is a read for the woman ready to take a long, hard look in the mirror, and then get real with herself."
ADIBA NELSON, author of *Meet ClaraBelle Blue* and *Ain't That a Mother* (Blackstone, 2022)

"In one of *Swing's* early chapters, the author describes her morning routine as a young figure skater in vivid, sensory detail. I was there in the locker room and out on the ice, tracing the perfect circles and figure 8s, wincing at the gash on my leg. I could relate deeply to the author's feeling of trying so hard, checking so many boxes, and yet failing at fulfillment ... hard-won wisdom about what constitutes a meaningful and happy life, and how to cultivate one's relationship with self."
DANIELLE SIMONE BRAND, author of *Weed Mom – The Canna-Curious Woman's Guide to Healthier Relaxation, Happier Parenting, and Chilling TF Out*

"*Swing* is sexy and fast-paced, relatable, and engaging ... a wake up call to all of us ... "
RONIT PLANK, author of *When She Comes Back*

"Like the beautifully choreographed transitions on the ice, Renard's execution of her own emotional transition is breathtaking to watch and oh so satisfying in the end."
DIANA KUPERSHMIT, author of *Emma's Laugh*

"In *Swing*, Renard takes us from ice rinks to home-schooling mommy circles, always swept up by her need to perform perfectly. It's a relief for her—and the reader—to find that the answer lies, not in a sex club or a secret affair, but within herself."
STEPHANIE **W**EAVER**, author of *The Migraine Relief Plan*

"Clever, funny, and raw. An inspirational and beautifully weaved narrative about marriage, being enough, and taking no prisoners in the pursuit of what matters most: loving yourself."
JAMIE **M**C**G**ILLEN**, author of *The Rainier Series*

"If you're seeking a deeper knowing of yourself or needing self-care—you may as well do it while laughing wildly and being turned on! *Swing* is the book to take you there. You'll read it over a weekend, think about it all year, and take the lessons with you for a lifetime. While you begin to fall in love with Ashleigh, you'll leave loving yourself."
STEPHANIE **H**OPE **D**ODD**, author of *Good Baby, Bad Sleeper* and *The F*cket List* (forthcoming)**

"Charming, hilarious, and deeply wise, Ashleigh Renard's remarkable debut is that rare thing: A memoir that both entertains and instructs."
JOANNA **R**AKOFF**, author of *A Fortunate Age, My Salinger Year,* and *The Fifth Passenger* (forthcoming)**

SWING

ASHLEIGH RENARD

Published by MW Books, an imprint of Manitoba Woman Media, LLC.

For more information please contact: pr@manitobawomanmedia.com

www.ashleighrenard.com

ISBN 978-1-7365968-8-3 (paperback)

ISBN 978-1-7365968-9-0 (ebook)

ISBN 978-1-7365968-3-8 (audiobook)

First edition

Publisher's Cataloging-in-Publication data

Names: Renard, Ashleigh, author.

Title: Swing / Ashleigh Renard.

Description: Philadelphia, PA: MW Books, 2021.

Identifiers: LCCN: 2021906838 | ISBN: 978-1-7365968-8-3 (paperback) | 978-1-7365968-9-0 (ebook) | 978-1-7365968-3-8 (audio)

Subjects: LCSH Renard, Ashleigh. | Renard, Ashleigh--Marriage. | Marriage--Biography. | Married people--United States--Biography. | Families--United States. | Sex customs--United States. | Sex in marriage--United States. | Parenting--Humor. | Conduct of life--Humor. | Women--Conduct of life--Humor. | Sex--Humor. | BISAC BIOGRAPHY & AUTOBIOGRAPHY / Personal Memoirs | FAMILY & RELATIONSHIPS / Parenting / General | HUMOR / Topic / Marriage & Family

Classification: LCC HQ536 .R46 2021 | DDC 306.81/092--dc23

Cover design: Chris-Anne and Valentina Abusabbah

Author photo: Carlyn Dixon

For Manny

Chapter 1

"Hi, my name is Peter."

"Pardon me?" I raised my voice above the music.

"Peter ... like the first apostle."

This was the second strangest thing I had heard in a sex club.

"Oh, hi. I'm ... in line." I shook his hand and gestured toward the bathroom. "Maybe I'll see you later." I turned to face the front of the line. I wasn't interested in talking to Peter. I needed to pee.

Waiting in line to use the bathroom in a fancy New York City sex club is just like waiting to use the bathroom anywhere else. Well, anywhere else that people walk around half-naked. And anywhere else that a stilt walker or fire performer may squeeze past you. And anywhere else that you must send in a headshot and a full-body photo before being added to the invite list. Besides those things, it's like waiting in line for the bathroom anywhere else.

I was in a cramped hallway, halfway down the long, narrow Manhattan loft that served as the site of the party. The people were beautiful and rich-looking. I wondered if I had accidentally entered a casting call for *The Bachelor*. I shifted my weight back and forth from one stilettoed foot to another. *Man, I love these shoes.* The door to the women's room swung open. I was inches away from finding relief when a skyscraper of a woman knocked past me, ducked inside, and locked the door.

"She jumped right in front of you!" a British accent cut through the noise.

I turned and saw a sexy man with sparkling green eyes. He was outraged on my behalf, and it made him cuter.

"Ugh, that's okay. I do really need to pee, though."

Another thing that is different about waiting in line for the bathroom at a sex club is that if a sexy man with an accent invites you into the men's room with him out of kindness and concern for you peeing yourself, you may say yes.

He introduced himself as Ravi, and we squeezed into the tiny men's room and closed the door. Our tryst was scandalous, even for a sex club. We were pleased with ourselves, until we realized there was no toilet, only a urinal, hung halfway up the wall.

I turned to him. We're invested. There is no going back—I planted the plan in his head.

"You'll help me?" I asked.

"Of course." He laughed.

I hiked up my dress. It was a short dress, therefore a short hike. I propped one foot against the wall and briefly admired my shoes. *Damn, I really love these shoes.*

Sexy, British Ravi boosted me up until I was in a spider climb position, one foot against each wall of the tiny bathroom. I felt that American Ninja Warrior contestants might have, in that moment, marveled at my athleticism. Inexplicably, my panties were down but not awkwardly stretched out. I was at the perfect angle to pee directly into the urinal without splashing and without exposing myself to my new British friend. I already considered him a close confidant, partially because I grew up singing "God Save the Queen" in my Canadian Elementary school, and partially because he was my accomplice in this feat of strength, absurdity, and somehow, sexiness. Because we had overcome laws of physics, we were both fittingly amused with ourselves. Forget American Ninja Warrior. Maybe this was the origin story of me becoming a superhero. He helped me down from the urinal.

I contemplated the square footage of the bathroom. *Six?*

I squeezed against him to get to the sink. He turned to pee, and his shoulder pressed against mine as he washed his hands.

We stood side by side, staring at each other in the mirror.

"You are so beautiful ..." He turned to me. "May I kiss you?"

I was already leaning in.

"Mm-hmm ..." Our lips were parted and soft as they met, coming together, then barely apart, then together again, before I slipped my tongue into his mouth, running it lightly across his teeth.

My hands traced the curve of his deltoids and up the sides of his neck. He squeezed my butt with both hands, lifting my skirt slightly. We laughed softly as we continued to kiss. I reached around the back of his neck and hooked his hair with my fingers. Muffled music vibrated through the bathroom door.

Breathless, we parted our lips but kept our bodies pressed close.

"Wow, that was nice." I smiled.

He touched my lips gently. "Your lips are chapped."

I died. Upon my reincarnation, we exited the bathroom. The club seemed so big and tall and loud.

"Thanks for your help." I smiled.

"Bye. Have a good night." Ravi smiled and walked away.

I scanned the crowd for my husband and my Chapstick.

"Long line?" Manny asked.

I applied the lip balm and told Manny about the stranger, the urinal, and the kissing. He laughed.

"Ready?" I asked, handing him the Chapstick.

He nodded. I grasped his hand, took a deep breath, and together we walked toward the tangle of naked bodies at the back of the room.

Chapter 2

I only recall my mom giving me two pieces of advice on men.

The first one was when I was seven years old and at a wedding reception. I came to her, very upset because a boy I liked hadn't asked me to dance. She said to me, "Ashleigh Brooke, if you want to dance with a boy, you go up to him, grab him by the tie, and say, 'We're dancing.'"

Secondly, when I was a teenager, she told me that I would be crazy to ever marry a man without living with him first.

So when I met Manny and found out he was expected to marry a Greek virgin, I honestly didn't know that the topics of ethnicity and virginity were concerns outside the Taliban.

I was the liberal kind of sheltered, idealistic enough to believe the world had progressed further than it actually had. I grew up in the least religious family in the least religious town in the world. There are about 3500 people living in my Manitoba hometown when the price of oil is high, and a multitude of empty hotel rooms and bank overdrafts when it is not.

The terrain was ironed flat, shades of brown and beige. In Spring, it was briefly green, then, as if a militia of fairies had risen up to embroider during the night, the fields would explode with the sunny yellow of canola and the lavender of flax. We cherished this briefly, as soon, if there wasn't too much rain, the crops would be harvested, and everything would be dry and brown again.

Fall was extraordinary and lasted for one glorious day. In the morning I'd feel a slight breeze; *summer is over*. I'd pull out a sweater. I'd notice the leaves were turning. By afternoon, a ferocious wind stripped the trees bare. The trees were accustomed to being used. Most of them were planted decades before, in utilitarian rows to act as shelterbelts. On the north and west sides of each farmstead, small shrubs stood stoutly to act as a snow trap, followed by lines of tall deciduous trees to direct the wind upward, then conifers closest to the house. On the night of the first and only day of autumn, snow would fall, and winter would begin. The earth slumbered under its great duvet as the aurora borealis set the sky ablaze all winter long, a majestic backdrop for the never tiring pumpjacks.

My high school had a curling team and a rodeo team. Our town had one stoplight, which made us the big town. Driver's education classes from other towns came to our town to practice going through the stoplight.

When my mom told me that there was nothing a woman couldn't do that a man could, I took it to mean that women had already achieved equality. I felt relieved that I had been born in the right century. I knew I couldn't live through the stress of a women's rights movement.

I was the oldest of four children. By the time I was eleven I had two jobs. The first was as an assistant instructor in our town's learn-to-skate program. I knew if I worked diligently, I would be rewarded with my own group lessons the next year. The second was a regular shift at my parents' grocery store. Every Sunday morning, I got myself out of bed and walked the two blocks and let myself into the still dark building that had just been unlocked by my more senior coworker. As the fluorescent lights flickered and the freezers whirred, I deeply inhaled the sweet smell of linseed oil on the old hardwood floors and got to work cleaning the produce cooler.

Manny and I took the same job out of college in New Jersey, even though I didn't know anything about New Jersey. I had never watched *The Sopranos,* and my move predated the debut of *The Jersey Shore* on MTV. When I looked at a map and saw the capital was called Trenton, it reminded me of King Triton in The Little Mermaid, and I thought, *this place sounds pretty.*

When I visited for my interview, they told me they had just met with a Greek football player from Philadelphia and were likely going to offer him a position. I thought, *Greek football player ... interesting.*

When Manny was there for his interview, they told him that they were flying down a Canadian figure skater the following week. He thought, *Canadian figure skater ... interesting.*

In Jersey (in a little town far from Trenton but still very pretty), I was offered the job and accepted on the spot, with a start date of a month later. It was a quick turnaround, considering a few weeks earlier I had no plans to leave Manitoba. I might still be there today if it weren't for a particularly awful day of weather in June. Of course, the weather in Manitoba can be brutal. In the winter, you often get a brain freeze from breathing through your nose— the rush of biting air icing up each hair in succession until the piercing pain hits your hypothalamus. But June? In any humane location, it should have felt like summer. But Winnipeg makes no promises of being humane. I was being pelted by sleet and hail.

I had just graduated with my bachelor's degree in exercise physiology, and I had plans to continue competing with the synchronized skating team I co-founded at my university. I had what I considered to be an exceptionally exciting job for a twenty-one-year-old, working as a strength coach with the Team Canada women's volleyball team. I had plans to begin my master's degree in exercise physiology in the fall. But, as the precipitation assaulted me, I wondered, *why do I live here?*

I sent out resumés that night, and by the next afternoon twelve companies had responded. The demand for a female strength coach was high in collegiate and private settings. With my background as a competitive figure skater and my experience training elite athletes, I was a worthy candidate for the open positions. The owner of the gym in Jersey was the first to offer to fly me down for an interview.

After accepting the job, I loved the impressed look people gave me when I shared with them the news that I was moving so far away, to a place where I knew no one. I felt undeniably grown-up. Really, it was about time. The only thing I had ever wanted to be was grown up. I remember, at seven years old, sitting in the stairwell of our old house, looking towards the high window. Sunlight streamed through the window, warming a patch of carpet to my left. Dust particles danced through the air in a way that should have seemed peaceful or magical to a child, but I was angsty, too angsty for one who was still years away from double digits. I contemplated how long my life had felt so far and how much longer I must wait to be an adult. It hurt, a burning kind of agony that crisscrossed in fiery paths across my chest, up the sides of my neck, over my ears, and traced a matching double helix pattern down my back. I thought the waiting would kill me.

Remarkably, I had survived, and I was certain I was nearing the promised land of adulthood. I printed out the MapQuest directions to prepare for my drive through one province and seven states to get to my new job and my new home. My mom made the drive with me. The thirty hours of self-improvement audiobooks I brought lulled her into a slumber. The trip was 2000 miles. She slept for all but twenty minutes.

I met Manny when I arrived. His jet-black hair was clipped uniformly short. Thick brows and lashes framed eyes the color and sheen of melted chocolate. As he shook my hand, pillowy, kissable lips gave way, in a crooked smile, to display perfectly straight teeth, definitely the products of modern orthodontics.

His smile was not the only thing that seemed to be carefully crafted. His body looked to be carved from fine Grecian stone, every muscle studied in my anatomy classes confirmed under his silky tanned skin. As he demonstrated deadlifts to a client on that first day, I wondered why my slew of anatomy professors failed to exalt the exquisiteness of the hamstrings muscle. Forget a three-headed dragon, I wanted to hear all about the Greek myth where a three-headed muscle group evoked in maidens the urge to supplicate for permission to trace each muscle from its origin to insertion point. Before my mom flew back to Canada, I was certain to introduce Manny to her, just in case I would be telling her about him later.

He was my only coworker, and therefore, my only friend. I did not want to judge my new job and new country based on a relationship, so I intended to remain just friends for as long as possible. My resolve held until we were hanging out at his apartment during one of our breaks. Of the high school and college athletes we trained, some of their parents worked out with us, as well. That morning, just as he did every Monday, Manny trained Caren, a mom of three boys, and herself almost fifty. "I just hope she's not self-conscious," he said. "I hope she knows how beautiful she is." With that, he turned and walked toward the bathroom to take a shower. I sat with my yogurt cup, spoon frozen halfway along its journey to my mouth. I was reflecting on the layers of awareness and tenderness in his statement when he walked back across the apartment, this time with only a towel tied low on his waist. Occasionally, I gleaned a sliver of his midsection when he used the hem of his shirt to wipe sweat from his brow after an insane and impressive conditioning session. Now, completely shirtless, chest shaved, summer tan lingering, of course I saw his high, firm pecs, fully cut abdominals, and the sexy inguinal ligament that traced a V from the top of his hips to his pubic bone. But my eyes were drawn to his serrates anterior, the tiny muscle group laying like three perfectly shaped fingers, diagonally between his pecs and abs. I made my move shortly after, transforming a friendly goodnight hug into a steamy kiss in his two-seater Tacoma. Instead of pulling back fully from the hug I let my face linger close to his. I paused there, the sides of our lips touching so faintly that it was hard to decipher whether they were really making contact or if the commingling of our body heat just made it feel that way. He had been playing it so cool that I wasn't sure if he was into me. Thus, I didn't know if my affections would be reciprocated. When he didn't pull back, I turned my head slightly, offering my mouth to his, which he took willingly. Tongues meeting, my hands on his face, his hands in my hair, the friend charade was officially over. Within a month, I had used my lips to diligently chart every muscle on his body. But, on the night of our first kiss, we didn't know we would end the night as more than friends. If we would have known it was going to evolve into a date, maybe we would have been more cautious about our movie choice. Instead, we saw *My Big Fat Greek Wedding*. In between snort laughs, I choked, "Is your family actually like that?" He assured me not. *Of course*, I thought, *no family could actually be like that*.

Two months later I was packed into a tiny row home in Philadelphia and his aunts were spitting on him.

Among the countless superstitions held by the Greeks, one of the strongest is the fear of the evil eye. Envy is a dangerous thing to provoke because you never know who possesses the curse of the evil eye. If they have this power and they become jealous of you, they can cause harm just by *looking at you*. It's like the dark magic version of the stink eye. The fear has evolved in some Greek families to the point that anyone can unintentionally curse a person, usually a child or baby, by gazing at them adoringly or over-complimenting them. Luckily, there is an easy way to counteract the sorcery summoned by a compliment: legit *spit* on the person you just gushed over. Yes, gushing is undone by salivating. It's Greek science magic. To avoid getting arrested and to prevent the spread of cold and flu germs, a modern, fake-spit has now become commonplace. It sounds like "ptoo, ptoo." The spit only works if you were the one who dished out too many compliments. If people out in the wild are complimenting recklessly, the counterspell is different. Manny's mom has a favorite phrase that she mutters under her breath to undo this type of hex. It translates to "garlic in your eye."

In my family, when you sneeze, no one will say, "Bless you." Even though they are Canadian, possess exemplary manners, and will apologize if you run over their foot with a shopping cart, they let the awkward silence reign, no one willing to surrender to the superstition.

When Manny brought me home to meet his family, it meant one thing. He wanted to marry me. That is the only reason you are allowed to introduce someone to your family when you're Greek. Conversely, in kindergarten, when the teacher turned her back to write on the chalkboard, I would kiss the boy beside me, call him my boyfriend, and introduce him as such to my parents.

In my single-minded ambition to be a grown-up, securing a life mate was definitely a sign of maturity, so I had no objections when things got serious between us quickly. Our sexual chemistry was hot, but everywhere else, we were just cool. We did not fall head-over-heels in love. We fell into stride with each other, walking one-foot-in-front-of-the-other in love. It was straightforward. I liked him. He liked me. We thought we should be together. There was no game playing or uncertainty about commitment. A couple weeks in, he asked me how many kids I wanted to have and before I could answer, he answered the question himself, "Two or three," while nodding his head. He was twenty-two years old and ready to be a grown-up. Within a few months I had moved in with him because neither of us could find the practicality in paying rent on two apartments.

Our certainty was equally matched by Manny's mom's uncertainty. She wanted a Greek daughter-in-law. She thought her son deserved a Greek wife. I didn't know what that meant, but I'd soon find out. Incongruent with her plan, I was the only woman being brought around. Manny's older brothers were single, in addition to every male cousin of his generation, on both sides of the family. I could see the wheels turning. *She's not a Greek woman. But, technically, she is a woman.* If she had dismissed me, it could've been a while before another woman came around. She cautiously decided to give me a chance.

Manny's cousin recommended a book called *Greek Customs and Traditions in America* to help me learn about Greek culture. It was written by a non-Greek who married into a Greek family, and I found it extremely informative, as it provided the "why" behind customs that Manny could not explain. Although enlightening, it had weirdly named sections like "What to Name your Baby," (because it's not really your choice) and "Greek Weddings Sparkle" (even though the bride and groom are not allowed to speak). I was halfway through when I realized I was reading a 400-page ass-kissing to Greeks and Greek culture. On every page the author subtly pleaded, *like me, please.*

I was reeling.

And I wasn't the only one. The fact that I had moved 2000 miles away from my family to a place where I knew no one had Manny's mom reeling. She also left her country for a new life when she was about my age. As was customary for her generation, her marriage was arranged. She and Manny's dad were from the same village, but he had been living away for years, having taken a job on trans-Atlantic freight ships when he was only thirteen. At the time that their families decided over letters that they would marry, he was living in Philadelphia and working in a restaurant. She was working in a fine crystal shop in the city of Chios. He flew back to Greece two weeks before their wedding, and they spent their "honeymoon" in Athens, completing her immigration paperwork. He had to get back to his job in the States, so she stayed with an uncle until her visa was ready. She then boarded a Lufthansa flight alone to leave behind everything she had ever known. The fact that I had left my family, by choice, as a single woman was baffling to her. I was certain she likened me to a leaf fluttering in the breeze, untethered, unsheltered, and this was the real reason she didn't actively protest against us living together. *If Manny doesn't take care of her, who will?*

A saving grace was that at least she and I had one thing in common.

We weren't from here.

She knew what it was like to be in a new country and know almost no one. She held a certain tenderness for me and for my family, imagining how much we must miss each other because she still tangibly recalled how she ached with loneliness for her own mother when she first moved to the US. Her village back in Greece only had one telephone, located at the post office. She would dial it from her home in Philadelphia and ask to speak with her mother. Then she would hang up and wait. Twenty minutes later she would call back, hoping that her mother had been successfully fetched from wherever she had been in the village. She loved hearing her mother's voice but longed to see her face, to possess the magic required to see her through the phone. She was seven years married and pregnant with her second son before she took her first trip back to visit.

Her found tenderness for me could not quite match her adoration for her youngest son. He was her whole heart. I pieced together quickly the reasoning behind the preference for a Greek wife. She felt life would be easier for him if he had a wife who had fewer of her own ambitions, who would require little from him—a woman who accepted that her destiny was to make life comfortable for the men and children in her family. She reluctantly accepted that he loved me and we planned to be together, but promised to treat me like a daughter only if I followed the Greek traditions. She also could not resist pointing out that every girl in the US and Greece who met Manny loved him. They loved him the moment they saw him. And the girl he chose is this Canadian girl. *And you are so lucky.*

I learned quickly that in a Greek family, the requirements for being a good wife were pretty complex. They were expected to cook and clean, of course, but the standard of cleaning made my head spin. The legs of coffee tables were dusted. Pots and pans were scrubbed on the outside until they showed no signs of use. I also quickly learned that in a Greek family, the requirements for being a good husband were pretty simple. Bring home a paycheck. And don't be a drunk.

Manny was a hands-on partner from the start. And despite the fact that he never lifted a finger growing up, he scrubbed our house top to bottom before we hosted every party. He learned to clean through osmosis.

None of this escaped his family's notice. When our oldest son Jack was born, Manny's competence as a father was cause for wonder and celebration. When Jack was a few days old, Manny knelt on the floor to buckle him into a car seat. Manny's yiayia nudged Manny's mom to behold. Behold the man, the man on the floor. The man on the floor who knows how to buckle his offspring into a rear-facing five-point bucket seat. Behold this incredible man. At that moment, and weekly ever since, a parade broke out in Manny's honor, filling the streets of their home village in Greece, recognizing him as the best dad in the history of Greek civilization.

His prowess was so enthralling that they even forgot to spit.

Chapter 3

My passport indicated I had been granted access to the US as a professional under NAFTA, but some days I wondered if I was a social scientist who had entered a parallel universe. For the first time in my life, I met people who "weren't sure" about evolution or climate change but were straight up certain that taking a boy to ballet class would "make him gay."

I was in the country a few weeks when I went to my first Major League Baseball game—Red Sox vs. Yankees at Yankee Stadium. That scene was emotionally charged on a good day, but it was made overwhelming by the fact that I was at the game alone with a client who kept asking me what I thought was hotter, lesbian sex or anal sex? He wouldn't accept my answer of "neither" and all day continued to press me to provide details on how I came to that conclusion.

The people I met in New Jersey were rich, much richer than the people who I thought were rich from oil money back home. It was there that I first heard the term "blue collar." Prior to that I just thought work was work. I knew no distinction. The people were so rich that my paycheck from training their children made me feel like I was on my way to becoming rich, too. Manny and I worked six days a week, early mornings, afternoons, and evenings. The gym was busy, and we were the only trainers. My hourly wage plus the fact that the exchange rate of the US Dollar was 1.6 times the Canadian Dollar meant that I would pay off my student loans in six months. I thought America was a magical land where a Trader Joe's winked at a Whole Foods from across every street until I took a drive to the social security office. It felt like a museum ride chronicling the class differences in America. I got on the ride in front of a house undergoing two million dollars in renovations, and two miles later, I realized that this little pocket of white New Jersey affluence I had dropped into was not characteristic of the whole country. Clearly, they couldn't even keep it up for two consecutive townships. I suddenly felt self-conscious about my fat paycheck. I assuaged my guilt by reminding myself that I had no benefits. My only health insurance was knowing I could fly back to Canada if I really needed to see a doctor.

I was startlingly homesick but reluctant to admit it even to myself. Over the years I had seen hundreds of young women bid adieu by my mom as they graduated high school and moved away. As their skating coach, she was like a second mother to many of them. I had learned that the ones who demonstrated immediate independence were the ones deemed mature. I wanted to believe that I actually possessed the maturity that everyone assumed I had, but I desperately wanted my family to come see me. Finally, seven months after my move, my little brother and sister were scheduled to visit. Awkwardly, I had moved to the suburbs of NYC coming up on the first anniversary of 9/11. On what was supposed to be the day of their flight, George W. Bush announced that the US was invading Iraq. Homeland Security's terror alert thermometer was raised to red, and my mom refused to let her youngest children board a plane to Newark. As bombs landed on Baghdad, I collapsed onto my bed in heavy, heaving sobs for mostly selfish reasons.

The complicated feeling of trying to fit into a new culture was countered by the straightforwardness of being with Manny. We worked together all day and worked out together on our breaks. The affluence of our clients resulted in us being gifted a lifestyle that would otherwise be beyond our means. We enjoyed free tickets to every major sporting event in the area and many Broadway shows. We ate at beautiful restaurants and quickly decided our favorite date was coffee at a bookstore. We continued down our path of sane, practical love. A few months after moving in together we decided buying was smarter than renting and invested in our first piece of real estate, a two-bedroom condo in the Philly suburbs, close to his parents, with the five year plan of moving to a larger place and keeping the condo to rent out.

We aimed to handle everything with this pragmatism. Manny had a joke. "I told you once that I loved you. Unless I tell you otherwise, assume I continue to love you." It wasn't exactly funny, but I did like the practicality of checking off the list of must-haves for adult life. *Agree on money? Check. Good sex? Check. Got love? Check.* We agreed on most everything, or at least we were savvy about avoiding arguments when we did not. Early on we established a protocol for broaching a discussion related to a grievance. Completely lacking nuance, we inquired, "Is the Complaint Department open?" and gave the other person the chance to answer yes or no. Most often it was open, and the complaint would be warmly shared. If we really didn't feel like hearing a suggestion or request at that time, we'd simply say that it was closed. And then we'd giggle, agreeing the gripe needed to be shelved for another day. All of it felt undeniably mature, secure, like we could already grasp the idea that being right mattered not in the long run. Often, I attributed it to us both being Libras, symbolized by the scales, eternally optimistic that justice would always be attained. We both abhorred confrontation and swiftly prioritized harmony in every conflict. We could not imagine anything more grating than someone escalating a tense situation just for the sake of argument. While others seemed to get a rush from a verbal altercation, I felt like my insides were a reverse gyro machine, a blade slicing thin layers of flesh off my organs with each argument offered. This was not a sensation I chose willingly.

When we got engaged, we immediately decided to have two weddings. Choosing one location and upsetting one entire side of the family was unconscionable. We would have a wedding in each country. As an unexpected bonus, when I couldn't decide on some aspect, *all white flowers or bright orange and pink? Hair up or hair down?* I did both, one at each venue.

My family is not religious, but oddly, I had a baptismal certificate from a ceremony my parents had for me when I was three years old. The fact that I was one of those baptized in my family was enough to appease the Greek priest, sort of. Before we met with him, my mother-in-law said she was sure I was going to like what he had to say. And then the first thing he said was that trying to be a good person for the sake of being a good person made me no better than an animal. This pitying superiority exploded a tight bud of resentment living low in my stomach. It rapidly unfurled into the shape of a giant oak leaf in my torso, the apex stretching to my throat, lobes reaching into my anterior deltoids, anesthetic running through its wide veins like ice water, numbing me from the inside, and freezing my tongue in place.

I couldn't defend myself with an ice block tongue, so I burst into tears. He offered no comfort, no counsel for navigating a marriage between people of different backgrounds. One biting remark was all he had for us. I decided in order to make it through future visits to this place, including the wedding, I would pretend I was an actress playing a visitor to a Greek church. And when I greeted the actor playing the Greek priest, maybe, most of the time, I'd forget my cue to kiss him on the hand and offer him a firm handshake instead. After the wedding we'd find out that he had accepted a position at a parish in Florida. While we were preparing to be married, he was already phoning it in. Maybe motivated by golf games or mai tais, he did agree to marry us in exchange for the envelope of money that would be passed to him on the afternoon of our wedding. After leaving that meeting where I burst into tears, out of relief, or stress, or uncertainty of what the hell else to do to recalibrate after an encounter like that, Manny and I pulled into a deserted park and had sex in the cab of his truck.

We had two beautiful weddings, with the closest of our family and friends attending both events. Our first, in Canada, was outside in a courtyard in the evening, with about fifty people in attendance. My cousin sang, and we exchanged personally written vows. Afterwards, more guests joined us for a cocktail party. We danced the night away, the playlist consisting of the classic rock songs played by my parents throughout my childhood and most often belted out around the campfire, under the clear night sky.

Eight days later, we were married again, this time in a Greek Orthodox church outside Philadelphia. The guest list quadrupled. The ceremony was mostly in Greek, everything repeated in triplicate, as is the Orthodox tradition. The reception kicked off with the traditional Greek wedding dance, the Kalamatiano, where all the guests take turns dancing hand in hand with the bride while other guests throw money in the air to encourage the band to keep playing. Many people think the money is for the bride and groom, but the modern tradition is for the band to collect it at the end of the night, as their tip. Lamentably for the bride, the dance usually lasts for eons. Within the first minute, my heel ripped through the underskirt of my dress, keeping my ankle bound uncomfortably for the duration of the spectacle, as each guest, even the Canadians, took their turn to dance with me, the actress sufficiently playing the role of the Greek bride.

Even with my dress holding my leg in bondage, the magic of the ritual was breathtaking. As the Greek Traditions in America ass-kissing book promised, this part of the wedding really did sparkle. My father-in-law displayed his uncanny ability to project a folded wad of dollar bills high into the air with a swift flick of his wrist. The night sky appeared above our heads as the money formed constellations, hovering, temporarily ignoring gravity in favor of the hypnotizing strings of the bouzouki. My eyes scanned the room, taking it all in. There was my family, Manny's, the clients from New Jersey who had become friends, the new group of skating colleagues I was growing (my future), and Manny's childhood friends (his past). After months of planning and weeks of whirlwind travel, this was the first time I realized everyone had come together to celebrate us, to signify that the two of us were starting something new together, to give their stamp of approval. It all felt remarkably supportive and remarkably grown-up.

The next day we flew to Italy for our honeymoon. As we soared high above the Atlantic Ocean, we recounted, with relief, how we were able to pull off two weddings in two countries, without disappointing any members of our respective families. I drifted off to sleep, relieved we were able to avert disaster. When we landed, we found out that Hurricane Katrina had made landfall over southeast Louisiana.

The wedding wasn't the end of trying to fit in with the Greeks. What I thought was some sort of finish line, I realized quickly and wearily was something very near the beginning. The expectations were strange and demanding. I hoped desperately they would like me. But neither of these things were new to me.

I grew up in figure skating.

I was two years old the first time my parents laced me into skates. By elementary school, I was on the ice five days a week. In the mornings, with the world lit by moonlight, I rolled from my warm bed, already wearing my skating clothes, a time-saver my mom insisted upon and practiced. She and I padded quietly, accustomed to maneuvering through the darkened house. We turned on no lights, save one mounted under the upper cupboards of the kitchen that remained on all night, as not to wake the rest of the family. Cereal boxes and bowls sat on the kitchen table, laid out the night before. The room was filled with the smell of coffee. My mom took her coffee black, in a tall aluminum travel mug, with two ice cubes, rinsed under the tap before being dropped in the coffee and dissolving quickly. In just a few hours my mom would rinse the filter and fill it again with grounds, pouring water from a plastic pitcher until it reached the max fill line, resetting the coffee maker for the next morning.

The frigid air struck me only briefly as I dashed to the warm car. My mom joined me after unplugging the extension cord from the block heater, the cord of which flopped out from under the car hood all winter long. The drive took two minutes. The soles of my feet were still tight from sleep as I walked methodically over the thickly packed snow of the rink parking lot, rolling from heel to toe, letting each icy peak massage away the sleepiness through the soles of my heavy Sorels. My hands stuffed deep in my pockets and my shoulders high in an attempt to cover my ears with the collar of my parka, I shifted my feet back and forth as my mom unlocked the door. The key was on its own ring, slung through a roughly drilled hole in a slice of thick, white plastic left over from the dismantling of the old rink boards. I was familiar with the persistent coolness of the plastic, the way my fingers felt when I ran them perpendicularly over the grooves and slices permanently etched on it. I knew this key, but I wasn't sure if we possessed a key to our own house. I carried nothing —everything I needed was kept inside the locker room. The locker room, which in just a few minutes would be warmed in equal measure by space heaters and the exuberant chatter of pre-teens who cared not that the clock had yet to strike 7:00 am.

Each day began with forty-five minutes of figures. We called it "patch" because we each chose a section of clean ice on which to practice our patterns. Over and over, the rink silent and the lights bright, we traced figure eights. Forward and backward, and with turns as we advanced, it was my favorite part of training. Some of my friends skated haphazardly over their own patches, impatient to practice their jumps and spins, but I was in no rush. My patch was meticulous.

On test days, heavy-booted judges stood on the ice to watch us skate our figures, each pattern traced thrice before completion. Without fail, at least one of them squatted down close to the ice to wipe away snow with a sheepskin-lined leather mitten. This is the world's most perfect mitten. No other style could keep a hand warmer nor compete with the volume of applause generated when they were clapped together. The latter attribute motivated me, before every high school hockey game, to dig as relentlessly as a terrier to find a matching pair in the storage compartment mounted under the deacon's bench at our front door.

The judge wiped away the snow to see my tracings more clearly. They were looking for flats. As I watched their assessment of my work, I silently prayed that they wouldn't find them. Flats were bad. A flat's presence on the ice divulged that my body lean had been weak and weight placement on the blade incorrect, resulting in two shallow, parallel lines. As the judge crouched lower, their widening knees threatening to pop the zipper on their full-length parka, I hoped they'd see only single, deep grooves on the ice, indicating I maintained a true edge around each figure eight and on the entry and exit of every turn. I appreciated the simple integrity of being assessed based on the prints my blade left on the ice. A tracing does not lie. A landed jump may be considered better by some if it's higher or if the flow across the ice is maintained on the landing edge. A figure tracing, on the other hand, was an inalterable record of performance, the perfection of which was directly proportional to the focus employed. It was one part story, telling the tale of the balance over the blade, and it was one part math—a correctly laid out and executed equation.

I have one flat that I'll carry with me forever, carved accidentally into the skin covering the medial edge of my gastrocnemius. It, and the other sixteen visible scars on my left leg, was the result of a habitually poorly placed free leg on the takeoff of my double Salchows. Oftentimes, I grazed my leg with my right blade and briefly thought I had escaped injury because my tights were not torn. Most often, I was reminded of the truth I learned too young: human flesh is more tender than any material man-made. I pinched my two layers of Mondor tights and plucked them away from my skin, breath suspended as I waited for a count of three. If a growing scarlet patch did not appear during that time frame, I set up for another double Sal. If blood did appear, I followed my solitary protocol of retreating to the locker room, pulling my dress and tights down to my ankles, dress inside out and draped like a splayed chicken over my still-tied skates. I dabbed the cut with a tissue and covered it with bandages, one to three, depending on size, all the while my head upside down, nose running due to the temperature change, mucus pooling in the top curve of my nostrils with an excruci-ating tickle. I pulled up my dress, wiped my nose, and returned to the ice in my blood-stained tights. Of the seventeen cuts that left scars, the flat is my favorite. The rest were small, some merely nicks. Many were originally deep, but this one was long. On the day of the injury it measured three inches, slicing clean through my double layer of tights, which gaped instantly, framing the cut like labia. Two tiny rivulets of blood sprang from the skin, running parallel until they pooled together in my boot, the skin between the incisions pink and pulsing, astonished that it remained untouched. Even in scar form, both edges remained clearly shown over its full length, a perfect flat. It puzzled me afterwards, seemingly impossible that I contorted my foot into the dorsiflexion required to brand myself in this way. But a tracing does not lie.

I didn't have to wait for test days or competitions to stand on the ice as the judges displayed their scores. I could apprise myself each day. Perfectly shaped figure eights, tracings all within an inch of each other, each new pattern set up ice one blade's length from the last. Years of report cards with straight

A's. A stack of notebooks, holding a decade of records, calories in and calories out, reps and sets completed, miles run, food allowances, weight-loss goals. Collectively, a memoir of my discipline. Collectively, an assurance that I was living a correctly laid out and executed life.

Some may say perfection is unattainable, but figure skaters know different. Every day we ventured closer to the inevitable. There would be a time when all the work, the early mornings, the bruises upon bruises that created a spectacle of color that put most canvases to shame, the steam rising from our sweaty heads as our toes turned a buttery yellow from the cold resulted in a performance that struck all who were watching as both effortless and beautiful. It would be declared, "Yes, you did it. It was perfect, and everyone likes you."

We would be awarded the 6.0.

Chapter 4

Within a year of meeting Manny, *My Big Fat Greek Wedding* was no longer just a movie or a funny first date story; it had become my life. Manny had left the gym to manage his family's restaurant. His older brothers were still living at home, but the fact her baby lived so far away (seventy to ninety minutes, depending on traffic) had resulted in his mom's heart, according to her own description, being "filled with blackness." After almost a year of pining for him, he returned to the family business when we bought our condo in PA. I continued to commute to Jersey most days of the week. Each time I re-entered Pennsylvania I puzzled at how I ended up in a place that, as a child, I found to be the most unfortunately named state. *It sounds like Transylvania,* I thought, *creepy.* To my surprise, Pennsylvania had ample sunlight and a remarkably low population of vampires. In addition, it was exquisitely beautiful. Lakes, and orchards, and covered bridges, oh, my!

Manny left the gym at a time of big expansion. Three male trainers were hired in his place. When we were set to attend a weekend conference and found out that our boss was footing the bill for the conference registration, but not for the hotel room, the four of us easily decided to share a room. We were comfortable with each other and had few reservations, and Manny was relaxed about the situation, needing no check-ins or assurances during my weekend away. During the conference a similar line of questioning came from everyone we met. They'd glance at me, the three young, buff dudes who were my constant side-kicks, at my engagement ring and then inquire, "You're staying with these guys? And your fiancé is fine with that?"

"Uh, yup. He's fine with that." I'd shrug. My co-workers shrugged. And then, shrugs apparently as contagious as yawns, the inquirer shrugged, too.

I arrived home late Sunday night, tired from the four-hour drive, and left my suitcase at the top of the stairs. I kissed Manny on the forehead and dropped onto the couch at the opposite end, stretching back and considering falling asleep right there, without taking out my contacts or brushing my teeth. He asked how the weekend went and, as an afterthought, asked who I shared a bed with while I was away.

This jolted me out of my near-slumber, and I turned toward him, squinting, trying to judge the sincerity of his question from the expression on his face. I saw that his nonchalance was authentic, eyes locked on the TV as if he had already forgotten that he asked a question. "Uh, no one."

He pulled back, stiffened, snapped out of the TV trance. "You made someone sleep on a cot?" His wide eyes were fixated on me and his mouth hung open in disbelief, as if I had just announced I had been transported around all weekend on a palanquin.

I couldn't help but laugh. My unflappable guy was, for the first time, flapped. I kissed him again on the forehead, told him he was absurd, and went to bed. That was the moment when I figured out that his claims about really not being jealous were clearly genuine. He'd already demonstrated that he did not have a vengeful bone in his body, so the next day I told him that from now on I would refer to him as a turn-the-other-cheek-but-I-don't-mind-if-you-covet-my-wife-kinda-guy. He didn't object.

When I was rested, I realized I had more questions about his bed-sharing assumption. Why, exactly, had he expected that? I asked him, and his answer was, plainly, "Because you're a nice person and cots are uncomfortable."

"Nice?" I asked, confused as to what nice had to do with sharing a bed with a colleague.

"Well, you know, you don't mind being close to people. You're not scared of germs. You clean public bathrooms." This last part was added with a touch of exasperation as if this action for humanity proved I would do anything to make others more comfortable. And it was a fact. I routinely cleaned public bathrooms, picking up paper towels, wiping counters, and, as needed, unclogging toilets.

"Okay, but weren't you thinking that something may happen if we shared a bed?" I pressed. He elaborated, saying that he thought it was likely that my co-workers could be attracted to me, or even me to them. But, if two of us wanted to hook up, we had the whole weekend and would have created an opportunity to do so. The sleeping arrangements, in his mind, were inconsequential. Furthermore, if I was falling for one of them and didn't want to be with Manny any longer that would really (*and don't take offense,* he said) have more to with me than with him. How was that within his control? And why worry about something that was not within his control?

Honestly, the man made some good points.

Rather than satisfying my curiosity, his clearly thought out argument made me wonder more. Over the weeks that followed, I continued to press further into this line of questioning. Treading carefully, I inquired, if something had happened between me and one of the guys, something minor, would he want to know? Well, he told me, if it was a coworker then it was likely that there was probably emotion behind it, but if it had been some random guy at the conference who I'd never see again, then no, he would prefer not to know. I thought about it and agreed. In the event that he was out with friends and something happened with another woman, a kiss on the dance floor, a touch, I didn't think I'd want to know either. Bringing home the news of a one-time thing would do more harm than good.

One night when we were preparing to host friends, I was setting the table as Manny chopped cucumbers for the veggie tray. I casually told him that if I had to categorize myself, I would say I was a "reluctant monogamist." I watched him out of the corner of my eye to gauge his reaction.

He replied, eyes still on the cutting board. "Well, isn't everyone, if they are being honest with themselves?" He looked up at me and shrugged. What I thought had the potential to be a grand confession now seemed banal, an obvious truth that begged to be formed into words, a truth that most people left hanging in the air, unsaid. If people knew it wouldn't ruin their relationship, or their reputation, or their health, would anyone actually choose monogamy? We were committed to each other and building a life together. That was undebatable. And monogamy did offer stability and predictability. But we had already experienced how monotony and the lack of novelty contributed to the almost inescapable decline in lust. Predictability seemed to be the antithesis of desire, and we agreed that this may be the one and only drawback of a committed relationship.

Periodically, we'd have pseudo-conversations, throwing a vague idea into the air to see what the other would do with it.

Maybe I'd be open to trying something different.

Yeah, maybe I would, too.

And then we'd go on with our day.

Finally, we'd had enough of these discontinuous, tennis-like "conversations" to be certain that we were open to exploring experiences outside our bedroom. We agreed that we certainly did not want to involve any friends or people we know. That exchange went like this.

Yeah, but uh … not like people we know, right?

Uh … no, definitely not.

Change of subject.

Even though we were discussing shaking things up a bit, this new level of honesty made our relationship feel even more secure. In considering our options, we agreed that the best and most private option was to attend a party at a swing lifestyle club, and we found one in Philadelphia. Spontaneity was not in our blood, so we did not decide to go on a whim. Even after joining the mailing list, we puzzled over it for months, pouring over each arriving email and rechecking the website. We wondered if the whole thing was a hoax. It seemed too good to be true. How could there really be enough people as sexually adventurous as we wished to be (even though we hadn't explicitly discussed what we were each wishing) to necessitate an actual brick and mortar establishment? Would there really be other people there? Was this for real? Finally, we ran out of questions to toss into the air and decided to go.

Manny spent five minutes purchasing the required annual membership and tickets for the party, and I spent weeks puzzling over my attire. I wanted to wear something sexy, but I had never been a provocative dresser. I had lived most of my life in the rink. And it's cold there.

I did have some lingerie. And I had a sewing machine. I picked out a white lacy pushup bra, a matching garter belt, a tiny white thong, sheer thigh-high stockings, and platform heels I guessed I had purchased for a Halloween costume in college. I felt I was off to a good start. I bought the shortest skirt I could find in the juniors' department and shortened it four inches. The result was fascinating. My move to the States had signaled the end of my competitive skating career, but the beginning of the hardest training of my life. Aiming to properly demonstrate every lift and drill we did with our athletes, within months I was squatting 225 pounds and had mastered rope climbs. Standing in front of a full-length mirror in a mini skirt and heels showed me exactly how fit I had become. When I turned around my glutes presented themselves like a perky round shelf. The backs of my thighs were not flat, rather, my hamstrings bulged out in a defined curve, and a slight bend forward showed where they dove deep beneath my glutes, highlighting the exact spot I had drooled over on Manny's body the day we had been introduced. The skirt fit perfectly low on my hips and showed how effective the medicine ball and rotational cable drills had been at bringing out the definition in my obliques. I was shocked by the surface area of human body visible when clothing was this minimal. And I liked it. I didn't want to cover more skin than this. I cut the bottom off one of my t-shirts and fashioned it into a crop top.

On the drive down to the club we were jittery, equal parts eager and skeptical. We made our way to South Street Philly, found parking and then set off on foot in the direction of the address that had been emailed to us. As we passed people walking on the street, I felt nervous. Would they know where we were going? Would they wonder why I was wearing a trench coat? Did I look like a flasher? At last we saw the fake sign the email had told us to look for: *Señor Rattler's Cantina*. We paused, looked up, and each took a deep breath. "Okay, let's do this," Manny said.

We stepped inside the building we had looked at online for months. It looked just like the pictures, except now it was packed wall-to-wall with people. Heads turned as we walked in and everyone gave us matching, welcoming smiles. We checked in at the front desk, handing them our confirmation email and our IDs so they could check our membership status. Right on cue, a male host magically appeared to greet us as we surrendered our coats and cell phones at coat check.

"Welcome," he said, face beaming as he warmly offered his hand to each of us. "I'm Chuck. Follow me."

As he led us through the throng of people on the main floor, I noticed that everyone was smiling. The crowd parted for us. Everyone acknowledged us as we walked by, raising their glass, nodding, or giving a little wave. The cheeriness made me feel like we were walking the iconic path in the opening credits for

Sesame Street. *Suuuunny day, sweeping the clouuuds awaaay ...
Coooome and play everything's aaaaa-okaay.*

We were unavoidably carrying the mark of newcomers. Not
only were we being led through the club, but we were wide-
eyed, blinking, exhibiting the curiosity of newborn baby deer.
And, my goodness, we must have looked young. Manny, with
his Mediterranean blood line could grow a five o'clock shadow
by 10:00 a.m., but he was still just a couple years away from his
college football prime. And I had yet to encounter an instance in
real life when I didn't get carded. Our rookie status could not
have been clearer, even if a neon sign hung above our heads
flashing "Fresh Meat." Despite this, or maybe because of it, the
treatment we received felt like an authentic welcoming. It did
not feel like the creepy, predatory type of attention I sometimes
experienced when I was out in the world as a woman. From a
mile away, these club-goers could tell we were first-timers, and
they wanted to assure us of the same thing they wanted to be
assured of on their first visit.

*Hi! Welcome! We are so glad you are here. No need to be nervous.
We are all just normal people.*

And they seemed to be. On the outside, they were all remarkably normal-looking people, the same variety of which we'd
encounter at the grocery store. As our host gave us the tour, I
tried to guess everyone's occupation as we walked past them.
Tattoo artist and hair stylist. Librarian and accountant (or something equally serious). Chuck led us through the main floor,
flanked on one side by a long bar, and on the other it opened up
into a restaurant, set up with a buffet. Manny and I had already
discussed that seeing someone grab a plate of food was the
grossest thing we could imagine witnessing at a sex club.

We squeezed through a mob of people to make our way to
the staircase at the back. It twisted up to a landing and to the
second floor. Through the low lighting we saw a sea of
mattresses, outfitted in sheets of dark purple and blue. Uniform
walking paths were visible between the row of mattresses and

punctuated by towers of clean dark sheets and white towels throughout.

"This is *the pit*," said Chuck. Following him, we continued our journey up another flight of stairs. The third floor held another bar, a dance floor, locker rooms and showers, and a platform with a dancing pole. Above the platform hung metal hooks anchored into the ceiling. I didn't wonder for long what they would be used for, as a dominatrix set up shop for the evening and a line began to form for her services. Chuck wrapped up his tour, showing us the change rooms, lockers, and showers. After he bid us adieu, we went back to the third-floor bar where we had left our wine, and each got a glass.

"Cheers?" I asked, amused, and still a little hesitant to believe this was all real, and raised my glass to Manny.

"Cheers," he agreed, and we each took a sip as we looked around. We had purposefully arrived late, after 11:00 p.m. and as we took a walk again around the third floor, we saw that the club had filled considerably since we began our tour with Chuck. I saw a banister framing a large open area and ushered Manny over to see what was there. As we got closer, we realized it looked down onto the sea of mattresses on the second floor, what Chuck had referred to as *the pit*.

"Don't worry," said a voice from behind, "that will be packed later in the night." We turned to see a smiling, earnest blonde couple behind us. He was tall and broad-shouldered, with hair cut short. She was petite with a sleek bob.

"I'm Morgan," she said, extending her hand first to me, then to Manny.

"And I'm Tony," he said, extending his hand first to Manny, then to me.

"You guys new here?" asked Morgan.

"Yup, first time," I said, trying to stay cool talking to a real-life swinger. "What about you guys?"

"We usually come once a month," said Morgan, "for a couple years, right, babe?" she looked to Tony for confirmation.

"Yeah, we've been coming for right around two years," he agreed. "But we are starting a new production and won't be back again for a while. That's why we are here tonight: a last hurrah before all our energy goes into our show."

"Show? What kind of show?" I asked and took another sip of my wine. They explained that they were actors, had first met when they were cast in the same play, and they were starting a new stage production that would take every waking minute of their time for the next six months. As we chatted, I noticed the music was lower than at a regular club, which made conversation much easier. We decided to take our conversation to the dance floor. The DJ was just starting a game where three women were blindfolded. They used their hands and their mouths to identify their partner on the dance floor. I thought this was a spectacular idea. I excused us to get another drink. As I leaned over the bar to ask for a glass of wine, Manny pressed himself against me. He wrapped his arms around my waist and spoke into my hair, "I'm horny."

I turned to him and replied through a kiss and a smile, "Me, too."

We took our wine and walked hand-in-hand around the bar. Looking over the banister, the mattresses were indeed filling up. The lights were low throughout the whole club, but we could see darkened bodies positioning themselves beside and on top of each other, mouths and hands beginning their search. Behind us, along two walls of the third floor, was a wide, L-shaped bench that served as a giant sectional. We turned and leaned our backs against the banister, surveying the partygoers perched along the bench. In front of us sat a man with a woman sitting sideways on his lap. She leaned back to kiss him, and he slid his hand high up the front of her skirt, deep between her thighs. To their left was a foursome, two men and two women. The women were kneeling on the bench and kissing each other as their partners flanked them, sipping on their drinks. We watched as the women stood and began to peel off each other's clothes. They returned to the bench, the men shifting outwards to make more room, and positioned themselves for 69, one woman lying flat on her back and the other snugly on top of her, each cupping her friend's buttocks and burying her face in her crotch.

I felt blood rush quickly between my legs, immediately causing a sensation of fullness and wetness. I decided that I'd had enough watching. "Let go sit there," I said, motioning toward the corner. We walked hand in hand to my chosen location. I grabbed a towel for Manny to sit on, with his back to the corner. I climbed on to sit facing him, straddling his legs with mine. My back was arched, and when Manny reached around and his hands touched my butt cheeks instead of my skirt, my suspicion was confirmed. My ass was visible to the whole club. As I kissed him firmly, he squeezed and ran his hands up my back, flipping my skirt up completely. I kissed him harder. Out of the corner of my eye I saw the actors, Tony and Morgan, sit down to our left. They motioned for us to join them. I shook my head and mouthed a "no, thanks" and they replied with "no problem." I felt Manny hard between my legs, and I rubbed against him as we kissed. He ran his lips down my neck and to my right I saw the 69'ing women had reconfigured with their partners and now the men were in on the action, each one of them going down on one of the women. With Manny's face in my boobs, I whispered to him, "I'm going down on you." I slid off him and between his legs. I knelt, white stockings on the floor, and undid his belt and pants. He propped himself up slightly so I could move them down low enough to access his already hard penis. I swirled my tongue around the tip and looked up at him as I took it in my mouth. He looked down at me and scanned the room. As I slid my mouth up and down on his shaft, I gave him a sly smile. I knew the visual and physical stimulation was enough to make him nearly lose his mind.

"Get on top of me," he offered. I giggled as I stood up, dizzy from the excitement. I turned around, reached behind me and pulled my thong to the side. Manny licked his fingers and reached around the front to put them inside me. I leaned into him, laying my back against his chest. He fingered me as he kissed my neck, and I looked out at the dance floor. On the spanking platform, a woman fingered herself as her handcuffed husband was flogged by the masked dominatrix. Beside us, the foursome were now having sex from behind as the women kissed and fondled each other's breasts. Tony was fingering Morgan and licking her clit, and she looked like she was about to climax. And then I realized so was I.

"I'm close," I whispered. Upon hearing this, Manny steadied the rhythm of his palm over my clitoris, keeping his fingers inside me. I closed my eyes, needing to focus on the building heat and intensity in my body and block out everything in my gaze. My body clenched, every muscle tight, as my orgasm exploded like a volcano, sending torrid streaks up my chest and over my ears. I stretched back, my cheek against Manny's and told him I was coming. Eyes pressed shut, I saw a rainbow explosion, a kaleidoscope of color that kept spinning behind my eyelids. I fell limp on top of him and looked toward the ceiling. My vision was foggy, but I felt Manny's body beneath me and the bass from the music rattle through the bench under our bodies. Finally, I let my eyes drift down and my vision quickly sharpened. The sex scenes around us seemed to have doubled. Everywhere I looked I saw different configurations of mouth and flesh.

I turned my eyes to Manny's. "I want you inside me, now," I insisted. I put my fingers in my mouth, scooping saliva to stroke down his penis. I positioned myself and took him inside me, lowering until my glutes pressed against him, spreading to his hip bones. He grasped my waist, fingers on my abdomen and each thumb lateral of my spine, allowing me to feel the contraction of my back extensors under his thumbs as I arched back and forth on top of him. I rose to my toes and pressed my hands on my knees, my arms pressing my breasts together as I rode him, all the while continuing to watch the scene in front of me unfold.

Chapter 5

Luckily, I-95 was quiet so late at night, so we safely navigated our way home, even though I had my hand down Manny's pants and his seeking hands kept my skirt pushed up around my waist. With his pants still unzipped, he pressed me against our front door, and I thought we might have sex right there standing up. But, then he fumbled with the keys, and we made our way inside. In an unusual side-crawl/make-out that looked like it was choreographed for a music video, we made our way up the stairs. At every wall on our way to the bedroom, Manny pressed me against it or I pressed him, mouths searching and hands discarding clothing. We were like pinballs bouncing off the walls of our condo, becoming progressively more naked in the process. We found our way to our bed and had wild, frantic sex. And again the next morning. And again before I left for work.

I couldn't get the scene from the club out of my mind. I kept replaying the sexy bar games and inventing my own far more scandalous versions in my head. I imagined a set-up akin to an on-stage magician. Three women laid on tables on the stage. A curtain hung from the ceiling so that they could not see what was happening on the lower half of their bodies. Their partners had to identify their lady only through oral sex. Oh, the fun! And maybe the women had to guess their partner by guessing which one of the men, number one, number two, or number three, was their guy.

And then the men were laying down and the women are blindfolded, and the game was repeated. *Can you identify your man just by the feeling of his penis in your mouth? Can you identify your lady by the way your penis feels in her mouth?* Oh, the excitement!

Or, what if it was just one woman lying behind the curtain? And a line of gentlemen was assembled to perform oral sex on this one woman. Now, in this scenario, the men are not trying to guess anything. They are competing to execute the most pleasureful oral sex. The woman lays there, being pleasured by each man. She cannot see their faces because: curtain. She holds a buzzer, used when she wants to excuse a man. She chooses the winner solely on her level of satisfaction. And the winner has sex with her! Maybe still with the curtain separating them, or maybe she sees his face. The possibilities were endless.

I didn't share my fantasies with Manny, but I was certain he was running a parallel set in his own mind. We both had sex on the brain and our hands on each other. When it came to whether or not we would be attending the club again, we needed no conversations to assert our intentions. We would be going back early and often. It was, hands down, the most fun we had ever had together.

Just three weeks after our best night ever, we sat at opposite ends of the couch watching Seinfeld reruns. Manny ate chips, and I perused sewing blogs looking for new purse patterns. During a commercial break there was a teaser for the Philly evening news.

"Local Sex Club Shut Down for L&I Violations."

We turned to each other, aghast, both thinking the same thing, but neither daring to utter it aloud. *It couldn't be.*

During the remainder of the show, we alternated between

tensely sitting and flustered pacing, freezing every time it broke for commercial, straining our ears and eyes to absorb every clue from each news promo. We demonstrated the vigilance and confusion that many people experience watching the returns on election night, as if our fate hung in the balance.

And then, the truth: it was our beloved club. As soon as we saw the *Señor Rattler's Cantina* sign, I sucked in a huge breath that felt like ice wind. I felt the full surface area of each alveolus as my capillaries snapped and sizzled like frozen little twigs.

Immediately we checked the old school message board linked to the club's website. Other members (later I found out the club boasted a membership of 8000 couples and hundreds of singles before it closed) were posting right after the news story. Many promised that they would not let the legacy of the club die here, that they would fight to reopen. There was much outrage. There was much disbelief. But, after months, there was still no chance the owners would be able to, or even any longer were interested in, reopening the club.

And then, after we had almost surrendered hope, we saw a post about a great new club that had opened farther away from the city! And they were hosting a sexy back to school party! And yippee, I looked adorable in pigtails!

We cleared our schedules in order to attend. There was no membership fee, which made sense because it was brand new, and we assumed we would just pay a cover at the door. We were so excited as we approached. It was opposite the direction of the city and the traffic was nonexistent. Wow, I thought, if this works out, this is going to be great. It's even closer to us, and the drive is so easy!

When we pulled into a parking lot that was as treacherous as ski moguls, my enthusiasm began to wane, quickly. The only building in sight was a ramshackle motel.

"Yeah ..." said Manny, double-checking the address, "this is it."

"Ugh," barely able to access my usual obsessive optimism, "I guess we could check it out …" my voice trailed off as I looked at the black woods surrounding the building. This would make a great on-location shoot for a horror movie. We could also be putting ourselves in a situation to become the next riveting local news story: YOUNG COUPLE MURDERED TRYING TO GET THEIR JOLLIES. That would be such an embarrassing way to die.

I looked at Manny's face. I knew we were both considering just turning around and going home. But we were already there. Plus, my outfit was killer. Hidden under my trench coat, I was wearing a tiny plaid skirt, low on my hips and high on my butt, white stockings, and a miniature white cardigan, tied high and tight under my breasts, which were popping out of said cardigan with the mechanical assistance of a very padded pushup bra. I had never worn a school uniform or even entered a private school, but online searches for "sexy schoolgirl" had provided ample inspiration for my outfit, as well as a low simmering concern for the state of our society.

We nodded at each other. We had come this far. We would continue. He held my hand as I navigated the mogul-like mounds in the parking lot. Manny pushed open the heavy, metal door and we walked inside. We were barely over the threshold when the door closed behind us with a screech and a slam, announcing our arrival. My eyes adjusted to the darkness, the dingy streetlights outside now seeming downright luminescent in comparison to the dusty lightbulbs that hung dubiously from the sagging ceiling. An old man, indisputably a local, drank a draft beer at the bar. He looked at us briefly and turned back to the blurry TV. Down the bar from him, a man and a woman were perched on barstools, their jumpy eagerness an easy tell that they were the organizers of the event. The door was barely closed before the male organizer bounded from his chair and rushed to greet us. He was eager to play the role of party host, so eager that I ascertained we must be the first guests to ever attend.

I wished we had just turned around in the parking lot. We feigned interest but could not muster enthusiasm while the host welcomed us and excitedly shared all of his plans for the place, including leading us up narrow, rickety stairs to show us the tiny, dirty motel rooms that he planned to convert to playrooms.

Minutes after we arrived, the door swung shut behind us again, having hastily bid our hosts (and the old dude at the bar) farewell and excusing ourselves. I stomped to the car indignantly and awkwardly in my platform heels, yanking out one pigtail and then the other. *I guess that's what we get for trying to find a sex club in Allentown.* Clearly, fun wasn't in the cards for us, so we got back to the work of being responsible adults.

Manny and I did all the mainstream things that were expected of us. He ran his parents' business. I ran my business. At twenty-three, I had started my own skating organization, and soon it had me on the ice seven days a week. And I stopped my commute to the gym in New Jersey. We had babies. For the first year after each of them were born, I was at my rink in Philadelphia and other skating rinks all around the country with a baby on my back. We had paid off our mortgages and had held onto the condo, per our first five-year plan, and had developed a reputation as gracious and reliable landlords. Most often, when we had a tenant move out, they recommended a friend to move in. In all the years we had owned it, it had only sat empty for a couple weeks. We were undeniably meeting the markers of adulthood.

I had competed as a singles skater, but my main love, and the discipline I pursued through university, was synchronized skating. Twelve to sixteen skaters on the ice seamlessly and simultaneously executing every movement, it combines the loveliest edge work of ice dancing with formations that fully appeal to my geometric and symmetrical way of thinking. Even though synchronized skating was big in Manitoba, mostly due to my mom starting the first organization there when I was a toddler, people in the Philadelphia area had barely heard of it. Although my twelve original skaters could skate, few of them had any competitive individual experience, and none of them had ever participated in synchronized skating. I had to teach parents and skaters about the sport, train the skaters technically, choose music and costumes, create choreography, negotiate ice times and rates with the rink, and learn the US rules and terminology for a sport I had learned and coached in Canada. I also had the rare experience of recruiting for a sport no one knew existed. Everyone was familiar with singles, pairs, and ice dancing, but unless people knew someone who has competed in synchronized skating, they were always surprised to hear that it was even a thing.

Like synchronized swimming ... but the water is frozen, I joked, part of my sales pitch.

I needed bodies. For many years, that was my main concern when fielding teams: get enough skaters. I brought skaters up from my beginner teams to much higher levels and trained them like crazy and several times even qualified for Nationals. My main goal was to spot potential. And I fell in love with potential. If I placed skaters where their work ethic dictated, they would excel, but I would not have enough athletes to field my highest teams. Instead, I placed them with rose-colored glasses, at the level where they could perform if all the stars aligned and they decided to train with the intensity of Michael Phelps. For this reason, I often suffered the heartbreak of investing in unrealized potential.

I labored to make my organization one of the best in the country, but the reality was that, for many of the families, this was just one of the many activities on their child's docket. Each season there were a handful of families with higher aspirations, and I pledged to them that I would work harder to try to bridge the gap. I spent hours reviewing practice video and planning each training session. I re-choreographed to make it easier when they did not practice enough on their own. I insisted the athletes perform and I taught them how to do so. I made every program as entertaining as possible, and my athletes could most often pull it off. What they lacked in technical experience they made up for in performance value. Many coaches created beautiful programs; mine were clever.

Skating and skaters are high pressure, but nothing compared to skating parents. I had a combined role of saleswoman, accountant, school principal, lobbyist, strength coach, sports psychologist, marketing expert, friend, mentor, and choreographer. Some thought I was too tough on their kid. Still, others thought I was too soft to ever be successful. Everyone required something different from me in order to commit to my organization, and I committed to being everything for everybody.

Some of it was comical, but time-consuming, like the mom at the beginning who insisted that we promote the fact that we were "Philadelphia's First" youth synchronized skating team, because Philly was the home to many of the "firsts" in the country, like the first library, the first hospital, and the first daily newspaper. No matter how many times I explained to her that being the first in Philly was different than being the first in the country, she didn't get it. She was convinced we were missing a massive opportunity and that I was ineptly short-sighted.

There was the mom who tried to plan extra practices for the team when I was out of town. After far too many seasons of her trying to sabotage me, but me never turning her daughter away, she took her to another team, and they medaled at Nationals the first season she left. I was at home refreshing the scores online and the moment they were posted, my phone rang. Her name showed on the caller ID. I jumped from my chair as a glacier slid down the slope of my trachea into my chest, breast to breast, icing the upper lobes of each lung. I stood staring at the phone, each ring seemingly louder as if she were amping herself up to jump through the phone if I refused to answer. A biting breeze rose off the mass of ice, back up my throat, through the roof of my mouth, burning behind my eyes. I shut them tightly. The ringing stopped, but it would be another ten years before I could think of that moment without feeling the icy pain between my temples.

Every season, there were girls who lied to their parents about things I said in order to get sympathy and to get in their parents' good graces in relation to another situation but didn't realize while taking the heat off themselves they put me in the impossible situation of regaining trust with their parents after their slander. Many times, skaters confided in me that they did not feel strong enough to be on the roster, but because their parents were footing the bill, they told them that they were heartbroken about not being able to skate. So, in these countless situations, I was left to try to rebuild a relationship with a kid I couldn't trust and stay on the good side of parents who didn't trust me.

There was the dad who took issue with my unpaid, four-week maternity leave after Jack's birth. He was a doctor and found it flagrantly irresponsible that I had two other coaches covering the teams' practices during that time. He insisted that he *never* left his business in the hands of anyone else after the birth of his children. Regrettably, I was too deep in my nursing fog and postpartum confusion to realize at that moment I should have pointed out to him that he had also *never pushed a baby out of his fucking vagina.*

Jack flew out of mine after only two pushes. Well, actually after 34 hours of unmedicated labor, and just a few minutes after my midwife told me I was only four centimeters dilated and assured me the baby would be born by "dinner time." I looked at the clock—10:30 a.m. I spent five minutes silently hoping that someone would just shoot me with an elephant tranquilizer so I could get out of the whole ordeal, then inexplicably, started grunting on my hands and knees which caused my midwife to ask, "Honey, are you pushing?"

I looked over my shoulder and said, "I don't know. Can I?" When the contraction was over, she flipped me onto my back and checked my cervix.

"Ten centimeters!" she exclaimed.

Then, he flew out after only two pushes.

Luke was born twenty-two months later, carefully planned to coincide with a lull in my skating season. By this point, the daughter of the dad who had given me a hard time about my maternity leave had graduated, but he had been replaced by a mother who wrote a thesis on the back of her contract every season about how she disagreed with every decision I made but still paid to have her daughter on the team. She never signed the contract, and she continued to talk behind my back all season, spreading rumors about me getting other coaches to do my work and stealing the credit. My anxiety increased any time she would walk in the rink, my heart pounding so hard that it plugged my ears and her eyes burning into my back for the duration of every practice. I smiled eagerly when I saw her, begging some invisible force that someday she would like me, and this excruciating stress would fade away. I spent my days creating choreography for the skaters while my own personal choreography was constantly sidestepping any reason she could use to stage a coup.

Jack had been tiny at birth, and hence, I let him nurse on-demand in those early days, forming a habit that led into the later days and all the nights. When I got pregnant with Luke, Jack was still nursing every two hours during the day and every forty-five minutes at night. Intent on improving upon chronic sleeplessness, we were determined to not repeat the same breast-feeding pattern. Instead of nursing him to sleep, I planned to stop nursing Luke when he was obviously sleepy, then walk or sway with him until he fell asleep. Then we would lay him gently in the crib in our bedroom and attempt an army crawl to escape. But, as soon as he was set down or, best case scenario, when we were face-down on the carpet, halfway out of the room, he screamed as if he had been set on fire.

The only way I could get Jack and Luke to sleep at the same time was to strap them both to my body in baby carriers and vacuum the house. I attempted this multiple times a day. If it was successful, I would lay down and extricate myself from the baby slings with a dexterity that rivaled that of Catherine Zeta-Jones in *Entrapment*, but with none of the sexiness. Only sometimes they slept, so often I held two crying babies, standing on extremely clean carpets, and looking towards the door, thinking, *when is the* real *mom coming home? This can't be up to me to deal with. I am clearly* not equipped *to handle this.* Just as often, I bundled up both those babies and took them to the rink with me. Luke was on my back and Jack was watched in the rink's upstairs lounge by a revolving door of gracious skating moms. I traveled across the country to competitions every other weekend in the fall and winter, and if the babe was still nursing, he would join me, while Manny's mom watched the remaining child at home, and Manny picked up extra shifts at the restaurant to cover her absence. When I got home, the re-entry period was always intense, the babies not having seen either parent for days.

During a regular week, Manny didn't get home until 9:30 or 10:00 each night. He was still diligently working at the restaurant, but his heart was not in it. What he had always wanted to do but had pushed aside in favor of supporting the family business was to trade in the stock market. When Manny had the opportunity to train under a friend who was a successful trader and just starting a new hedge fund, I pushed him to do it. I didn't know how much longer I could handle his late nights. I had one of my most stressful groups of skating parents, and my nerves were fried. It would be a long period of transition, but I needed to know there was a light at the end of the tunnel. He worried that his absence would increase the workload on everyone else at the restaurant, but I pleaded with him to consider the workload that was already on us. My job was stressful and physically demanding and competitive, but I truly loved it. I wanted him to have a job he loved, as well. He was terrified to talk to his parents about it, distressed that they would see this move as an indicator of a decrease in loyalty to them.

"Babe, nothing is more important to your parents than family, right?" I asked.

"Exactly," he said, exasperated, thinking that I was proving his point.

"This," I motioned around us, to the infant on my hip and the toddler eating frozen peas at the table, "this is your family, too. We need you to do this."

Finally, he understood that the opportunity for him to change careers and have a schedule that suited us was one that we couldn't pass up. Within weeks, he had shifted his schedule, working four days a week at the restaurant and spending two days a week, unpaid, training under his mentor and friend.

I could now imagine a break on the horizon, a relief in the difficulty. Perhaps in a few months, Manny would be fully transitioned to his new schedule. Maybe he would be home by 5:00 p.m. Maybe Luke would be sleeping through the night. But things got worse.

Manny's back had been hurting him since Luke was born. He had thrown out his lower back in sports many times, but this was different. It was a deep, piercing pain between his shoulder blades. He assumed it was related to carrying a toddler and a baby, and he followed his own rehab plan to try to get some relief. It didn't get better. It just got worse. When Luke was five months old, it was finally so excruciating that Manny decided to see a doctor.

An MRI showed a tumor in his T4 vertebra.

My mom was on the next plane to Philadelphia, planning to stay with us while we went through the next rounds of tests. She tended to the kids and tended to Manny. I tried to put out fires at work and cover my teams so I could stay home during the upcoming competition. The next month involved scans, blood work, a 24-hour urine collection for testing, and a lot of waiting. Manny's usually olive complexion was waxy and pale, blanched from fear. He moved through our house like a zombie, and I moved at twice my usual speed.

Finally, after ruling out every possible type of cancer, doctors concluded that it was an osteoid osteoma. This type of tumor was benign but puzzling to every doctor we saw because it was extremely rare to find in the spine. It was usually found in long bones, like the femur. Always painful, the location of Manny's case made it increasingly so. The mass took up a third of the vertebral body in which it had grown, essentially creating a compression fracture, causing pain to radiate from his spine, around his rib cage, to his chest. Despite the threat of chronic pain, we were told we should not attempt an excision. The location and risks of the surgery could cause more issues with mobility than the effects of the tumor. He was not limited in activity, but he had to figure out a way to deal with the incessant pain. Doctors had little advice for him except to take aspirin to try to manage the discomfort. The unusual characteristic of an osteoid osteoma was that the pain intensified during sleep. For a year after his tumor diagnosis, he had an activity to keep him busy during his nighttime pain and sleeplessness. In an attempt to help Luke sleep, Manny walked in the dark, with Luke's head nestled against his shoulder, up and down our hallway, every night, all night long.

Chapter 6

I knew Manny's pain was there, but for the next few years, I didn't hear or think much about it. Our life became a daily triage. As Luke started sleeping at night, his days became nearly impossible. Things as simple as putting the wrong sock on first caused epic meltdowns that lasted hours. If he became hungry or overtired, there was no going back. It was a matter of *try again tomorrow*.

Jack, showing resourcefulness even as a toddler, found noise-canceling headphones that Manny used for mowing the lawn and put them on every time Luke had a tantrum. Afterwards, Manny would often ask me what started it. I'd stare at him blankly, having no clue, like I'd just experienced a trés mal seizure.

Jack was a very thematic kid, becoming obsessed with one thing after another, fire trucks, construction, sports. When he was in the middle of one of his longest obsessions, marine biology, we learned that the frilled shark had the longest gestation period of any invertebrate, three and a half years. And then everything about Luke made sense. He had simply expected to be a frilled shark in this incarnation. To be born after a mere nine months of gestation was not acceptable. As a result of being booted from the womb prematurely, he had to live the first three years of life on my hip. When he got a little older, he matter-of-factly informed us that he was able to hear anyone in the world speaking at any time. All he had to do was think about them. I gave birth to a clairaudient frilled shark —like I said, it all made perfect sense.

Even though our experiences in the first few years of parent-hood threatened to kill us, either from accidents caused by sleep deprivation, or tumors, or slow-reaction time with crazed sports parents, we somehow still agreed that we wanted more children. By the time Luke was three, he showed signs of being ready to step out of his intense neediness, and we thought being a big brother may give him a space to grow into. Many people cautioned us that Luke would be jealous if we had another baby, but my mom thought the opposite. "You will never have to worry about that baby if Luke is in the room," she said. "He will watch them like a hawk."

And it was true. Our sensitive little frilled shark was growing into an intensely thoughtful little boy. If a friend left a toy at our house, Luke would be the first to notice and put it in a safe place. And then he would remind me to take it if I was going to see the friend's mom. When I told him I was pregnant, his eyes got wide. He put his hand on my belly, paused for a few seconds, then looked up at me and said, with certainty, "That baby really likes me."

And the baby did really like him. With blond curls, amber eyes, and golden skin, Niko was like sunshine from concentrate. Jack and Luke were instantly enamored and would fight over who got to kiss him first each morning. Resembling my youngest brother, who looked like a big, huggable Canadian lumberjack, by the time Niko was six months old, he was as big as the other boys had been on their second birthdays. He was a cuddly mass of pure love.

Even with this new little love monster, every day was a blur but felt a hundred years long. Manny was trading full-time, and we were master tag-team parents. He would come in; I would go out. He left the house at 7:00 a.m. and walked in the door at 5:00 p.m., a huge improvement over his 10:00 p.m. return when he had been running the restaurant. He was finally doing a job he loved, but it came with intense pressure. Some of his trades were shorts, betting against a stock. Even lifetime traders think short-sellers are a special kind of crazy.

I continued to work, two steps forward, one step back, struggling to keep the numbers to field my teams every year. Finally, I saw an opportunity for more support and proposed a merger with another organization, run by my friend Kati. Their full docket of lower-level teams fit perfectly with my higher teams. The size of my organization nearly tripled overnight. With it, I got an expanded coaching staff and Kati as my co-director. I could place skaters more appropriately on team levels, and even if many walked, I would still have enough skaters to maintain our teams. I could finally coach the way I wanted to coach without begging people to stay or placing them where they didn't belong. As a bonus, our main practice rink was five minutes from my house. I pinched myself at my good fortune.

While I had increased support, my responsibilities also increased. I was now at the rink more than ever. We went from busy to busier. Even so, Manny and I still met up a couple times a week for sex. The boys all slept in our room, so we would rendezvous on the couch or in the guest room. We would start with oral, a little back and forth, then I would get on top and come two to three times, then he would finish from behind. Afterwards, he would get a snack and I would go to bed, falling asleep quickly and deeply, as if I could average out his sleepless-ness. One time we forgot our vibrator in the guest room, and the next day, I heard Luke declaring, with pomp and circumstance, "I haaaave the trophy!" I peeked around the corner and saw him hoisting the dildo over his head, with the pride of an Olympic torch carrier.

Even after we learned to safely hide our sex toys, our days

seemed like one long, drawn-out episode of *Punk'd*, crazy occurrence after crazy occurrence. Some days it all seemed too intense and persistent *to not be orchestrated*. Toys would be dumped immediately after tidying. Ready to walk out the door, one child would pull down his pants and pee on the floor, and then belly flop on the puddle in an attempt to clean it up with his clothes. Tandem freakouts would occur in a manner that I was certain was choreographed.

The threat of being recorded by hidden camera and the promise that Ashton Kutcher may pop out from around the corner made me determined to be the perfect modern mother. This meant I spent most of my time and energy trying not to yell at my kids. All generations prior to mine considered yelling to be their form of "gentle discipline," but Generation X really upped the ante. One friend even went as far as to tell me that yelling was "the new spanking." It sounded impossibly difficult to parent without yelling, so of course I tried it. I even challenged myself to go a whole year without yelling.

I could make it a few days. Several times I would get as far as twenty days and then lose it. The most memorable time I broke my no-yelling streak was when I took the boys on vacation to visit my parents' lake house in Canada without Manny. On this vacation, Jack and Luke, already potty trained for practically a hundred years, kept shitting in their pants.

There is more than one way a kid can shit in their pants. There is the macro shit, where the child needs a bath and you seriously consider throwing away the clothing. Then, there is the micro shit, and if you are a total rookie you will think this kind is better and maybe even give it a cute nickname like "shart."

A shart does not mean they are done. It means they have barely begun. The rest of the shit is harbored inside a child who has shown total disregard for their bodily functions that day. So my boys just kept shitting in their pants, three or four times a day each. For a week. And no, they were not ill.

They were effervescent with wellness.

My cousin Jordelle was visiting with her two children. As far as I could tell 0 percent of her children were shitting in their pants. After a week of this, solo parenting, and trying to discreetly handle the cleanup and laundry around everyone, I yelled at my boys. I really, really yelled at them.

And I then I quit the challenge for good. Instead of trying to reduce the frequency of my yelling, I resolved to simply apologize to the boys after I yelled. Still, for years I told myself and others that I simply hated yelling at my kids, until one day when I was holding an enormous, cumbersome car seat, waiting for Niko to open the car door for me. He was bouncing around in the car, oblivious to my request, and in that moment I stayed calm. I saw the joy in his face, and I realized that my request had not registered with him in the slightest. He did not know I was standing there waiting for him.

"Hey, buddy."

He looked and saw me standing there and scrambled to open the door.

"Sorry, Mom."

Rationally, this is a much better scenario than yelling at him, but in that moment, I noticed something.

I felt like a junkie who had just missed a hit.

Clearly, my body was ramping up for the expected surge of endorphins, and when it didn't come, I felt physically uncomfortable.

I missed the physical sensation that accompanied yelling.

I missed yelling.

Cognitively, ethically? I hated yelling. *But physically, physiologically?* My body loved yelling.

One of my superpowers is attracting brilliant friends. One of them is Sheila, and one day as we sat at the creek and our children waded, looking for tadpoles, I mentioned that my yelling was probably screwing up my kids.

"Oh, yeah, you are definitely screwing up your kids," she agreed, skipping a rock on the water. "But you're also rocking it at the same time. That thing that you think you are rocking, well, that's probably what's screwing them up. And that thing you think will screw them up?" She looked me in the eye with certainty and said, "Well, that's probably what will make them super dope."

I considered what she was saying. I considered that maybe there wasn't much value in judging my parenting play-by-play. The timing was helpful because at this point the judging system for figure skating had changed. No longer was perfection indicated by a 6.0. The new highest score was infinity.

When my boys became school-aged I could think of no good reason to send them to school, so I didn't.

I homeschooled, using a blend of unschooling and Waldorf education. I was introduced to Waldorf when Jack was a year old, and I quickly implemented many of the recommendations in our home. Wooden toys, no screen time, baking our own bread, lots of time outside in nature, and so much fucking humming. Parents and teachers are encouraged to memorize stories instead of reading them and sing songs instead of playing recorded music. When you've repeated the same cleanup song forty times and the cleanup is not yet finished because your brain is numb and your voice is tired, you hum. If you think you know anything about Waldorf, triple the amount of humming you'd assume occurs and still, you are not even close.

Humming aside, I was grateful for it, as I was the perfect overachieving candidate to become a Baby Einstein/My Baby Can Read Mom when I encountered Waldorf. And there was something remarkably soothing about slowing down, baking bread from scratch, singing to my babies, and having them participate in household chores. Because, really, nothing makes me prouder than child labor.

We were part of a big homeschool community; longtime friends and new friends had enthusiastically embraced the homeschool trend. We had playgroups and rock-climbing classes. I started a wilderness school and brought in an instructor trained by The Tracker Tom Brown who taught the children how to build shelters, start a fire with a bow drill, and filter water with cattails and sand. I even hired a Lego tutor, who used the bricks to teach the boys multiplication and division, as well as building to scale and building in symmetry.

In addition to building a usable chess set out of Lego pieces, my preschoolers grew their own vegetables. Anything we could not grow ourselves was delivered by farmers I knew personally. This simpler, back to the earth living made me feel connected to some of my favorite stories from my grandmothers, raised on the Canadian Prairies. For most of their lives, they hung all their laundry out, even when temperatures plunged to minus forty. I loved hearing how my Grandma Yvonne would bring in the cloth diapers, frozen like little blocks of wood, and put them on the wood stove to soften them for her babies. And how she always slept with her babies cuddled close to her chest because their stone house was much too cold for a baby to safely sleep on their own.

My Grandma Betty told me how her mom would bring in her dad's frozen trousers and stand them upright in the corner of the kitchen, like a parlor trick, until they melted and fell to the floor. I asked her repeatedly to tell me the story of how she saved to buy her own pair of skates. She was twelve years old in 1946 and idolized Barbara Ann Scott, who would go on to win Canada's only women's Olympic gold only two years later. My grandma had an older sister and five brothers who all played hockey. There were plenty of pairs of brown or black skates kicking around her house, but she desperately wanted white skates so she could feel like a true figure skater. There was no skating coach around, so she and her friends taught themselves. She saved her babysitting money, twenty-five cents a night, until she had the required $13.98 to purchase the skates from the Eaton's catalogue. Three times a week at 8:00 p.m., the mail was delivered by train to her little town. Her Aunt Anne was the postmistress and called her on the evening they arrived. I picture my grandma running across town in the dark in her pajamas to get those precious skates, but each time I tell her that, she assures me that she would have been dressed properly, "Because it was wintertime, you know."

I was glad to have modern conveniences and one-day shipping, but I thought if my grandmothers had managed to be so self-sufficient, even during Canadian winters, I could surely do it in a climate that rarely got under freezing. My craving for a greater understanding of what my grandparents had been through, or maybe even ancestors further back, compelled me to persuade Manny to travel to Maine for a long weekend where we paid top dollar to stay in a tent and learn how to live off the grid. We were shown how to identify medicinal herbs and forage for our dinner. We learned the delicate art of water conservation and helped to remove chunks of ice from the icehouse to place in our coolers during our stay. We took all our trash out with us, as they had no garbage collection on site.

Our hosts had built their own tiny house. We hadn't heard of a tiny house before this and *whoa*, it was tiny, smaller than our master bathroom. Our kids still talk about it. Even the doorways were built short, a suggestion from Grandfather, the indigenous elder who taught them. It was important to him that people were forced to bow as they entered their homes, as a method of keeping themselves humble. And humbled I was, every single time I entered their home and hit my head on the door frame.

Upon arriving home, extremely humbled and slightly concussed, I wanted to implement everything we had learned. I wanted to convert our shower to solar-heated hot water. I wanted to gather rainwater for hand washing. I spent weeks researching and prototyping a reusable alternative to toilet paper and realized that the best I could do was rinse down with a squirt bottle. We expanded our garden, and we had each of our boys tend their own vegetable bed. I canned forty quarts of tomatoes in one summer. *Radical Homesteading* and *The Complete Book of Self-Sufficiency* became my bibles. I seriously considered the daily time commitment required to start a dairy cow share with friends, and I got a little teary-eyed every time Manny refused to even get a goat. I was this close to building an outhouse in the back yard with a composting toilet because, I mean, who does not want to turn their shit into blueberries? Then Manny vetoed that, too.

Manny's experience with food differed from that of our own children. Even though they ran a restaurant, his mom cooked from scratch every day of his life. His mother's fear of her children starving drove her to allow Manny and his brothers to eat whatever they wanted to eat, always making separate meals based on their preferences at the moment. This even included permission to add chocolate syrup to any "plain" cereal to make it more palatable. I have never been given the full dossier, but I know Frosted Flakes is one of the cereals that was considered "plain." I guessed it was because it wasn't chocolate and didn't contain marshmallow bits. I had married a grown man with a child's taste buds, suspicious of any food that did not come out of a box. To him, "real" food was processed, labeled, and underwent quality control to assure that it consistently tasted the same. Early on in our relationship, he complained to me that something was different about his Cocoa Puffs. He insisted something had changed, even though the packaging remained exactly the same. He brought it up every day and night (as cereal was his favorite bedtime snack).

"They changed something ... I just know they did," he mused.

He was insistent, and I was amused, so I reached out to General Mills for more information. They quickly confirmed via email that they had, in fact, started adding a small amount of whole grain flour in the production of Cocoa Puffs. And they sent us a whole lot of coupons.

Manny felt vindicated, certain that it was the attempt to make the food healthier that resulted in the reduction in enjoyment. Healthy food could not be trusted. He maintained that taste was always sacrificed with a healthier option, and he was not willing to sacrifice taste for anything. I eventually got him to switch to organic milk by scratching the expiration date off his regular milk and refilling the gallon with organic milk for weeks. Afterwards I asked him if he had noticed a difference. He had not. I confessed my scheme and he was converted, albeit reluctantly. The more committed I became to eating local, organic food, the more diligent Manny became in avoiding it at all costs in private, but he maintained the facade of a unified front for the kids.

Together, we indoctrinated them to believe that boxed cereals with colorful graphics were for grown-ups and Halloween was a holiday where children collected candies for their fathers. Manny hid his junk food high in the pantry and in front of the boys he ate—or pretended to eat—the healthier option served to them.

Local farmers would drop off their food at our house, and we'd store it in one of our three freezers. Friends, family, and total strangers would come and pick up their share. It was a mini-depot compared to the local food operation being managed by my friend, Megan. In case of apocalypse, everyone needn't worry. If Megan's porch remained unscathed, we'd all be fine.

Between our deliveries, eggs from our chickens, veggies, and berries from our garden, and visits to Megan's porch, I would only go to the grocery store once every six weeks. This was a part of my larger commitment to reducing our impact on the earth. I made our own cleaning products, used washable cloths for cleaning and cloth napkins at every meal. I dried all our laundry on the clothesline, in almost all weather. We cloth diapered of course, but much of the time I practiced elimination communication with our babies, which basically meant I developed supersonic hearing and could detect a change in their breathing patterns, even from another room, drop what I was doing, scoop them up, and hold them over the potty so they could do their business.

My mom always made it clear that very few things were

actually rocket science. The first time I recall her telling me this was when she was standing on the dining room table, holding a chandelier. I had returned home from school to find her there, and I was wondering what in the world she was doing. She was installing it, she told me. *It's not rocket science.* It had been sitting in the box for weeks, and she wanted it up and my dad hadn't done it yet, so she was just going to do it herself.

"So, you're like the Little Red Hen?" I asked.

"Precisely."

I nodded and retreated to my bedroom, as is customary for any self-respecting adolescent after a brief interaction with a family member.

This DIY sensibility continued in my family. It grew, actually, and looking back I can safely say that it began to border on the insensible. The list of injuries we incurred by doing things ourselves without the right equipment or training got longer each year. Manny and I used to fix our own appliances—until I lost a game of tug-of-war with a washing machine tower and ended up in the ER for stitches in my forehead, during a snowstorm, on Boxing Day.

I never had an awareness that this wasn't the way for everyone until my best friend's husband pointed it out in a way I couldn't forget. Rebekah's husband, Anthony, was curious about the part of Canada I came from. When I told him I was from Manitoba, he was very excited. He was a big hockey fan and knew all about Winnipeg, the story about how the Jets left and how the Jets returned. He had a lot of love for Manitoba.

Anthony was always impressed with my projects, noticing them and then remarking to Rebekah, "Bek, did you see what Ashleigh did/sewed/made?" But it was the time that they were having trouble with their aggressive roosters that my stock really rose in his eyes. In Maine, I had been taught how to process a chicken. Anthony and Rebekah's roosters had been attacking their kids, who were still quite young. They could find no one to adopt these little bantam roosters because bantam roosters are notoriously obnoxious. They fully exhibit the Napoleon Complex. And so, the day I picked up his troublesome roosters and fed them to my kids for dinner, he offered what would instantly become my favorite compliment of all time.

"That Ashleigh sure is a Manitoba Woman."

Chapter 7

I loved being pregnant. I felt strong and healthy, and productive. There is nothing quite like checking "growing a human" off the to-do list every day.

I also felt sexy. I hadn't actually worked out since before Luke was born, but I spent every waking hour on the ice, hauling wheelbarrows full of garden soil, or wrangling children, so I was slim and muscular. I loved the way pregnancy changed my body, softening it, giving me curves where previously there had been edges. Over the years, Manny would regularly bring up our old club experience, reminiscing, dreaming how sometime, someday, in another lifetime, maybe we would have that much fun again. But when I was pregnant, it was I who insisted that it was time to look for a new club. We should have that much fun again this weekend, tonight, right at this moment. *Yesterday, goddamnit. Take me to a sex club yesterday.*

"Are you kidding me?" he would ask. "Seriously, if I took you to a club with that belly, I would be arrested. We should both be arrested." He'd laugh, picturing it. It was a funny image, true. Regardless of the fact that I also thought it was a sexy image, he would not entertain the idea of escorting me to a sex club, even though my libido was high, and even though I resorted to begging.

Our lives felt like a pressure cooker, but we thought that it would someday pass. We thought it would get easier when our boys got a little older, and it did—sort of. The physical demands of parenting eased as the boys gained more independence. For a whole decade I had been pregnant, or nursing, or both. One night when I nursed Niko before bed just before his first birthday, I decided I was done nursing at night. When he woke to nurse that night, I told him, "No more milky when it's dark out." I pointed out the window.

"Dawtch ..." he repeated, looking longingly toward the sky, willing the sun to rise. Then he turned over and went back to sleep. He continued to nurse well into his toddler years, but this was the end of middle-of-the-night wakeups for everyone besides Manny. There had been the chance that the tumor would resolve on its own; it did in a percentage of cases. But his case was not one of those cases. The size had remained constant, and the pain often intensified, giving him bouts of intense pain followed by the reprieve of moderate pain. He had resigned himself to never sleeping soundly again.

Soon Niko seemed like he could handle a sleepover with the big boys, and Manny and I decided to take a weekend trip to the Pocono Mountains. The Poconos visitors' bureau website promised romance and relaxation. Just what we needed! On the drive up, I eagerly anticipated walks in nature and cuddling on the balcony, overlooking the expanse of mountains, forest, and lakes. I expected we would see other couples deeply appreciating their time together and we would all share in the collective enthusiasm. What we got was an empty resort. As we sat at dinner, the only people in the restaurant, I wondered why our silence felt so awkward. We had been out for dinner before. And then I realized, we always invited friends to come with us. We hadn't sat at a dinner table alone together in years.

"What do you want to do?" I asked.

"I don't know. What do you want to do?" Manny replied, smiling, looking up briefly from his phone.

I stared out at the golf course, my diaphragm stiffening. It crackled, icing up like the surface of a lake in winter. I tried to take a deep breath and the ice thickened.

Afterwards we walked back to the room, out in the fresh evening air. I hoped the cool breeze would help me get a comfortable breath. I reached for Manny's hand and it felt big and clumsy in mine.

I touched nearly a hundred hands a week: the hands of my boys and their friends, wiping before a snack, wiping after a snack, gently extracting a splinter, clipping fingernails, holding tightly in a parking lot. The hands of my skaters, to calm them after a fall, to adjust their grip on a teammate's shoulder, to ensure they were really listening when I told them something important, to close every practice, in a circle, with skaters wiggling to be the closest to me, smiling up at me as they slid their hand into mine.

"When was the last time we held hands?" I asked Manny. He shrugged.

I tried for another deep breath, but a stench pierced between my eyes. "Skunk!" I choked.

"Ugh, that's terrible!" We dropped hands and both broke out in a run, heading for the hotel.

It was hard to get the sting out of our noses and our eyes, even after we arrived back at the room. We both fell onto the king-sized bed. I lay, wondering if he would reach for me. Instead he reached for the TV remote. Every second the bed got wider and my heart pounded louder. Soon the sound plugged my ears. I got up and went to the bathroom.

My arms hung at my sides as I studied my face in the mirror. My pale skin looked grayish, the lines on my forehead deep, my lips drew a tight, horizontal line. My eyelids were heavy, the crease of my eye hard to find. I took a breath that only reached halfway down my lungs. I brushed my teeth. I touched up my makeup. I went back out and asked Manny if he wanted to have sex. We started with oral, back and forth. I got on top, came twice, then he finished from behind. Afterwards I fell asleep to the sound of the TV.

The next morning, we went for brunch at the same restaurant, still deserted. We walked back to the room. We flopped onto the bed. When I saw Manny reaching for the remote, I leaned in to kiss him, circling my hand over his wrist, holding the remote away. We had sex, the same as the night before, the same as always. Afterwards we lay on the bed, looking at our phones in boredom.

"You want to go home early?" I offered.

"Yeah, sure." He shrugged.

We took our two small bags to the car and started the drive back in blinding sunlight. I inhaled, willing my lungs to open, but they wouldn't. The bottom half of my torso was still frozen solid. I hadn't had a good breath all weekend long.

At home we returned to our regular routine. Compared to the awkwardness of being alone together, our tag-team parenting was a well-oiled machine. I would tag in and he would tag out, to work, to bed, or out with our own friends. When Manny returned home at five, I was already on the ice at one of my rinks. His mom was with the boys and she had usually brought dinner from the restaurant or cooked for us. When I got home at eight or nine, I watched practice videos while I heated up dinner, Manny putting the boys to bed while his phone dinged with Twitter updates in the background. There was a certain ease in our partnership, but as we became more skilled in our arrangement of alternating solo parenting, we became even clumsier at parenting in tandem. It was rare to have all five of us home at once. I craved togetherness, but when it did happen, it often felt uncomfortable. The kids didn't know who to go to for help. We didn't know what to do to entertain each other and the three little humans staring eagerly at us. We just putzed around the house, wondering when the fun and togetherness would start.

Oftentimes, if I was home from work on the weekend, Manny took the opportunity to run several errands a day, back and forth, in and out. The transition felt more comfortable for both of us than the inelegant attempts we made at togetherness.

Perhaps this is one of the reasons that we began to bring up our first club experience more regularly. It was the one time we could identify that we had gone out together in search of enjoyment, and we had found it. Everything about going to a sex club seemed that it should have felt awkward and embarrassing, but it had felt natural. Now, hanging around our own house often felt awkward, and the lack of grace, embarrassing.

We wanted something exciting. We wanted something fun.

The old club never reopened, but, unlike our search for another club a decade before, this time only a little searching online led us to several options for traveling parties and two permanent clubs in Philly. We decided to first try the larger one because what we liked best about our previous club experience was the large crowd. We felt there was the possibility for more excitement and definitely less pressure if the club was crowded. Our dismal venture to Allentown also proved that a small crowd was unbearably awkward.

In our searching, I was reminded that the "violations" that were cited in the closure of the old club really amounted to mattresses pushed too close to emergency exits. The City of Philadelphia License and Inspections department only visited after the news anchor snuck in a secret camera. I understood why exits needed to be unobstructed in any public space, but it was clear that the real motivation behind the hidden camera was to provide a sensational story.

This time around, the ease of preparation made it clear that a decade had passed since our last visit. Online shopping provided me with everything I needed. I ordered a half dozen dresses and tried them on at home. I bought tall black boots and sexy heels with straps crisscrossing around my ankles, planning to choose that night, depending on my mood. I ordered a waxing kit and self-tanner. I laughed when I thought about my makeshift outfit from our previous visit, pieced together from the juniors' department with help from my sewing machine. I bought new lingerie that fit perfectly under my chosen dress, a mini-dress from French Connection with a keyhole opening at my chest, and a cross-over skirt that hugged my butt and came even shorter at the front.

On the night of our chosen party, I started getting ready early. Taylor Swift had just released a new album, and I cranked it before getting in the shower and played it on repeat while I dried my hair and curled it into long, golden waves that hung nearly to my waist. I carefully applied my makeup, reminding myself of when I used to get ready to go to the bar in college. But, this time, I wasn't applying body glitter; I was applying colors from a gorgeous organic eyeshadow palette. I spent more time getting myself ready than I would usually spend in a whole week. The time alone felt remarkably indulgent. As I danced to the music blasting through my bathroom, I thought if I squinted and posed at just the right angle, I could pass for a twenty-something globe-trotting party girl. I was sure of it.

We didn't need to find street parking this time. The new club had a private, gated parking lot. It was easy to assume the size of the crowd as we made our way to the end of the large lot to find parking. As new members of the club, we were asked to wait at the entrance for an official greeting and tour from the host couple. Host couples are volunteers who are willing to spend part of their night showing new couples around and the people you go to if you have any questions. They are just like a Walmart greeter who you'll possibly see naked later in your visit.

We stood expectantly at the archway leading from the front hall into the club. Other members passed us as we waited, and we saw the club filling up. It was a huge, warehouse-type space with high ceilings. From where we were standing, we saw a large area with a half wall around it, a covered Jacuzzi, and a huge glass-enclosed shower.

A friendly and outgoing couple approached us, both in their early 50s, with dark hair. Leon and Liza introduced themselves, shook our hands, and asked if we had ever been to a club before. We told them yes, but not for a very long time. We gave the backstory of going to the old club before we were married and how it closed a few weeks after. They were awestruck as if we were a part of ancient swingers lore. We walked past a row of open rooms, each with a different theme. First, a large, wooden X with handcuffs and ankle cuffs. Second, a sex swing that we'd seen advertised in a magazine, but we couldn't think of an inconspicuous place to install it in our house. Third, an OBGYN table, complete with stirrups. That was a fantasy scene that had never, ever occurred to me. I was impressed by the variety.

Leon and Liza were relaxed and welcoming, but still, we were nervous and walked a little stiffly. I grabbed Manny's hand and gave it a squeeze. He squeezed back. On the way to the bar I saw that within the half-walled area was an array of mattresses. They took us to drop our wine off at the bar and I saw a small platform with a dancing pole. On it stood a woman in her 60s, swaying back and forth with her eyes closed, as her husband clapped adorably to the music.

Manny and I were each given a paper bracelet with the number 55, which meant we were the 55th couple to check in at the bar, and we were told to ask for that number when we wanted a drink.

There were big-screen TVs above the bar, playing different types of pornography. They were all muted and the only sound coming from the speakers was the music from the DJ.

Leon and Liza walked us past the buffet table.

"You probably know this, but don't have sex too close to the food," Leon told us.

We nodded and smiled tight smiles. *Obviously, eew.*

We were shown the back bar, with the larger stage and dancing pole. All along the way, every couple we saw gave us a wave, a smile, or a nod, and again I found myself strolling down

Sesame Street. *Suuuunny day, sweeping the cloooouds awaaay ...*
Apparently some things never change.

We walked back through the main room, past the covered
Jacuzzi, and into a back hall.

"These are the private rooms," Liza led us down a hallway,
past the bathrooms and a wall of lockers.

We walked past the linen depot and saw stacks of towels and
sheets, all wrapped in plastic. They were similar to the linens
that were delivered to Manny's parents' restaurant every week. I
desperately wished I could have been a fly on the wall during
the linen service sales meeting when the rep announced to the
company that they had landed the sex club account.

The private rooms were all different, some with bondage
equipment, but most with beds or sex chairs. Again, Manny and
I had looked at these in catalogues, too, but never could find a
place to put these s-shaped furniture pieces that wouldn't
betray to house guests our very private intentions for them.
There were a variety of wall murals, flames, castle scenes,
Mayan art, a buddha, and a cave. Leon showed us how to use
the dimmers on the light switches and let us know the rules of
the door.

"Door closed means you do not want company. Door open
means you are fine with other people coming in," he said.

"And people will just come in?" I asked.

"They sure will." He smiled.

Each room also had a window and a curtain.

"Curtain is up to you. Some people keep it closed." He
motioned to a room with a closed door and closed curtain. "And
some people keep it open," he said, pointing toward a room with
a closed door and a half-open curtain.

Manny and I peered in. There was a man on his back,
completely naked, with a woman on her knees on the floor, also
naked, going down on him.

"What's that?" I pointed to a large room at the end of the
hallway. The door was open. In the middle of the bed was an

enormous, mounted dildo that looked like it needed its own circuit breaker.

"Oh, thaaaat ..." Leon laughed. "That's Liza's favorite. You have to pay a deposit and clean up after you're done."

I then noticed the container of Clorox wipes on the side table.

"This is where she first learned to squirt." Leon added. Liza nodded and laughed silently, her eyes squinting.

"Squirt?" I asked, now very interested. I turned toward Liza. "Really? You can squirt?" She nodded, knowing that Leon would continue with the explanation.

"Oh, yeah," Leon assumed an expert posture, leaning back and crossing his arms, one hand on his chin. "Pretty much every woman can squirt." Manny and I exchanged a wide-eyed look. This was news to us.

"Oh, yeah, definitely," Liza continued, "In fact ..." She choked back a laugh and paused, looking at Leon, who's expression showed that he understood where she was going with this.

"You're not ... you're not going to tell them that now? Are you? We just met these poor people. They don't want to hear about that." He was feigning shock, but I could tell he was ready to play along.

"Oh," Liza's eyes were wide, and her face glowed with excitement, "yeah, I am." She nodded, and her smile widened.

"So, one night, it's late, almost time to get out of here, and we start talking with an *older* set of guests." Liza bat her eyelashes to emphasize the preciousness.

"*So old,*" Leon lowered his head and his shoulders shook from withheld laughter. "They were *sooo old.*"

"Yes, *so old,*" agreed Liza, moving on with the story. "And the sweet old lady tells us that she has never been able to squirt, and it's one of her fantasies."

Leon put his head in his hands as he continued to try to hold back his laughter.

Liza couldn't wait to get the rest out. "So, Leon here, Mr. Nice Guy, offers to *show her.*"

She paused. Manny and I turned abruptly, mouths gaping, to Leon. He stared at us with a sheepish smile.

"*And?!*" I asked, knowing exactly what was coming and also half dying from the suspense.

"And ... I did." Leon shrugged, trying to act modest, but his face fully revealing his pride and the recognition of the inescapable humor of the situation.

"And then he shows the husband, and the husband *makes her squirt, too!*" Liza threw both hands in the air, unable to contain her excitement.

Leon was over his embarrassment and finished off the story, impersonating the sweet, *satisfied*, little old lady, "And she says, *oh, sweetie. That was just the nicest thing to do for us.*"

Manny and I wailed with laughter. I clapped my hands. I pressed one hand on my chest and the other against the wall to keep from doubling over. Leon reddened and shook his head as he laughed. Liza wiped tears from her eyes, barely able to compose herself.

This was the strangest thing I heard in a sex club.

Despite being weird, I was impressed by the commitment, the willingness to help. These were the traits that were usually reserved for sensational neighbors, the reliable, friendly people who would be certain to offer help in any situation. If you locked yourself out in the middle of the night or needed help cleaning a stubborn gutter, these were the kind of people who would hop to it and dig right in.

When we emerged from the back rooms, the crowd had doubled, and the club was packed. We bid Leon and Liza good-bye. We thanked them again for the tour, and I thanked them profusely for the squirting story. Manny and I went to the bar and each got a glass of wine.

"Should we take a walk around?" asked Manny, taking his first sip. I nodded.

As we took our lap around the club, I made eye contact and smiled as we passed people, careful not to look for too long and give the impression we wanted to talk to anyone yet. About a third of the people were paired up with other couples, talking, laughing, or dancing. Another third were dancing with their own partners, and the remaining third were like us, walking around or standing on the periphery of the dance floor, taking it all in.

Some people were there to engage with others. I watched the people around us and made a mental note of the partner they started with, so I could tell when the dynamic changed, and the attention started crossing over to someone from another couple. Usually, it was the women who started it. The foursome would be dancing in a group, and then the women would get closer and touchy. Some started by grabbing the other woman's hand while dancing. Others leaned in to give a compliment and lightly stroked the other woman's hair. Sometimes the dancing got closer and they would rub against each other and soon hands were touching shoulders or arms or legs.

For most of the couples, things progressed quickly. After the initial contact, the women started kissing. I noticed two couples to our right. They looked more familiar with each other, as if they had come all together. While dancing, the first couple started kissing, and the other woman leaned in to make it a three-way kiss. Then the first woman left the kiss to make out with the other man, who had just been watching up until this point. The dancing and grinding and kissing would continue, the couples now swapped.

After another glass of wine, we were dancing. Quickly, as if on cue, everyone started getting frisky on the dance floor. There were hands up skirts and down pants. A woman beside us bent to her knees and unzipped her partner's pants, taking his penis in her mouth on the dance floor. It was like a way out of control grown-up school dance—everyone horny, zero chaperones in sight.

I leaned in close to Manny and whispered in his ear, "Take off my dress."

"Off, like right off? Like, right here?" He pushed himself close to me. His breath was hot in my ear.

"Yes." I inhaled deeply and gave him a wet kiss on his neck. I raised my arms as he pulled the dress over my head and slung it over the back of a chair.

I wore a tight, black lace negligee with hot pink trim, a matching black thong, and knee-high black boots. There I stood in a sea of a couple hundred people, in my underwear, for the very first time and yet, it felt entirely familiar. I resumed my dancing, trancelike, catching Manny's shining eyes and the faces and bodies of those around us. I moved my body to music every day, but in a choreographed, instructional manner, with thorough prior analysis to develop my lesson plan, often with sixty pairs of eyes looking to me for direction. As I danced, from deep in my belly, a whisper rose like a puff of smoke, a memory rising up. *I used to be a performer.* Even then, there had always a set of require-ments, a coach or choreographer telling me, *do this, not that.* As I surrendered to the music, I experienced a sensation long forgot-ten. I got to feel what it was like to let my body move me.

Manny kissed me hard, his hands in my hair and on my butt. "Let's go to the back," he whispered into my mouth. I nodded and grabbed his hand. He tossed my dress over his shoulder and followed me to the back, picking up a wrapped stack of sheets and towels on our way. The back hall was crowded, but we found a room that was open. He closed and locked the door and started to pull the curtain shut.

"No, open," I said, already kneeling on the bed.

With dim lights, the electric atmosphere, and the probability of people peeking in the window, everything was heightened, every touch from Manny's familiar hands and mouth, intensi-fied. I climaxed again and again with the awareness that my performance was not yet over.

It was after 3:00 a.m. when we were ready to leave. We saw Leon and Liza and they gave us a wave.

"Was the first visit a success?" Leon asked with a smile.

We both smiled widely, nodded, and picked up our coats to leave. As we were walking out the door, Leon asked where we lived. Manny told him. Leon's eyes widened with his grin, and he asked for more specifics.

"You know the area?" I asked, intrigued. He certainly did. They lived right up the road from us. We were basically neighbors. Manny and I walked out the door, laughing nearly as hard as we did from their squirting story. In the car, I leaned back, wiping tears from my eyes.

"Whoa, what a night." I turned to Manny with a smile. He was shaking his head in entertained disbelief.

"Do it again in ten years?" he joked.

"Sounds about right." I laughed.

As we left the parking lot, we started recounting our night.

"It was so packed. I can't believe it." I was still in awe.

"Oh, and the way you looked when you were dancing in your lingerie. Ah, so hot."

"Oh my God ... I *loved* dancing with my dress off. How can I find a place every day where I can dance with my dress off?"

Manny laughed and reached over to me, pushing up my skirt. Even though we had just had a ton of sex, it was impossible to keep our hands off each other. The drive home seemed to take forever, and when we were a few minutes from our house, I couldn't take it any longer.

"Let me go down on you." I leaned over the center console of his SUV. His eyes were wide with disbelief. Never, ever, had I made this offer, rejecting him even when he asked, refusing to sacrifice safety for sexual satisfaction whilst driving. I had told him early on I had a "No Road Head Policy."

"Ah, yeah, please." He was not about to pass up the opportunity.

Keeping my seat belt on, I leaned over, unzipped his pants, and pulled them down slightly as he lifted his butt up in the air and held his hands high on the steering wheel to let me get positioned.

I licked up and down the sides of his penis, moving my hair from my face, and wiggling to adjust the seat belt that dug into my hips and shoulder. More comfortable, I leaned further over the center console, my butt in the air. Manny reached over and stroked my back and squeezed my butt cheeks.

Suddenly, we hit a bump, and my head bounced up, hitting Manny's outstretched arm.

With my hand still around the base of his penis, I froze. *"What was that?"*

"A raccoon." He said with a shaking voice. "We just hit a raccoon."

Chapter 8

The lesson from the raccoon was pretty clear, but the next morning I googled "raccoon totem" just to be sure I wasn't missing anything. *Insatiable curiosity, exploration, having to take on different roles in different aspects of your life, adventures at night, keeping secrets.* It sounded like the raccoon could be the spirit animal of the swing lifestyle. *Sorry, little guy.*

Until Jack was born, I believed everything I needed to know could be explained by science. I was a skeptic, raised by skeptics, a science lover, and a logical decision-maker. Soon after I became a mother, the world felt a little different. Well, a lot different. I didn't anticipate that along with a child, I would also birth an increased sensitivity that allowed me to sense the energetic connection between all living things, past, present, and future. Sometimes, I could even see it, a vibrating, reddish energy, linking all that is. Somehow, this tidbit was missed in my pregnancy books.

It filled me with a calm, a steadiness, quieting my mind in a way I had never experienced. At first, I didn't tell anyone because it sort of weirded me out, and also because everyone around me knew that I rejected anything supernatural. It seemed hokey for me to announce to everyone, "Oh, yeah, you know that God thing that you've all been talking about, I get it now. All good." Because it wasn't all good. The experience was good, but I had trouble reconciling it with what I had learned about God through religion.

Some kids grow up in religious homes and stash a Playboy under their mattress. I grew up in a liberal home and under my mattress was a Bible. When I was little, I asked my parents questions about God, especially about how different people believed different things about God. My mom always said the same thing, "Whatever someone believes is right for them." And when I would continue to dig, "Please, Ashleigh, don't bother your [Catholic] Grandma with these questions."

And from my Dad, "Evolution, Ashleigh, I believe in evolution." He was a catechism dropout. And when I would persist, "The monkeys, Ashleigh. I already told you, the monkeys."

I considered my town to be de facto-Christian, based on the fact that most kids I knew believed in Santa and the Easter bunny. I knew very few families who were actually religious. But, periodically at school, I would be passed a little comic book from one of my classmates who was a practicing Christian, always with the same hushed message, "I really like you, so I think you should know …" Then their voice would trail off and off they would scamper. I'd then flip to the second last page and recoil, seeing the same thing as the time before, the little cartoon people burning in hell.

Clearly, I had no pressure to believe at home, but I could not shake the curiosity around why some people were so into religion. So, as soon as I started to drive, in addition to my secret Bible studies, I became an undercover listener of Christian radio. For years, whenever I was alone in the car I would listen, then be certain to change to a different station before I got out. I knew why I was keeping it a secret. Back then, I had no Christians in my life, and if my friends and family knew I was curious they would wonder if I was going to change and get all weird and pressure-y with them. Later, when I somehow had a ton of

Christians in my life if they knew they would get all weird and pressure-y with me. The truth was, even though I had these years of private contemplation, I still didn't feel convinced to buy in. Rather than experiencing the good news of the gospel, I felt I was being sold a pitch for a bad time share.

Christian Heaven Gatekeeper Timeshare Dude: Sign on the dotted line or you will regret it eternally. Yeah, it's not much now, but let me tell you about the upgrades coming in Phase 2. If you don't buy in now, you'll miss out on the eternity pool …

Me: Don't you mean the infinity pool?

Dude: No, an ETERNITY pool. It goes on FOREVER.

Me: Uh, yeah … that's … okay, never mind. *Notices pervert jacking off in corner* Wait, what is going on with that guy??

Dude: Ma'am, I'm going to have to ask you to cover your shoulders.

Not much of my secret Bible study helped me make sense of my new spiritual awakening. I mostly kept it to myself and tried to just pay very close attention. Soon I started finding spiritual books, friends, and teachers who shared the same experience. Preparing for unmedicated birth and breastfeeding had linked me into a natural mom group. Within that community, I quickly found friends with rich experiences and understanding. Many explained that their belief was that our babies each chose us as their families before birth. They choose the parents who are best served to teach them the lessons they needed to learn during this lifetime.

Still pretty sure I was on an extended episode of *Punk'd*, I committed to reconciling my mothering exhaustion with my new spiritual awareness. I shared with my yoga teacher that I often felt that I needed the real mom to come home. I was not equipped to handle this. She replied confidently, "Well, you know you can handle this because you're a mama this time around."

I didn't know if I believed her, but quickly I realized that I felt better when I pretended that I did. I felt calmer, more patient, and more content, basically an all-around better-functioning human being when I decided to pretend that I was put here, on earth, in my role, for a reason. It didn't matter if it was true or not. When I believed it, I felt more capable of dealing with the chaos. I felt like, *even if Ashton never shows up, I've got this.*

And this began my fake it 'til you make it approach to spirituality.

What would happen if I sent a question out into the Universe and trusted that I would get the right answer? What if I believed my intuition was linked to something broader, an intelligent energy that cared for me? I tested it out on big decisions and little decisions. Sometimes I would act on it; sometimes I wouldn't. Often my fear prevented me from following through, but I found that my gut always told me the right thing to do. When I ignored it, the situation would intensify until I eventually let my intuition guide me.

I figured out that if I got quiet and listened, I would always know what to do. Even if everyone around me had an opinion, I could trust myself to have the answer. I became more confident, believing that this universal energy I could sense was intelligent and compassionate. I carefully chose words to explain what I was experiencing: first Prana, because I had experienced the surging of life force energy in yoga, then the Universe, the Divine, and then, after many, many years, God—but only with close friends who knew what I meant. "God" meant something very specific to most people, and it varied depending on their geography. In any case, I wanted to avoid using the word and having people jump to all sorts of conclusions about what else that meant about me. And just like people assumed (incorrectly) that I must be a vegetarian because I ate organic food and I kind of look like Dawn from The Babysitters' Club, their assumptions about what I meant by "God" and what else that meant about my views would likely be way off.

When I was pregnant with Niko, I found a lovely meditation teacher who said our experience of the Divine is similar to being blindfolded in a room with an elephant. Each one of us has our hand on a different part of the elephant, the tusk, the ear, the tail. And many of us insist that no one else is really touching the elephant unless they feel the same thing we are feeling. "We are all connected to the same thing," she said, "but experiencing it in different ways."

I love to oversimplify. If I can distill a complicated set of ideas down to one blanket idea, I do. But I was shown over and over that when I expressed something with absolute certainty it turned out to be more nuanced than I had assumed. I was certain one of God's favorite games to play with me was, *believe this without a doubt so I can spin you around and make you see it from the other side.*

When Manny and I first met, it was clear church was a non-negotiable for his family, and even though this was before I had any experience of the Divine, I offered to find a church that we could both agree on. I had two requirements: women were allowed in leadership and gay people were allowed to get married. Those items were the baseline for me determining whether a church did more harm than good. He was not interested but assured me that church would not be a big deal in our lives. We just needed to agree to get married in the Greek Church. He said his parents "wouldn't consider us married" if we didn't. I read my bookmarked pages on the Greek Orthodox Archdiocese website and confirmed his claim. He would be excommunicated, disallowed from even having a Greek funeral. Harsh, but okay, I guess I could go along, considering the repercussions for him. And baptisms, he said, we just need to baptize our children, and that's it.

I made it through the wedding playing a convincing version of a happy Greek bride, and I was relieved that it would be a while before I had to go back again. Then, just a few weeks after Jack was born, I sat on our bed, topless, nipples red and sore, nursing Jack on one side as milk sprayed out the other and I pressed a cloth diaper to my breast.

"We need to go to church next week," Manny said, walking into the closet.

I hoped the prolactin was making me hallucinate. "Pardon me?" I asked.

"For the forty days," Manny said matter-of-factly from the closet.

An icy stream circled my ears and ran down my shoulders. "Pardon me?" I repeated.

"It's just part of the baptism," Manny emerged from the closet and shrugged, but his eyes betrayed his nervousness.

He knew damn well that I knew it wasn't "part" of the baptism. We had discussed this when I read the ass-kissing Greek traditions book. Women were traditionally not allowed to go anywhere for forty days after giving birth, and only immediate family members would have contact with them because they were unclean. Historically, after the birth of a female child the mother would be considered unclean for eighty days, but in modern times it had been decided women could undergo the cleansing blessing at the church after forty days, whether they had a male or female child, for simplicity. I had read about it years before, relieved that I would not have to participate, and raging for every woman who ever had to undergo this archaic ritual.

I looked down at Jack, suckling and looking up at me with wide, blinking eyes. I wanted to scream. I did not want anyone in that church touching this baby. Not yet. I knew when he was about a year old, we would go through the baptism charade, but I couldn't do it yet. Not now.

"This was not part of our agreement," I said through gritted teeth, jaw set, eyes wet.

Exasperated, Manny looked like he was going to walk out of the room. He turned and said, "Look, Ash, if the only reason we go to church is to make my mom happy, what is wrong with that?" My jaw dropped, his simple inquiry freezing my ability to form even one word to begin to outline the layers upon layers of what was wrong with that. Then he walked away. A spear drove up from my diaphragm, piercing the roof of my mouth. My brain drained into my throat, and I swallowed it down. Later, I would shit out my brain.

So, I rebooted my role as the actress visiting a Greek church. Father Florida was gone and the new actor playing the priest was kinder. Also, the cast had been expanded with adorable actor babies playing Jack, Luke, and Niko. To keep my sanity during the scene, I pretended that it wasn't really my responsibility when they were taken from my arms, stripped naked, covered in oil, dunked in water of unknown temperature, and then given communion, even though until that point they had had nothing but breastmilk in their tiny mouths. If they cried, surely someone would yell, "Cut!" and the on-set baby-wrangler would take them, because there was nothing I could do. After each baptism, Manny and I hosted a lovely lunch at a lovely restaurant. I took lovely pictures when requested by our lovely guests but never kept a single one.

After Jack's baptism, I sighed in relief. I wouldn't have to go through that rigamarole again until we had another baby. Then Christmas rolled around and Manny told me that taking the baby for communion every Christmas and Easter was "part of the baptism," too. What I really wanted to say was, "You're drunk, and you are making no fucking sense. Having a baptism does not mean going at forty days and going for Christmas and Easter for the rest of our lives. That's not what it means!" Instead, I tried to bargain for a compromise.

"Babe, you know one of the things I hate the most about religion is that kids are treated like sheep, little drones, doing things that they don't understand. What if we waited and we took him for communion when he was older? We could make it something that is meaningful for us, having him give up something before he goes, teaching him about how lucky we are, and some people don't have as much. I am sure when he is three or four years old, he would probably be able to understand some aspect of it, then we could take him." Again, Manny would not entertain my idea. And this time I knew why. His mom had already told him that we should take Jack the next week.

"I'm out," I said.

"What?" His tone asserted his surprise.

"I'm out. If we have no compromise, if I have no input, I'm not going. I'm not going to watch our baby have something shoved in his mouth with no explanation. I'm not okay with it, and I am not going to sit there and pretend I am."

His jaw dropped, unable to form even one word. I walked away.

So, now I had a new role, the role of the mom who helps her children and her husband get dressed for church, then stays home. It was less awkward, but still pretty damn awkward. Every year or so I would again bring up the option of finding a solution we could both support when it came to church, but he would not budge; he was unwilling to even discuss it. Oddly and awkwardly, the deeper I got into my own spirituality, the tighter the gag order he and I had about all things related to God.

It's not that I had never had a meaningful experience in church. When I was seventeen, I was at my twin cousins' christening, and I was hungover. I sat next to my brother, Alex, who, indisputably, possesses the weakest stomach in our family, and maybe even the world. If you said the word "booger," he would gag. If there was anything subtly gross or if he exerted himself, as in hockey, he would barf profusely. Once, he up-chucked through the cage on his hockey helmet and my parents could not get it to cease to smell like pepperoni pizza for the rest of the season.

At some point in the service honoring the sweet cherubs, my mouth started to water, the surefire sign that I was going to vomit. I looked around, trying to figure out which direction to go to get to a trashcan or toilet expediently, but there was no escape. We were sitting too close to the altar, and the puke was coming quickly. If I would have tried to get there I would have certainly thrown up on the floor, causing a scene, disrupting the service, and horrifying my parents. Alex sensed my discomfort and looked toward me. His eyes filled with understanding and dread when he saw—even through poorly matched, teenage foundation—that I was turning greener by the second. He continued to watch in horror as I pressed my fingers to my lips, let my mouth fill up with vomit, cheeks full as a chipmunk, and swallowed it back down, once, twice, three times. Our mom, who was tasked with videotaping, looked toward us with a smile, as if to say, "Isn't this precious?" She then looked back at the cooing, drooling babes up front. But they weren't the only ones drooling. Alex shakily removed his vest and handed it to me so I could wipe the dribble off my face. As we exited the church, he threw the vest in the garbage outside the main doors.

Since then, the doctors have verified what he had always insisted, that he cannot help his weak stomach. It's because of an anatomical issue, a missing valve. There is only one word to describe his ability to control his physiological tendencies in order to prevent me from being grounded that day. Transcendent.

Despite the years of curiosity about religion and that experience of bonding with my brother in church, everything that I learned brought me closer to the conclusion that, although there were many others in these clubs, and the consequences of not joining were purportedly dire, I was just not interested in buying into any of the big box religions.

My faith in my own eclectic blend of spirituality deepened. I came to believe that things in my life were really happening *for* me, not just *to* me. Through consistent study, I came to appreciate that the physical world gives us many opportunities to work, play, and experience here, but the non-physical is what is actually real and unchanging. During my limited time at Earth School in my meat suit, I was certainly going to try to be the best student. I looked for the deeper meaning in everything, including every time I dropped something or stubbed my toe.

Universe, what is it? I'm listening.

Ashleigh, you just stubbed your toe. It's nothing.

Are you sure I wasn't thinking about something that was not in my best interest and for the greater good of the world?

Nope. You just stubbed your toe.

Okay, just checking. Want to give me any other tidbits while we are here in conversation?

Drink more water.

Okay, Universe. Divine advice. Thank you.

Chapter 9

Despite the terribly unfortunate incident with the raccoon, the sexual charge of our club visit lingered for weeks. Instead of getting out of bed to meditate or start the coffee, I would reach for Manny. We'd sneak into the bathroom and have sex on the counter while the kids played. One evening before dinner, we found ourselves in the pantry, Manny fingering me when we should have been making dinner. Even when we weren't having sex, we couldn't keep our hands off each other.

"Leaving the house at 10:30 …," Manny chuckled and shook his head. We were heading to the club a month after our first visit. "Who do we think we are?"

I tilted my head and fixed my eyes on him. "We're swingers, baby." I held his gaze with a sexy pout for only a moment until we both cracked up laughing.

The club was again packed. Leon and Liza welcomed us back. We felt more comfortable and talked to more people. We went through the standard greetings. *Are you new here? Are you new to the lifestyle?* We told them our weird swingers origin story, that we had visited the old club in Philly just a few weeks before it was shut down and hadn't been to a club since. Everyone had heard of the old club, but none of them had been there. We were granted instant legend status, as we provided the oral history of the club actually existing. We were living proof that the myths were true. We were total rookies that were looked at with reverence, like we were wise beyond our years (or experience).

We were struck again by how friendly everyone was. Three for three, swingers' clubs had provided us with a welcoming atmosphere. (All memories of the club in Allentown had been cleared from our brains, thank goodness.) All couples were male-female, likely because gay and transgender people had a club scene that was more established than this. The swing lifestyle club, although seemingly racy, is just a shade past vanilla. It's how straight people from the suburbs take a walk on the wild side.

I noticed that most people were not there to engage with other people, rather more for the atmosphere so they could engage better with each other. Undeniably, the atmosphere was electric. Although it was sexually charged, I considered it to be charged in a way that was much healthier than what I have experienced at regular bars. Instead of women sizing each other up as competition, they actively complimented each other. The women's bathroom was a downright praise-fest, females fawning all over each other about hair and shoes and dresses. The dynamic was more comfortable with the men, too. Instead of feeling like I had to guard myself from unwanted advances, I trusted that people were there to act like responsible adults, not sleazebags.

It has become a matter of course that anywhere I go in regular life where there is a crowd of people, men often feel the need to put their hand on my back when they "squeeze" past me, although they successfully move past other men without having to touch them. Fascinatingly, at sex clubs, I rarely experienced that. On the contrary, if we were in tight quarters and a man needed to move past me, more often they would say "excuse me" and make eye contact, lifting their hands to make sure they didn't accidentally graze my body while passing.

Finally, I was in a place where men could not feign ignorance about what equaled consent and what did not. And none of these men had gone through required sensitivity training as a requirement of membership. They used common sense. When it's a rule to act like you care, you figure out how to care.

My youthful partying days had been short; I had met Manny when I was twenty-one, and besides that one club visit years before, we had no nightlife. But, while in university, I perfected the art of the "toss back." Every time I would be dancing, inevitably, I would feel a hand on my body from some stranger who I couldn't even see. I would pick up his hand and toss it back to him. Men who were particularly dense may have felt entitled to try again. I would repeat my gesture and toss it back again, this time with a sharp "no" and eye contact. Then I would migrate my group of friends to another part of the dance floor. Men exhibited the standard "if you're here for a good time, I'm guessing that good time includes me" sort of attitude. Conversely, at this adult club, it was more of an "if I want to figure out if your good time includes me, I know I have to start a conversation like a regular, respectful human, and talk to you and your partner, and gauge interest and negotiate interactions beforehand" kind of attitude.

I could be myself, be flirty, be sexy, and feel confident that no one would act like I owed them anything. To have that freedom when I would normally be worried about the opposite made me feel remarkably at ease.

Most people had a drink in their hands, but very few were visibly intoxicated. We didn't see any drug use or even smell weed. The most offensive thing in the club was the cigarette smoke. Because it was a private club, smoking was allowed. It was a big place, but still, our clothes and hair carried the smell after we left.

There was a dress code, so everyone was dressed up (or undressed, depending on the time). We saw a couple we recognized from the month before. They looked like straight-up grandparents, easily in their late 60's, both wearing glasses. She was in her white garter belt and stockings, on the platform, swaying slowly in front of the dancing pole. He stood on the dance floor, looking up at her, also swaying to the music, with a gold crucifix hanging outside his mock turtleneck t-shirt and a big 'ole smile on his face.

Manny and I had made no decisions about interacting with other people, but by this point, I had scoured swing lifestyle websites for information, and Google knew all my curiosities. My two most pressing concerns if we were to hook up with another couple were health and safety. First, I did not want to end up tied up in someone's basement. That would be bad.

Secondly, I didn't want to catch anything, not even a cold. But, the annual count of how many swingers experience the common cold wasn't something that Google knew the answer to, so I focused on the STD information. According to my research, the myth that non-monogamous people have the most STDs didn't turn out to be true, and it seemed to be perpetuated by the same people who say your sex life will be super-hot if you wait until marriage.

I had read that people who cheat rarely use protection during the infidelity or with their primary partner. Through my digging, and through what we had seen and heard so far at clubs, I discovered that people in consensual non-monogamous relationships were more likely to use condoms with their partner and any others they engaged with than people in monogamous relationships. They were also more likely to be tested for infections and discuss their sexual activity with everyone involved. The long and short of it was, irresponsible sex leads to more risk of disease, even for the partner who is not straying. Planned, negotiated sexual activity, even if it involved more people, involved less health risk.

The club was considered a "swing lifestyle club," but it was really a blanket term, and a term that was becoming more antiquated by the day, especially considering that many of the couples there would not consider themselves swingers. Swinging referred to the swapping of sexual partners. There was soft swap, where there was no sexual intercourse, and full swap, where there was. Although mainstream Western culture is somewhat obsessed with intercourse and considers it to be the most intimate physical encounter, and the way you go "all the way" with someone, the people we met in consensual non-monogamy had a much more nuanced understanding of intimacy. Some couples considered kissing or oral sex to be more intimate than sexual intercourse. I met more than one woman who shared that she had intercourse with her partner before and more often than oral sex, because even in a committed relationship she didn't always feel comfortable doing the latter. So, even though the lifestyle seemed like a more open subculture, it was by no means a place where everyone said, "anything goes." The understandings between partners and with the people they met were detailed and involved.

Open relationships are a sub-set of consensual non-monogamy that people outside the lifestyle are usually the most familiar with. In this arrangement, one or both partners are free to be physically intimate with others, and it is not usually done together. People in these types of partnerships may have the agreement that their primary partner needs to be informed before or after the engagement or not at all. Everyone we met had their own rules.

Increasingly more common is polyamory, where in contrast to the two examples above, the focus is not just on casual sexual engagement but also on emotional connection. In polyamorous relationships, individuals are in committed relationships with more than one person. Sometimes it is a third person who joins an already committed couple, and the three of them formed a triad, all in relationship with each other. In other situations, each individual is free to establish a committed relationship or relationships with other people. In polyamory, it is most common for all people involved to know about all sexual partners and even to vet them beforehand.

A newer term, coined by Dan Savage, is "monogamish." It designated people who were classically monogamous on a day-to-day basis but had some agreed-upon exceptions to the rule. It seemed to me that most people at the clubs would fit under this designation. In real life, they were monogamous. At the club, they were not. Some had been married for fifteen years and had never been with a person other than their spouse before they ventured into the lifestyle. Most people we met were married, and most had been together for many years. Some were just dipping their toe in this scene, trying to figure out if they liked it, after years of talking about it. Others had been coming to clubs for five to ten years, and it was a regular part of their social life. I liked the term. "Monogamish" is how I would categorize our marriage, too.

Even though this was only our second visit, I had already established my customs. After a few laps of the club, some conversation, and a couple glasses of wine, I had my dress off and was dancing in my lingerie when a couple approached us. They had caught my eye when we walked around the club earlier in the night. I think it had been because he was tall. He caught me with a cute smile through a sea of people. His wife was adorable, curvy with silky brown hair and full, pink lips. They were definitely younger than us. They introduced themselves as Jillian and Kevin.

"You look really hot," Jillian leaned in to tell me in my ear.

"Thank you. I love your dress." It was black and strapless, and her rocking body filled it out beautifully.

"It's my standard sex club dress. I think I wore it last time we came, too." She laughed.

"We came over to you because you look like the most normal people," Kevin shared, talking to Manny. We laughed. Everyone looked like normal people, but I understood what he meant. Couples who partnered up usually did so with other people who looked like them. They shared that they had been in the lifestyle for a couple years, the same length of time they had been married, and they were both in their late twenties.

The dance floor was packed, and Jillian and I danced together while the guys did the standard thing that non-dancing guys do: hold their drinks and sort of sway back and forth, looking very busy paying attention to watching the women dance—therefore too busy to actually bust a move themselves.

Jillian was sexy and a good dancer. I was having fun with her when the DJ stopped the music and announced a kissing contest.

"We should do it!" Jillian exclaimed and grabbed both my hands. I looked to Manny and Kevin. They were both nodding as most heterosexual men would when faced with the prospect of women kissing. Usually, I find this double standard annoying and stupid, but in that moment, I was actually more in the mood for a kissing contest than a debate. So, I said yes.

Hand in hand, we made our way into the line of contestants, all women. Jillian whispered to me, "I'll go down on you so we can win."

I laughed and choked out the words, "No. We are not doing that. We are sticking to the rules, just kissing."

"Okay, okay," she waved me off and laughed equally hard in return, even though her offer had been sincere. We waited our turn.

Jillian was not the only one with the idea that oral sex should win the contest. There was a whole lot more than kissing going on up on that stage. But when it was our turn, we abided by the rules I had set, and we just kissed. I was struck by how soft her skin was. It was amazing to kiss someone who did not have some degree of stubble on their face.

Our crowd applause was light, likely because we were the only rule followers. We went back down to meet Manny and Kevin, who gave us rousing applause.

The music resumed, and we continued dancing. I don't know how or when it happened, but suddenly I noticed Jillian's dress was pulled down and her breasts were out. And they were glorious. Now, large breasts have always been a mystery to me. I find them so confusing. Although I have faked having larger breasts with push up bras for most of my life, I'm naturally very small-chested, and the only time I had actually had breasts was when I was pregnant or nursing. When women are neither growing humans nor feeding humans and have large breasts, I can't wrap my brain around it, especially when they are petite, like Jillian.

With the sight of the large, beautiful, can't be photoshopped because they are right before my eyes, twenty-something breasts, I looked at Jillian and asked, "Do you guys want to go to the back?"

I am really pretty straight, so it's not that I even wanted to hook up with Jillian. It's just that the breasts helped me access the truth that I was really pretty horny.

Everyone nodded, and I didn't take a survey, but I guessed that meant they were turned on, too.

We made our way to the back, through the crowd of people. We walked down the hall that led to the private rooms. All the doors were closed and many of the curtains, too. We got to the very last room. No one was in there, unless you counted the dildo machine, and I didn't, even though it certainly had a commanding presence.

"This one is empty," I told the other three. "But, it's the only one open."

I turned to Manny and asked him, with very few words, but a questioning expressing and some quick gesticulating if he was okay sharing the room with them. He nodded. Then, I turned to them, like the director and choreographer that I was, and checked to see if they were comfortable.

"We're good," nodded Kevin.

I made a rushed and mumbled comment about us being new, and Kevin responded with both hands in the air, "We'll just follow your lead."

Then I went to the linen depot window to explain that we

wanted the room but were not planning to use the machinery and asked if we could just move it off the bed and onto the floor. Permission was granted, and I was handed sheets and towels.

When I got back to the room, Kevin was moving the dildo machine, with both hands, to the corner of the room.

"Whoa, that guy is heavy," he laughed.

Jillian and I each grabbed a side of the sheet, giddy as if preparing for a sleepover. We stretched it over the king-sized bed, letting it drape over the sides of the rubbery mattress. Previously curious about the linen service, I now wondered where they sourced these wipeable mattresses, but now was not the time to go digging for answers.

Jillian and I stood, and for a moment all four of us just stared at each other, like kids tasked with playing seven minutes in heaven and not knowing where to start. But we weren't kids, well, Manny and I weren't. Jillian and Kevin nearly were, smoking hot little millennials. Kevin pulled the curtain shut and dimmed the lights just slightly.

"Good?" he asked, scanning the room to gauge everyone's comfort. We nodded and I took a step toward Manny. I pressed my lips into his and he laid me down on the bed. Kevin slipped Jillian's dress off as she unbuttoned his shirt, hands twisted, lips locked. Manny unbuttoned his shirt as I lay, taking it all in. My dress was still somewhere on the dance floor. Jillian, wearing her heels and a black thong, laid beside me on the bed. Manny found his way on top of me and Justin on top of her. Within minutes both men had found their way between our legs and Jillian turned to me. Her eyes sparkled and she reached for my hand. Her hand was small and soft. She leaned in to kiss me and stroked my stomach and hip with her hand. She took my hand and moved it toward her leg, where I stroked her thigh and then cupped her butt in my hand. Her skin felt exactly like silk, and I pledged to start using body lotion the very next day.

The thrill of having Jillian and Kevin in the room with us, cool, fun, soft, sexy people right there beside us, was incredible.

We mostly did our thing and they did theirs, with hands crossing over to the other side, with bodies leaning against each other. Right before we finished, I was on top of Manny and Kevin was on top of Jillian and our faces were close. He caught my eye with a sexy smile and wouldn't look away. I leaned into him, and he put his hand in my hair, wrapping his fingers around the back of my head. We kissed long and hard and he whispered, through the kiss, "You are so hot."

For the days and weeks that followed, many of the things we had seen and experienced came into my mind and reminded me of the excitement of that night. But the memory that repeated the most frequently, on a loop that made me feel warm from head to toe, was what Kevin had told me.

You are so hot.

I couldn't recall the last time in my life someone had told me that.

Chapter 10

Our research this time around had uncovered three main types of lifestyle events. The first: a permanent club like the one we had visited, usually held parties three nights a week and had an annual membership, as well as tickets for each event. The second: hotel-takeover parties, where a ballroom and several floors of the hotel would be blocked off for partygoers. Usually these had a theme and people were encouraged to dress in costume. The rules on the website stated that nudity was allowed in the ballroom, but there could be no sexual contact. In the halls reserved for partygoers, there was a green light. Most doors were open, and couples hosted others in their room, just like when parents travel for sports and take the opportunity to party, but not exactly. The third option, more exclusive and more expensive, was to join the mailing list for traveling private parties, held mostly in New York City, at various secret locations. In order to be added to the guest list, couples were required to undergo an application and approval process that included sending in photos and a bio with details about their relationship.

I guess it was unfair to say that Manny and I hadn't done anything for fun in a decade, because about every five years we attended a concert. It had been approximately that long when we caught wind that Atlantic City would start hosting concerts on the beach. Since we had also heard there was a club down there to check out, we decided to do both on the same weekend. After making a life as boring homebodies, we were now party animals, clearly.

The AC club was a little run down, as is the case with most properties close to the shore that do not have buckets of money poured into them. In addition to the club, it had a hotel, a 24-hour pool, and a huge deck, surrounded on all sides but open to the clear night sky and the ocean air.

There was also a Jamaican DJ who wore a mask, and a loin cloth-type thing, who danced wildly for most of the night. When requesting songs, I had to proceed with caution. I have always attested to being comfortable with nudity, but I can clarify that a whirling penis does make me a little uptight.

My favorite feature was found far below the main level of the club. Late in the night, we embarked down a labyrinth of stairs. The music became progressively more muffled as we made our way lower and lower. Soon we could only feel it pulsating as we descended the twisting stairways and stopped off to explore each level. Some were small, with only a landing and a bath-room. Some were large, with a hallway and private rooms. But, *Raiders of the Lost Ark* style, we kept venturing further. I wondered if we would find the Ark of the Covenant at the end of this quest. And then, we had it in our sights, what we had ventured to discover: a long rectangular room, with mirrors on all walls and on the ceiling. Many may assume that because we were frequenting sex clubs, our sex life at home must have been remarkably kinky, and it would have taken more than a mirrored ceiling to make us lose our minds. They would be wrong.

Down at the far end was another couple. We now considered people three mattresses away to be practically in a different zip code, so we grabbed the last stack of clean sheets and set up home base at the other end, feeling like we had the room to ourselves. Maybe it was just because the low lighting was flattering, or because we had developed a slight partiality to exhibitionism, or because we were so sexed-up after hours of dancing and chatting and drinking, but having sex under those mirrors was the hottest thing, ever.

So hot that I think we may be failing as a species by not having mirrored ceilings in every master bedroom. I propose that it should become part of building code for new homes. I predict it would reduce the sedentary lifestyle, screen time, and divorce rates. Overall, it would constitute an enormous financial and emotional savings for our society. Clearly, I could not do something as outrageous as asking our handyman to install mirrors on our bedroom ceiling, and I am sure others may have similar reservations. If mirrored ceilings were a standard installation, it would save all of us embarrassment, allowing us the option of experiencing the humanity-strengthening awesomeness in our very own homes. If anyone is interested in politics, please feel free to run with this idea. I think this has the making of an outstanding platform.

The mirrored room was a definite highlight of our lifestyle exploration, until we found ourselves at a private party in NYC that looked like a casting call for *The Bachelor*.

We were, laughably, considered veterans of the lifestyle due to our historic tale about the old club in Philly, but we were still curious to experience the modern options. This led us to apply to an invite-only mailing list for events in NYC. We submitted a short bio along with photos and waited to see if we would be deemed suitable. We quickly found out we were approved, communicated through a gushingly sweet email from the party host, Susie.

In addition to the party, Susie was hosting a pre-party event on a private floor of an uptown restaurant. A belly dancer undulated through the crowd, enticing and loosening up the guests. Great food and drinks had been set out. We broke our rule about not eating at sex clubs because technically we were still at a restaurant. We met Susie and her boyfriend and several of the couples who would be making their way to the club afterwards.

Maybe I was naïve, but I viewed all conversations with people in the lifestyle as friendly, non-invasive attempts to get to know us. In other words, I did not assume everyone who approached us to talk was hoping we would get naked with them. Manny and I were there for fun, not pressure, and the reality was that we were mostly there to do our own thing. Sometimes people would ask us outright if we were interested in hooking up, which was a much less awkward exchange than you may assume. On this night, a hot Italian couple in their late forties stopped by the restaurant. They were on the mailing list but planned to make it an early night, their weekend very busy with sporting events for their teenage children. They were stopping by the restaurant for a drink but not coming to the club.

But, after meeting us and chatting for a few minutes, the man glanced at his wife and said, "You know, we could reconsider and come to the club," motioning to us. "If you guys are interested." She nodded her agreement, sizing up Manny, who looked like a younger version of her Italian husband. Clearly, he was her type.

I waved them off, kindly giving them my standard answer about us "being rookies." They accepted our rejection gracefully. Before leaving, they extended an invitation for us to come stay at their place in the Hamptons. Apparently, they had a restaurant where Billy Joel often came to play and their house had plenty of room, so we should "bring the kids."

Swingers were proving themselves to be the funniest people we had ever met. Even if you're not into the sex, you could hang out at sex clubs just for the comedy.

It was not that these people were not attractive. They were very attractive. Accidentally finding our way into sharing a bed with Jillian and Kevin had been one thing, but we weren't at the point where we could promise early in the night that we would later jump into bed with total strangers. We decided jumping into a car with total strangers was no big deal when a few minutes later, a darling Russian couple offered us a ride to the party.

We were greeted by a doorman and showed him our IDs so he could check the guest list. He pointed toward the elevator and told us the floor to go to. The loft was amazing: high ceilings, exposed brick, lovely furniture, and lighting. The DJ and bartenders were professional and friendly.

Not surprisingly, considering the pre-screening process, everyone was gorgeous, but it was the first crowd that was genuinely culturally diverse.

It was like the United Nations of Hotness.

You could say it was proven to us that you get what you pay for. This place was awesome. The belly dancer had followed us from the restaurant, and every half hour another professional performer joined the party.

Because this was not a permanent club, there were no themed rooms, no sex swings (not that we had ever used them), and no walls. There was only one large play area at the end. "Play" is the general term that lifestyle couples use to indicate sexual interaction with others. And I guessed it was due to the fact that the main purpose, in the minds of the people we met, was pure fun. To be in a place that prioritized fun for *grown-ups*, well it felt implausibly frivolous, yet there we were.

We walked to the end of the loft and took in the scene. Couches and mattresses were pressed together, with walkways in-between, like the room was set-up for an epic game of "The Floor is Lava." Everything was draped in sheets, with stacks of clean towels throughout, so even without the sprawling nudes you would be able to guess that this scene had been constructed for a more grown-up type of play.

The action had already started. Licking, touching, reaching, hands and mouths explored. It occurred to me that these people could use a little instruction.

Hey, you … leg up … more extension.

And you ... head down. Aaand, arch.

Work together.

Don't rush.

Anticipate the movements of your partner.

Yes ... that's better!

I kept the coaching in my head, all the while snapping my fingers to the cadence of the music. I truly possessed the required skill set to get this orgy into shape. Perhaps I missed my calling as an orgy choreographer.

In all honesty, I may be taking too grand of a liberty in calling what I saw an orgy. People were in very close quarters, naked, engaging in sexual activity, and there was some touching or kissing that linked many of the partners across the great sea of multi-colored nudity. Personally, I considered this an orgy, but I do not want anyone to think that what I witnessed was a debaucherous free-for-all like you may see in pornography. For those who don't already know, most things that happen in pornography never happen in real life, even at sex clubs.

I spotted an open place in the far-left corner. I pointed and led Manny, hand in hand, stepping carefully to avoid the outstretched arms and legs. Without the playrooms that other clubs possess, the action was extremely concentrated. Manny slipped my dress over my head, and it was the first time I realized that I had made it this far in the night without taking it off.

I laid back, and he started going down on me. I turned to take in the scene around me and realized we were very close to the people next to us. I recognized them from earlier in the night, having noted how cute this man was when I first saw him. He had shaggy, curly hair past his ears and clear blue eyes. His face was close to mine, and our eyes met. I smiled, and I slowly leaned in to kiss him. He turned his face away, which I understood to mean that he didn't have the green light to kiss other women. I looked up at his partner with a smile, and she leaned down to kiss me softly. Our lips met and then our tongues. She pulled away and nodded to her husband, whispering, "You can kiss her." And he did. Because there were people on all sides, and we were all basically a pile of sexing sardines, I did actually consider this to be an orgy. So, I would say that in kissing that couple next to us, I crossed something off my bucket list. I didn't even have a bucket list. But in that moment, I thought maybe I should start one. I did enjoy making lists and including things I could already cross off.

The party was clearing out, and I found Susie to thank her for hosting. She gave me a tender hug. "No one ever says thank you," she said, eyes brightening.

"Well, they should start. This was awesome." I hugged her again, and we made our way down to the street. The air was still warm, with that distinct New York smell that I love in very small doses. We decided to walk for a bit before we got a cab, and even though my shoes were comfortable, my clothes felt cumbersome. I wished I could take my dress back off.

I forgot about the dress quickly. On my phone was a message, a match from a swingers' app I had just installed. Her name was Jessica. His name was Brad. They had four children. And they were from Philadelphia.

Chapter 11

There was a time in my life when I really struggled with my sexual identity. It was during the week that I was making our profile on the swing lifestyle app. I couldn't decide whether marking me as straight, bi-curious, or bisexual would get us the most matches.

I would soon find out that I didn't really need to worry about matches. Manny and I staged a little photoshoot with me wearing a black and pink lacy garter belt and threw some pictures up on our profile, and the messages started rolling in. Invitations for dinner, to go to a nudist resort up in the Poconos, to go to Atlantic City for the weekend—these were all requests we got within the first twenty-four hours of making our profile.

Truthfully, our club experiences of just doing our own thing were super fun, but our interaction with Jillian and Kevin had stuck in both our minds, and we were curious about what other possibilities may be available if we had another couple whom we trusted and considered friends. Manny would have preferred to go to clubs every once in a while and just see how the night played out, but I still had concerns about health and safety. If we could keep things spicy but avoid late nights at smoky clubs with total strangers, well, that seemed like a far more responsible approach.

I turned down every invitation we received, feeling nervous, but also because a certain profile had caught my eye and had stuck with me. She was my age, and he was almost ten years older. Their names were Jess and Brad, they lived close to us, and they had "four beautiful children." There was something about that line that made me unable to forget their profile, even as I hemmed and hawed about what info to put in ours. Immediately, the thought of interacting with a couple who also had little kids and big responsibilities made me feel more secure. I felt that we could trust them, and due to our shared family situations, we would more easily understand each other's lives. We all implicitly understood the break, the release, the fun that we were looking for in the lifestyle. I knew for certain that they would be the first people I reached out to when I had our profile up and running.

In most decisions in our life, I was the one who wanted to go all-in right away. I wanted to get married, have kids, and move to our big house sooner than Manny did. I always wanted to buy the bigger bulk order of everything. If we were painting a room, I wanted to paint the whole house. And I wanted the garden to be bigger, much bigger. I was the one with the big, flashy plans. Manny balanced me out. He pulled me back. He suggested we do half of one-quarter of 10 percent of what I had suggested. He reasoned that the idea was great, but it was just a little *too much* or a little *too soon*.

Our usual perspectives held true when we ventured into the lifestyle. Even though Manny had been the one to bring it up more frequently in the past decade, once I was in, I was all in. I was the gas, and Manny tried to be the brakes. With Jillian and Kevin, I had been extremely turned on because there was just so much going on in one room. Problematically, I had also been unable to have an orgasm that night because *there was just so much going on in one room*. That led me to believe that what may be the most satisfying for me would be a separate room full swap. The separate room part was because I wanted to minimize distractions. The full-swap part was just because I liked going all in. Why not? The fantasy of being with another man was a huge turn on for me, and the thought of Manny being with someone else was also a turn-on. Manny was not offended or upset, but he did think it seemed a little extreme. Separate room full swap was like the double black diamond run of swingerdom, and we were barely off the bunny hill. He ventured, "Hmm, maybe we could start with kissing other people?"

On the train home from New York the next day, I showed Jess and Brad's profile to Manny. He shrugged and went back to Twitter. I messaged Brad, and he was shocked that I was running our profile. I guess he was used to other dudes messaging him back. I flirted and told him about NYC and asked what he was into. He laughed and told me we would all need to be on a group chat together before he could talk about any of that, so we exchanged numbers. The four of us started texting and quickly made plans to go out for dinner in a few days. They also opened up the private section of their profile so we could see more photos. We added face shots to the private section of our profile and granted them the same access.

Brad wasn't my usual type. He was six feet tall, with light brown hair, an easy smile, and a face that would certainly take days to produce stubble. Before Manny, I dated men who looked like Manny, with dark hair, sideburns, and who could grow a beard in a minute. Because of this, Brad's All-American look felt a little exotic to me. He looked like a high school math teacher. But he wasn't. He was a veterinarian. Jess was my height, athletic, tanned, with wide-set blue eyes and curly blond hair, all criteria that made her attractive to Manny. She ran a moving company that had been in her family for three generations. Since taking over, she had expanded it to six states. Their "four beautiful children" were two little girls about the same age as Jack and Luke and older boy-girl twins from Brad's first marriage.

We met at one of our favorite restaurants, a place where we had met other friends before. But this time it was nerve-wracking. Would the hostess ask if we needed to be seated in the Swingers' Section? Luckily, when we said another couple would be joining us, the hostess acted like that was the most normal thing in the world and not at all scandalous. The other customers in the restaurant paid us no mind. It seemed that we were not emitting a swinger vibe, and we were relieved.

Brad and Jess arrived just a few minutes after we did. Friendly and easy to talk to, over the next few hours we went back and forth, sharing how we met, our jobs, and funny things about us as a couple. Whenever we meet new people, I always lead with the same few jokes: Manny's habit of putting chocolate syrup in frosted flakes, how he is suspicious about any food that doesn't come out of a box, how we met as trainers but never work out, and how I laugh really hard at my own jokes. They shared how they met. Brad was working for Jess's family's company when he was going through vet school. His marriage was breaking up at the same time that Jess's mom was diagnosed with cancer, and they found comfort in each other. They got close very quickly, as quickly as Jess's mom passed. Soon Brad had moved in with her and her dad while he finished vet school. Jess's dad welcomed Brad's twins, then toddlers, as his own grandchildren immediately. A few years later, Jess took over the family business, and she and Brad were married. Now the twins were teenagers and lived with Brad and Jess most of the time. Brad's ex-wife lived close by, and their arrangement was flexible.

"Teenagers are crazy," Brad said, "but they make great babysitters."

They told us about their lifestyle experience. They had been going to clubs on and off for about a year but had started actually dating another couple just two months prior. This was a new experience for them after only casual interaction with couples at clubs previously. Gina and Cory were the first couple they had actually dated.

In their profile on the lifestyle app, couples indicated what level of interaction they would be interested in. Brad and Jess's profile had said they were up for soft swap, maybe more. From that, I had surmised that they were rookies at the lifestyle, like us. That was another part of my attraction to them. It quickly became clear that they were a tad more experienced than their profile let on. They had recently graduated to full swap with Gina and Cory. I didn't know what to think because, even though I had my own lofty and premature full swap fantasies, I felt terribly out leagued by their surprise veteran status. The unanticipated information just kept coming. They shared that within a few weeks of meeting Gina and Cory, they had begun seeing each other on a regular basis, even having playdates with their kids and barbecues with their extended families.

I could not wrap my head around how all that actually worked. It wasn't that I thought there was anything wrong with this, per se, but I had questions. *Where did you tell your parents that you met them? Do you ever steal a kiss in the kitchen, or is it all after hours?* My eyes were wide as the questions started tumbling out, and Jess could sense my actual, singular question behind them all. *Why? Why take this extra-curricular, sexy, side thing and incorporate it into your regular family life?* She liked being able to hang out with Gina, just the two of them, and have playdates with their kids. It made everything feel more comfortable for her, like everyone understood there were marriages and lives involved. This relationship was for fun, but it was not something that was going to jeopardize their marriage. She also liked that it wasn't all about sex. She liked that they were all really friends. Brad and Jess had not expected the relationship to evolve like this, but it had all happened so quickly. Before they knew it, they had become fixtures in each other's friend group and family. Jess elaborated that, for her, she appreciated a more polyamorous approach to the swing lifestyle. Brad, on the other hand, admitted that he didn't mind that they were friends; he genuinely enjoyed hanging out with them but preferred to keep it more in the physical realm instead of the emotional.

I had always been fascinated by polyamory, so I had a lot of questions. To be fair, just because I was fascinated by something did not mean I wanted to participate. I am a curious soul. I have researched many things I would never engage in, including furry culture, inceldom (a disgusted, "watching a train wreck" type of curiosity), and Pokémon Go. But, polyamory? It offered the security of a committed partnership with the added excitement of receiving attention and affection from others. It wasn't all late-night, smoky club type action. I imagined it to be walks with the dog, shared grocery shopping trips. I guessed it was like the stability of marriage with the excitement of dating. Manny, on the other hand, had always cited that it looked like trouble waiting to happen. For him, it wasn't a stretch to separate love and sex, but to have this kind of closeness with many different people at once? That seemed much too complicated. Manny had always struggled keeping up with the communicative and emotional needs of just me. One of the early perks of this adventure was that it had given us more to talk about than we had had in years.

That night with Brad and Jess, we were in a public place and had no plans to go to another location afterwards. This night was not about sex, but we all knew we were meeting under the pretense of examining the possibility of some sort of intimacy in the future. In all honesty, these kinds of conversations were a hybrid of a first date and a job interview. *Here is our experience. Here is what we are looking for. Let's all consider whether or not we are a good match and circle back.*

Since they were already dating another couple, I was curious as to why they were even meeting with us. Their schedule of barbecues and playdates and nights out on the town seemed to have them quite busy. Their answer involved some skirting around my question but, in the end, seemed like an honest attempt to not insult their friends. It was clear that Jess and Cory had a great connection. It was also clear that Jess and Gina had gotten to be very good friends and the kids loved hanging out together. The sticky spot seemed to be between Brad and Gina. "It's not that we are *incompatible*," Brad started.

"She's just sometimes hard to deal with ...," Jess trailed off. They both started touting the greatest things about her personality, then mumbled and stuttered around the less desirable. *Moody, unpredictable, insecure.*

"But she has such a good heart," assured Jess. "And she's *beautiful.*"

"Yes, she's definitely beautiful," Brad agreed.

Time flies when you're sharing sexcapades, and we realized we needed to wrap things up because the restaurant was closing. I would have liked to see them again just to have more conversations like this. It all fascinated me. We agreed that we would figure something out on our group chat to see each other again in a few weeks.

When I got home, I had a message from Brad, not on the group text, but individually.

It was really nice to finally meet you. We are fine with texting privately now if you and Manny are okay with it.

"Man, are you okay with us texting directly, out of the group chat? I have a message from Brad." I asked.

Manny shrugged, "Yeah, why wouldn't I be?"

"Okay, well, text Jess. Tell her it was nice to meet her, okay?"

Manny nodded, "Okay."

The next day during our texting, Brad and I looked at our calendars and figured out a day that they could come to our house to hang out in a couple weeks. We were free for the upcoming weekend, but their Cory-Gina responsibilities meant that we had to book at least two weeks out in their calendar.

In the meantime, I was curious about the other club in Philly, the smaller one Manny and I pushed aside in favor of the larger. When we were out for dinner, Brad and Jess had told us that they much preferred the smaller one. It was nicer looking, and there was no smoking allowed, which was a major selling point for me. Mostly, though, I needed something to keep my focus while we were waiting to see them again.

The next Saturday, I mentioned my curiosity to Manny. "Isn't it smaller?" he asked.

"Hmm, I think so. But Brad said it was nicer and newer. And you can't smoke in there." Manny looked distractedly at his phone and hadn't answered me. "So," I prodded. "Do you want to go?"

He looked up to see that I was staring at him. "Oh, like, you mean ... tonight?" he asked.

"Yes," I nodded, still looking him in the eye.

The boys were already slated to sleep over at his parents' house that night, and we had been planning to go out for dinner.

"Oh, well." He looked around. "I guess." He nodded. "I'll take the boys. You get ready and buy the tickets." He paused. "I guess we'll need to buy the membership, too." I nodded and agreed to look at the website and get it all taken care of.

He left to round up the boys, and I took my phone and Bluetooth speaker to the bathroom, blasting my Taylor Swift. Waiting for my hair to dry, I went online to buy the tickets. The website made it look nice, definitely more of a lounge feel than the other club, which looked just like a nightclub in a warehouse, because that's what it was. I was feeling excited, and when I came back downstairs, I decided to text Brad to tell him we were taking his advice.

Guess who's going to the little club tonight ...

I got a text back immediately, but it wasn't from Brad's number. It was from Jess. *Are you shitting my husband?*

My head fogged, completely confused. I responded, *No.*

My phone rang.

I answered and spoke to Jess on the phone for the first time. First, the hello, hello, pleasantries, then right to the reason for the call. They also had plans to go to that club, and they were not going alone. They would be there with Gina and Cory. Gina and Cory did not know Brad and Jess were talking to us, and if they found out, especially Gina, she would freak.

"Oh ..." The dots were connecting.

She asked if we had already bought our tickets. I told her yes, just a few minutes prior.

"Oh, crap ...," she groaned.

"Okay, what do you want us to do?" I asked her.

She paused to think. After several seconds, she said, "I guess we'll just have to pretend we don't know each other."

"Hmm, and how hard will that be? I mean, how small is this place?" I wondered.

It was small, she said, but it would likely be crowded, so it wouldn't be too big of an issue. She paused again, and I wondered if she was reconsidering. Then she told me that the plan would work. I agreed that we could pull it off. We both laughed, like we had built a small bridge of camaraderie. And the truth was, if I had met her anywhere else, I think we would have become fast friends, independent of our husbands. She was funny and a damn smart businesswoman. She also juggled motherhood and step-motherhood with what seemed like a lot of grace.

Manny returned, and I gave him the lowdown. He looked at me like I was crazy, or I was making it up, or like maybe we were both crazy.

"This seems complicated, already more drama than I'm looking for."

"It will be fine," I assured him.

Then he shrugged and walked away. I took that to mean that he agreed that we could pull it off.

We arrived first. We got a tour from the hostess, dropped off our alcohol at the bar, and found a place to sit. It was definitely a nicer place, smaller, cozier, and more upscale decor. The main floor was a small lounge, and there were private rooms and an open area downstairs.

When the four of them came in, I tried to act nonchalant, but this idea of pretending we didn't know each other had already had me turned on. Jess entered first, looking like she was intentionally leading the way. She scanned the room, found me, and gave me a little nod: *We've got this.* Gina and Cory came in next, laughing and talking, in their own world. Brad came in last. His eyes scanned the room in the same way that Jess's had. I caught his gaze and held it. Locking his eyes on me for as long as he could, he blushed, turning away, smiling, and shaking his head a little. From across the club, he looked back at me and mouthed, *Whoa,* exhaling slowly.

Even though the place was remarkably small, Manny and I kept our distance. We each had a drink and danced a little. Not long after they arrived, I went to the bathroom. I hadn't been there a minute before Jess flew through the door. Hugging me tight, she started talking quickly.

"Okay, I think this is going well. We are doing it. And I just have to tell you, I have never seen Brad like this about another woman before. I mean, he is just so into you. He likes you so much."

I felt surprised, taken aback. I didn't expect this and didn't know what to say, especially since she was talking about her husband. "But he barely knows me," I said.

"Yeah, but he already thinks you are so hot and funny. He really thinks you are so funny."

I felt surprised, confused, flattered, but mostly excited.

"Okay, I've got to go before Gina comes in here." She hugged me again and left.

Later in the night I saw Brad approach the bar, alone, and I motioned to Manny that Brad was up there, and I was going to get a drink. As I crossed the dance floor, I imagined this was exactly what it felt like to be a real-life secret agent. As I closed in, I could smell something. I was certain it was danger.

I stood close to Brad but looked straight ahead and ordered my drink. He also kept his gaze directly at the shelves of bottles behind the bar. "Hey, stranger," I purred, as is the policy of any self-respecting spy approaching an informant at a bar. I'd seen enough James Bond movies to know how this was done.

"Wow," he said slowly, "you look so good." I saw him smile out of the corner of my eye.

We simultaneously took a deep breath. The forced relaxation of the exhale brought our hands close enough to touch. A jolt of energy from my little finger zapped into my chest, down to my toes, rocketed to my head, then settled as a deep ache in my pelvis. It intensified, radiating outwards. I instantly grabbed him around the neck with both hands. My mouth found his, the softness of our lips made softer by the hardness in his pants and the bar pressing into the small of my back. He hoisted me onto the bar and pushed my skirt up around my waist. I leaned back in ecstasy as he buried his face and fingers between my legs.

Actually, no. After our hands touched, I kept my eyes straight ahead, frozen, and I started babbling. "Oh my God. Did you just feel that? Oh, wow. Wow. Oh. My. God." His shoulders shook from stifled laughter. I mumbled goodbye and walked away in a fog.

Chapter 12

I had always been in a hurry to reach any milestone that proved I was getting closer to adulthood. I had my period when I was eleven and couldn't believe I'd had to wait so long. Marriage was a substantial marker of adulthood for me, so I had considered every boyfriend in my life to be my future husband. I was always on the lookout for my one and only. So, when the boyfriend I found when I was twenty-one materialized into a husband, I thought I had hit the jackpot. I could not fathom why anyone would want to be single or dating.

Manny and I had been together seven years when his best friend, Chris, started dating a woman he really liked, named Tina. He is a photographer, and they met at the opening of one of his shows. When Manny told me that Chris had met someone new, I felt really happy for him. Immediately afterwards, I realized that they were now, maybe even right at that moment, experiencing something that Manny and I would never have the opportunity to experience again: New Relationship Sex. I wondered what life would be like to sit on the couch, watching a movie, wondering if I would be getting any action? How in the world could we keep up that kind of ripe and intoxicating anticipation in a relationship that was no longer new? This is one of the questions we were trying to answer with our foray into the lifestyle. And even before we decided to go back to the club scene, when we were only just considering the possibility, the desire in our marriage increased. Writer and relationship coach Esther Perel says that we can quite intensely "relish in the buzz of transgression." Manny and I had simply been discussing ditching societal norms, and we were both already turned on. Our choice to go to lifestyle clubs may seem extreme, but on every issue, everyone draws the line *somewhere*.

It is easy to assume we mostly have the same ideas of what is acceptable and what is not in our society, in our relationships, in our families, but the continuum is much broader than most people realize. I am not a parenting expert, but I certainly consider myself an expert on parents. After two decades of coaching hundreds of athletes, I've had over a thousand parent conferences and have been privy to the inner dynamics of many families. I also spent years straddling two worlds—the competitive, glitzy world of competitive skating and the hipster world of radical unschooling. I have seen enough to know that each family decides for themselves what is allowed and absolutely not allowed and that there is a huge range.

I've heard parents say (about little kids), "Well, it's not like you can *force* them to eat something they don't like." In the next moment, another mom was telling us exactly how to force-feed a child. It had something to do with plugging their nose and blowing in their face. I know moms who laid out their children's clothes until they were twenty-eight years old, and I had a homeschooling friend who considered it optional that her four-year-old brush his teeth.

Even though most people think what monogamy is and what monogamy isn't is pretty straightforward, it also exists on a continuum. What people consider acceptable varies from couple to couple. Everyone has different views on watching pornography, reading erotica, lap dances, being friends with exes on social media, and flirting. I've even heard that some people expect their partners not to fantasize about other people, which I found hilarious until I realized they were serious. Then I found it disturbing, like when I heard children in North Korea were taught that the government can hear their thoughts.

I appreciated that in the swing lifestyle, partners discussed what they considered acceptable, in monogamy and in consensual non-monogamy, before getting into an actual situation with an outside person. Most couples we encountered in the lifestyle seemed to have had many nuanced conversations about sex, intimacy, emotional connection, and honesty. It was clear that communication was a prerequisite for even considering dipping your toe in the lifestyle.

Every conversation we had with other couples in the lifestyle got deep and personal very quickly. I love words. I love talking. And I loved when people opened up to me and shared things that were usually kept secret. I loved having a window into people's deeper thoughts. I firmly believe we were all more similar than different, and the range of intimate conversations validated my assumptions. I loved to see the other person soften and sink into their own skin a little more comfortably. I loved that connection.

In general, the people we met in the lifestyle were incredibly forthcoming. There were few places in life where you could spill a deep dark secret or a hidden fantasy and expect others to listen without judgement. The people we met were trying to be real. They were looking for sexy fun, but also, many of them were trying to connect more deeply with themselves by expressing the aspect of humanness that is the most repressed, the most judged, the most taboo: sexual desire.

For some, their foray into the lifestyle was also an attempt to reimagine a part of their sexuality that was judged and labeled early on. A few women had shared with me that the first boy they had ever been with had told them or told friends something inexcusable about their bodies. They were too wet. They were too "into it." They had carried those things shamefully for years, but they were now examining and healing those early beliefs through a new experience of self-discovery.

The lifestyle was an opportunity for playing out sexual fantasy, but for many we met, it was also an opportunity for developing a new sexual identity. With like-minded adults and set guidelines, many were rediscovering their sexuality on their own terms.

The men didn't talk about past hurts or insecurities. Instead, they spoke about the present and almost singular fear of men in sexual situations, the one that we are reminded of with every Cialis and Viagra commercial. They talked about what happened when they were not able to get or maintain an erection. Obviously, a penis is not the only part of a man's body that can give or receive pleasure, so when this happened, we were assured that people moved right past it. It was no big deal. If men wanted to continue in the lifestyle, they had to quickly get over any belief that their contribution to a sexual encounter started or ended with their ability to get a boner.

In order for any of this to work, people had to be considerate. They had to communicate. They had to listen. There wasn't one person we met, male or female, who didn't obviously understand the vulnerability involved for everyone, the vulnerability of talking about desire, deep secrets, taboos, of acting out fantasies.

In addition to our monthly club visits, Manny and I had figured out that a consistent way to increase our desire was to text Brad and Jess. Though Manny was not as into it as I was, he tried to play along. I loved it. I asked Manny if he wanted to see my messages with Brad, but he declined. He seemed content with the fact that my increased desire was impacting our sex life in a positive way. Sometimes I would wake him up by running my lips along his chest or stomach. We'd have sex; then we'd both get up, have coffee, and he would be out the door to work.

All of the texting with Brad and Jess fueled our desire to get together again in person. We established that we would get together with them to hang out, nobody would be getting naked, but we would leave open the possibility of some interaction. Soon, we were sitting with Brad and Jess at a high-top table at the bar across the street from our house. Manny and I sat on the same side of the table. Jess sat across from him, and Brad sat across from me. A band was setting up beside our table, and I realized we were very close to the small stage.

Brad looked at the menu and remarked on how much he loved fried pickles. Jess looked at her menu and absentmindedly remarked that he was gross for wanting to order something so garlicky. He joked that anyone else who may be kissing him later would need to order them too. He winked at me, and I almost fell off my chair. I loved how cute he looked laughing at his own joke. Jess rolled her eyes at him like this was his usual schtick. She looked at me, and I tried to maintain my composure, although the color in my cheeks likely proved that I was eating this up. Manny laughed and studied the menu.

We got our appetizers and drinks just as the band started to play a decent but very loud Motown medley. "Maybe we should just finish these drinks and head back to our house," I said, above the music. Everyone agreed.

Brad looked me in the eye and smiled. It's a wonder I didn't melt and become a puddle on the floor. Another rush of warmth sprang to my cheeks, and an anticipatory ache spread over my whole body.

Cool summer raindrops, the kind that make you hold your breath when you are running through them, pelted us as we dashed to the front door. We shook off in the front hallway and hung up our coats.

"Beers?" Manny offered, switching into host mode. We all nodded.

We got comfortable in the living room, and Manny returned with our drinks.

In one particular way, a swingers' double date is just like a regular date between two people. You spend most of the night wondering who is going to make the first move. Except it was laid on the table at the beginning of this date that Brad and Jess had already discussed this and were in agreement on their prediction for how the night would go.

"So, it's always awkward, trying to figure out who will make the move, who will get things started," Jess said.

"You know, with two people it's 50/50, but when there are more, it's hard to figure it out sometimes. You don't know if you're going to have to be the one," Brad added.

"So, we talked about this earlier, and here," she circled her finger in the air, indicating the four of us sitting in our great room, "we don't have to wonder."

"What do you mean?" I laughed.

"It's you," Jess said. "I told Brad, 'it will definitely be Ashleigh.'"

"Definitely, Ashleigh," he nodded.

"Ha!" I laughed out loud, "What?" I tried to feign innocence. They didn't know the story about my mom telling me to grab the boy by the tie, but clearly, I emitted a vibe that told them all they needed to know.

Jess walked toward the kitchen to put her bottle cap into the garbage. She shrugged, "Sometimes you just know." She looked back over her shoulder, adding, "Oh, and it's already clear that we ..." she motioned to herself and to Manny, "are just interested in sex. But, you two ..." she motioned to me and Brad, "you two are all falling in love over there."

Brad chuckled and took a sip of his beer, blushing. I took a sip, too, but kept my eyes on Jess, nervously. She comfortably plopped down on the couch beside me and smiled a relaxed smile.

Soon they had us captivated, sharing all their lifestyle escapades from leaving a club with a couple to go back to their rooftop hot tub to being presented with a game of "swenga," a Jenga set fashioned into a sex game. Each block had an instruction to perform an act of intimacy, kissing, touching, removing clothing. I tried to focus on the conversation, but I had to forcibly resist my urge to pounce on Brad and rip his clothes off. I felt like a puppy who's being taught to "leave it." *Leave it ... leave it ... no, bad girl ... leave it.* I needed to keep reminding myself, lest my impulse took over, and I stripped him naked, mid-conversation, right there in my butterfly armchair.

"And this guy," Brad said, shaking his head, recounting the experience with the Swenga guy. "This guy was so into Jess, like he was completely *ignoring* his girlfriend."

Jess laughed. "You were so annoyed. You were pissed at him." She looked toward me and then Manny, continuing. "So, anyway, we didn't stay for that long because Brad was not having it."

"There's just got to be some balance," Brad explained. "It can't just be one-sided."

"Mr. Rules," Jess teased. "He's always got the rules. He's always got to be like the dad in the group."

I was figuring out she was the gas and he was the brakes. Brad just shook his head, not wanting to dig his hole deeper. And then he got up and gave a little stretch. The table in front of us was littered with empty bottles, and we had been sitting for hours, "Hey, want to give us a tour? Show me that bathroom," he added.

We cannot tell anyone anything about our house without mentioning our ugly master bathroom. Our house was built in the early 1990s, but by old people, which resulted in decor and fixtures that looked like they were installed in the seventies. We had renovated every other room in the house. But we couldn't bring ourselves to redo the enormous bathroom, primarily because we doubted we'd find another bathtub that was so amazing. To be clear, the bathtub was hideous but monstrous. It was forest green, deep and wide with square corners so it fit a ludicrous amount of water. It was so big that our boys had taught themselves to snorkel in it. Plus, Niko had been born in that tub.

I led the way for all four of us into the master bedroom. Our bedroom was built to scale for our bathroom, and it was a sprawling expanse of space. At that time, we still had it set up as a family bedroom with two queen-sized beds, a single bed, and a couple dressers, with still ample room to have a dance party. Brad commented that it looked like we already had it sex up for a sex party.

"Yeah, honestly, when the kids get older that would be a perfect use for a family bedroom." I laughed.

We peeked our heads into the bathroom, all four of us standing in the hallway. Manny and Jess turned around to head back to the great room, and Brad gently grasped my arm, indicating for me to stay back.

I assumed when they ended up in the living room and saw that we had not followed, they would figure out really quickly what was happening. Meanwhile, back in the hallway, Brad and I were standing face to face. Well, face to chest. I had to look up to meet his eyes.

All night of getting myself to *leave it* had me feeling weak. He smiled down at me as he put his hands on the sides of my face and wrapped his fingers behind my ears. He pulled me close, and I stretched up on my toes.

The kiss did not disappoint. Our lips shared the electricity I felt when our hands touched at the bar. It now flowed and reverberated through my whole body. My knees weakened as we pressed against each other and he wrapped his arms around my back to hold me close. I opened my eyes and sensed that his eyes had been open the whole time. He was looking at me and smiling as we kissed. I smiled back, continuing to explore his mouth with mine and running my palms up and down his back. He slid his hands down the sides of my body and grasped my hips firmly. He pushed them back, arching my back and I let out a small moan, while whispering, "Yes, yes, yes …," as we continued to kiss, harder and deeper. After another minute, I pulled back for air. He smiled down at me. His face was in focus, but everything else was hazy, like we had just created a steam room in our hallway.

"Whoa … I have been waiting all night to do that," I said.

He laughed and brushed a hair from my face. "I've been waiting weeks to do that."

Chapter 13

I felt grateful that our marriage was solid enough to head into this new adventure. Instead of every day feeling like Groundhog Day, we were finally entering a new chapter, where we could find excitement and connection, like we were coming back to life after a decade of hibernation.

As is the case for almost every mom, I had many needs that I had pushed aside for a long time. I longed to have Manny tell me I was pretty or that I was doing a good job, or to show some affection in front of the boys. Just simple things: a kiss when he left the house, or a compliment. I did not need a sonnet recited over our morning coffee. But he rarely did these things. Often, when I asked him a simple question, he would ignore me. When I objected, he pointed out that we had known each other far too long to necessitate small talk. The nonchalant confidence that was attractive at the beginning had become cocky. And annoying. Especially annoying, because I like words. Words are really my favorite. I was early to speak, early to read, early to write, and now no experience is complete until I put it into words.

However, there are few things in life that hurt my pride more than barking up the wrong tree, so instead of begging I mostly substituted with other things. I cultivated a group of amazing

friends, threw myself into work and homeschooling, and deepened my spiritual practice. But, every so often I would get really
fed up with the bar being set so low in this one area of our life
together when we pushed ourselves to achieve in the other
areas. Even though I tried to talk to Manny about it, he seemed
not to hear me.

I joked that growing up in such a traditional household had
effectively trained Manny to ignore the sound of a woman's
voice. This was not a funny joke. It was a joke that was even less
funny than his, "I told you once that I loved you; unless I tell
you otherwise, I continue to love you," joke. It seemed that the
only type of communication that would really get his attention
was loud, angry sobbing. This was the polar opposite of my
preferred method of communication, but throughout our relationship, every eighteen months or so, I would talk myself into
getting worked up, crying heavily for emphasis. Through tears, I
tried to explain that it was essential that we have more of the
simple, connective elements in our relationship on a daily basis.
It was good for both of us and good for the boys. He argued that
he didn't really need it, but if I really wanted it, he would try.
And he would, for approximately four days.

In the most critical ways, the foundational ways, our
marriage was solid. Manny was responsible and dependable. I
was also meeting all the markers of being an incredibly responsible adult. I had homemade soup in the freezer. I had carried no
credit card debt for a decade. The previous Christmas, I had
given handmade gifts to everyone on our list, including sewing
reusable fabric gift bags for each one. Even though it could probably be attributed to avoiding the hard conversations, Manny
and I never fought. Our children used fucking coasters. We were
hardcore adulting. A big part of this occurred because I could
trust him. Since we had met, I always knew I could trust him to
work things out with me. I trusted him to do the right thing, to
be levelheaded, to abstain from making rash decisions. Our
venture into the lifestyle was built on the fact that we would

always be honest with each other. We were both open-minded enough to try to come to an agreement. Unless I had talked myself into one of my semi-annual crying jaunts, neither of us would get worked up. There was nothing that we needed to hide.

And then I had a dream. It was the night after Brad and Jess had been at our house, and Brad and I had converted our hallway into a steam room of desire. In the dream Manny was having an affair with his friend Amber. In real life, I had met Amber a couple of times. They knew each other from high school and her office was close to his. I knew that they would often run into each other on the way to work at their morning coffee place. I stopped in on a weekend with Manny to get a coffee, and we saw her. He introduced me, and I recalled how she acted like she really knew who I was and really wanted to continue her conversation with me. When I saw her a year later at a friends' barbecue, I noticed the same thing. She was eager to talk to me, even excited to see me.

In the dream, I had stumbled upon the affair through Manny's phone, seeing unusual information about his location on his navigation app. Still in the dream, I confronted him. He reluctantly admitted there was something going on, but he was standoffish, and I knew I wasn't getting the whole story. I kept telling him that I knew he wasn't telling me everything. He kept brushing me off like we didn't need to talk about what had happened. Like I was being ridiculous asking questions about it. It was no big deal, and discussing it was unnecessary small talk. Minutia. Words, gratuitous words.

I woke up in a panic, my stomach filled with ice, and my cheeks wet with tears. I reached toward Manny for comfort, but he wasn't in our bed. My heart was racing, but I was also exhausted from the emotion of the dream. I rolled over and fell immediately back to sleep. When I woke again a few hours later, I felt like I had been hit by a truck. Although I had fallen back asleep, I didn't feel rested. I felt like I had been sobbing all night.

My eyes were red and puffy when I saw Manny in the bathroom the next morning. I asked where he slept, and he told me he had fallen asleep on the couch. He could see that I was not okay and knew immediately that something had happened.

"Babe, what's wrong?"

Sobs rolled out as I started to speak, "I had a dream. I had a dream that you were having an affair with Amber."

His face went white. "Oh, baby, oh, baby, no. You don't need to worry. Nothing is happening." He pulled me into his arms.

I leaned against his chest and continued to cry, "But in the dream you weren't telling me the whole thing. Tell me," I leaned back. "Tell me, really. Did anything happen?"

He put his hands on my shoulders and looked me in the eye, "No, no, baby, baby. You don't need to worry about anything. No, baby, we flirt, but I am not even going to do that anymore. We are flirty, but I am not going to do that. I am not going to flirt with her anymore. I knew we shouldn't be doing it." His hand flew to his forehead, and he whispered to himself, "*Damn it …* And I'm not going to do it anymore. I'm not going to do it, baby." He hugged me in again and put his hands on the back of my head, holding me close.

Confused, I let him hold me. It would have made more sense if he told me there was nothing, but he had seemed super guilty. He went to work. It nagged at me.

Later in the day I texted him. "I know there's more. I just know. Have you kissed her?"

"Yes. Twice."

Oftentimes in my life, I have asked questions and knew the answer I would hear. This time, I had correctly anticipated his answer, but I didn't know what to do. I was in shock.

The kissing was not the big deal. My new favorite hobby was kissing other men, and I was not entertaining the double standard that it was fine for me but not okay for him. That was not the problem. I was guessing that he didn't just grunt and wave to Amber at the coffee shop and end up making out with her. There had to be small talk, connection, compliments, flirting: all the things I had been begging him for year after year. And I was in the dark about it.

Manny had tried to convince me many times that I was imagining that he used to be more affectionate in the past. He resented that I was trying to change him. He had never been over the top affectionate, but he had been very attentive. I knew I wasn't misremembering it. My parents were still very affectionate with each other, and I had never dated anyone who was not. Confirming my suspicions, every time my parents visited, Manny would automatically switch into a mode where he was slightly more attentive, sometimes even sitting with me on the couch, putting his arm around me. Yet around his own parents, he barely spoke to me, mimicking his own dad's quietness and his parents' marriage dynamics. Manny's original level of affection had lasted until a little before our wedding and then tapered off year by year, until there we were, years away from the last time he told me I was beautiful, or even pretty. It had probably been five years since he had initiated an "I love you," and his most common response to me telling him I loved him had become "goodnight." I had stopped saying it very often because the sting of not getting it back was too hard to bear.

I had thought we were so evolved, but was he open to me connecting with other men just because he wanted a pass for whatever he was already doing on the side? Was he only interested in going to clubs because he was already involved with Amber, and somehow this made him feel less bad about it? How long had it been? How far had it gone? Had there been anyone else?

When Manny came home from work that day, we went straight to the bedroom to talk. I was furious, imagining him building intimacy with another woman while ignoring the basic requests I had of him at home.

"I feel like a fucking idiot," I told him. "Meeting all these new people, telling them our relationship story, like it's a fucking fairytale. Meanwhile, you're doing this bullshit on the side. Is that the only reason you are doing this with me?" I was livid.

"No, babe," he groaned, "I'm the fucking idiot. I am so sorry."

I had felt progressively less loved by him since we were married, and it hit me hard after Luke was born. I had told him this before, but I elaborated in a way I never had.

"I have fantasized about divorce for years," I told him, "but I knew I couldn't do it. Everyone would hate me. I would be the bad guy, the ungrateful bitch who left her perfect husband. Now? Now I feel like you have handed me a golden key out of our marriage. I could just say, 'Oh, he cheated on me and I just couldn't get over it' and I wouldn't be the bad guy."

Gone were the days when I had told him that if he kissed someone, he shouldn't tell me. That bringing home the information would do more harm than good. A lot had happened since then. A decade of marriage had happened since then. No longer was this no big deal. If I wanted to, I could make it a big fucking deal.

It was all at once strange, liberating, and terrifying. If I had left at any other time, even though I was not getting what I needed, people would have judged me. Even though it wasn't about the kissing for me, other people might freak and agree that I was doing the right thing by leaving him. It was like I had been handed an out, a way to exit my perfect looking life.

I also felt angry that Manny had fucked things up with Brad and Jess. We couldn't keep talking to them if we were this confused. I contacted them and told them we needed a break from the lifestyle, that we needed to work some things out. Clearly, our relationship was not as solid as we thought it was. I hadn't even considered that we were doing this because something was missing. I thought we were more evolved, less possessive, less needy than most. In between my regularly planned attempts at shaking things up and bringing more emotionality into our relationship, I diverted my attention and my energy in an attempt to convince myself that things were fine. I worked more. I spent more time with friends. I looked on the bright side. I had always felt that being emotionally needy was a hallmark of a weak, immature person, so I tried to minimize emotions in myself and stick to focusing on the next project or goal. Manny had always seemed to naturally have very few emotional needs. This left me relatively unburdened but also struggling to connect with someone who didn't seem to need connection and who seemed to be turned off by the need for it. Now I could see that he *did* long for more connection, but he wasn't trying to get it with me.

I felt paranoid that Manny was going to continue communicating with Amber, so I started snooping on his phone. Weirdly, after my dream, anytime my phone would vibrate, I hoped the message would be from him. This was after weeks of wishing every single message would be from Brad. With a little jealousy thrown into the mix, I clung to Manny more than I had in years, maybe more than ever. Furious, there I was, now wanting Manny to text me more than ever, wanting him to check in during the day, even though that was something we had never done. He was definitely making more of an effort. I could tell it was out of fear and some remorse, but mostly fear that I would go off the deep end with a very big, very extra idea and tell him to get out. And I was jealous about Amber, wondering when he would run into her again. And I was missing Brad, missing how thoughtful he had been in his messages to me and realizing how needy I felt when I wasn't getting his attention.

Manny willingly handed over his phone so I could further my investigation. I wondered if he was only willing because the juiciest messages with Amber had been via instant message on his computer, during the workday, after they ran into each other at the coffee place. He admitted, yes, the bulk of the messages were through IM. They had a text chain on his phone that went back a couple of years. She seemed to know about situations at his office. She checked in more than once to see how he was feeling about a work conflict. And they had inside jokes. All of these were things I had never heard of. My heart broke.

I found weird messages about me, talking about how she thought I was pretty. And she was disappointed when I didn't attend a party they were at together. I pressed Manny, and he said that they had talked about the three of us having a threesome. I wanted to kill him.

I hated Manny and at the same time felt terrified that I was going to lose him. I felt sick thinking about the special connection he had with Amber while I longed for the warm rush I got when Brad sent me a sweet good morning text.

"Hey, sunshine. It was killing me to wait for you to text." (This was at 9:00 a.m.) "Oh, and that funny thing you said yesterday ... I am still laughing."

And even though I told Brad and Jess we couldn't talk to them, I wondered if Manny and I were not wired for monogamy. Could we only really appreciate each other when we had someone on the side? And is it unfair to ask for our partner to give us everything?

There I was, hoping Manny would not be flirting with Amber but longing to get that connection with Brad. I was incredibly angry with Manny, but I also understood why he connected with her, why he let it go too far. There were so many demands on us. It was hard to give each other all we needed and still give to ourselves and our jobs and the boys. I had to be so many things to so many people at work and at home. How could I give to myself and give to all of them? How much should I demand Manny give to me?

I thought about the one time I had texted with Brad since I told them we couldn't talk. The day after I had told them we needed a break from the lifestyle because we had to work something out, I was home alone with the boys, wondering if Manny was going to see Amber on his way to work when Brad texted me. "How is homeschooling today?" And then, "I don't know if

I should be texting you. I just wanted to check in and see if you are alright."

I wasn't alright, and I couldn't stop myself from asking, "How often do you tell Jess she is pretty? How often do you tell her she is a good mom? How often do you tell her you love her?"

"Oh, I am good at that stuff, he said. It's other stuff that I have trouble with." I didn't ask what the other stuff was.

I told him that Manny wouldn't kiss me hello or goodbye, even though those were simple ass things to do. I went on to tell him how Manny never said I love you, his very unfunny joke about "I told you once that I loved you. Unless I tell you otherwise, assume I continue to love you." It felt unfunnier than ever before. It felt so sad.

"You are beautiful. You are a great mom. You are a great wife. You deserve to hear all of that," he replied.

We exchanged over 100 texts that day. I didn't tell him about Amber because I thought it would immediately disqualify us from seeing them again. Even though I was hopeful that Manny and I had experienced a catalyst that would move us into a better place, and I had considered that the better place could be a monogamous place, I wasn't ready to accept that I would never see Brad again.

I told him, "I really shouldn't be texting you. We need space to work this out."

Sadness weighed me down constantly. Manny had ruined my plans. He had broken the rules, so now I could not have the excitement I had been loving. The Amber revelation had snapped him into a place where he now went along with my demands to try to keep me happy, worried that I would leave him. I wondered if maybe we were just plain not cut out for monogamy. Maybe we both needed someone on the side in order to actually appreciate each other, and maybe this has been the missing piece for our whole marriage.

Half the time I was worried if Manny saw Amber that day or

was messaging her from work, and the other half I was obsessing over how much I missed Brad. Mostly I just felt confused. I also felt alone. So, less than two weeks after my dream, I told Manny I wanted to start seeing Jess and Brad again. He reluctantly agreed. I could tell he wasn't into it, but I think his guilt over Amber convinced him to go along.

Chapter 14

B rad and I picked up right where we left off, but with greater fervor. Our messaging became more frequent, and even though I didn't predict it was possible, it became much hotter. It was as if we worried that again our connection would be cut off, so we abandoned all caution in our communications. Out of the shower, we sent naked photos. He told me how he liked to change positions often. I told him I could only come if I was on top. He asked me if I liked oral sex.

My response was: "Yes, please. But, fingers, too." He often had his four-legged patients and their owners wait extra time in the exam room as he recovered from a particularly sexy text I had sent, which I found considerate. Nobody wants their vet to walk in with a hard-on.

All at once, I felt intoxicated and intoxicating. I felt drugged and like I was a drug. And I sometimes wondered how in the world he was running his business when it seemed that all he did all day was message me. His attention was such a rush, so fun, and so hot that I could almost put Amber out of my mind. At the very least, I could rationalize it. I understood the feeling Manny must have gotten from flirting with her. I didn't want him getting that from her anymore, but I could understand why it felt so good. I would rather he try to get it from Jess, and I encouraged him to text her. Even in the moment, I understood the absurdity, hoping my husband would connect with this other woman while hoping he would not connect with this other, other woman.

When Jess asked me out for dinner, just the two of us, her text was light and fun. I thought maybe it would be a nice break from the absurdity.

As soon as I saw her, I realized this was clearly not just a casual hangout, as her message had suggested. She looked stressed. As soon as we sat down, she opened up. She told me how everything had changed so quickly when they met us. How Brad was usually the one to make sure things didn't go too far, didn't get too serious, but he had been changing all the rules. Instead of being the brakes, he was now the gas. She was at a loss about what to do about this, so she decided to talk to me about it.

She gave me more of the story of why they started seeing us in the first place. It was because Brad sensed she had feelings for Cory. Even though what they were doing was much more like polyamory than swinging, the assumption had been that they would keep the emotions friendly, no deeper than that. When Brad recognized that Jess was developing a caring connection with Cory, he was jealous, but instead of calling things off with Cory and Gina, he had searched instead for someone to arouse similar feelings in him. And then he found me.

Well, I found him, as I was the first to message them on the app. And that had made the attraction even more intense for Brad. He had always had the upper hand in his relationship with Jess, most likely because of their age difference, Jess told me. But, my confidence, my assertiveness, it was all part of the Ashleigh Package he had created in his mind. It was something new for him, and he found it incredibly alluring.

"When you told us you couldn't talk to us anymore," Jess paused, her eyes heavy, "he was crushed." My eyes widened, taking it all in. "He acted like he was going through a divorce." She went on to explain that he had been a wreck and that she had comforted him because she thought we would never see each other again.

"But ...," she started.

"But here I am," I said, suddenly realizing what was really going on.

"Yup. Here you are." She looked like she wished she could make me disappear. And she looked like she felt badly about it.

We sat there staring at each other, both soaked in confusion about what to do next. I knew we had gotten ourselves into a unique embroilment, but I also knew we weren't alone in feeling this way. In that moment, I wondered if there was anything more confusing than being a woman in this world. Our shared confusion stemmed from an arrangement that, at face value, should have brought more freedom to explore our desires, but instead had become a complicated and burdensome responsibility. But I knew my feelings of confusion didn't start at that restaurant table or even a few months ago during our first club visit. I was always a bit uncertain about what was expected of me as a woman. Well, not uncertain. It was pretty clear that *everything* was expected of me. It wasn't that I thought Manny expected everything of me. It was that I thought the world expected everything from me. Even as a competitive skater and straight-A student, I didn't much compare myself to other people. I compared myself to the textbook perfect girl, the gold standard. In marriage and motherhood, I had done the same. Even when my upbringing and opinions about women being subservient to men halted me from taking over all domestic responsibilities, I still felt badly for not doing it all.

And there I was, sitting across from a beautiful, smart, hard-working woman—a woman who I knew in my heart would be a genuine friend if we had met in different circumstances. Two modern moms overwhelmed with what we thought was expected of us, and instead of shedding some of our responsibilities, we had upped the ante. We had taken the age-old pursuit of trying to do it all to a whole new level.

We were not alone. I saw it in my friends, all feeling the same unworthiness and lack of clarity. I had seen it play out in different ways countless times over my coaching career. I saw moms—brilliant, successful women, wracked by insecurity and doubt, intent on finding a way to shield their daughters from the same. Early on, many of them had landed on figure skating as a vehicle for providing their girl with a perfect sports experience. I could see in their eyes that they were certain that if they themselves had grown up as a figure skater, in the spotlight, with the associated beauty and prestige and physical abilities that they would not be in the position they found themselves in now, working so hard and yet feeling like they would never measure up. They imagined that anyone who grew up in the ice castle of figure skating surely wouldn't feel this badly about themselves.

Every time I told another coach or former skater my observation, they would almost fall off their chair in hilarity and resonance. They had seen it, too, even if they had not recognized it as such. The scrambling and micromanaging of modern sports parents, and the desire to make things perfect for their child. I could see that it was deeper than a feeling of accomplishment if their child won medals. Their actions were driven out of fear of their daughters not feeling good about themselves. Of course, almost all of us who grew up in performance sports are plagued by at least some remnants of disordered eating, distorted body image, and the incessant need to be perfect. Even though we loved the sport and many of us had continued on as coaches, having lived it and still bearing the physical and emotional scars of it, we were certain that achieving success as a figure skater was not the formula for self-love and assurance.

Years before, I had worked through a mindful self-care program with my friends. Our facilitator was Sheila, who later became a very good friend and the one who told me we were all screwing up our kids but probably opposite the way we thought we were. Sheila instructed us to pick one small, doable thing to take better care of ourselves. I went very small and very simple. I decided to go pee when I needed to go pee.

I desperately wanted to tune into my body's deeper knowing and get more in touch with my intuition, but there I was, ignoring, sometimes for hours, one of my most basic needs. I decided on that day that whenever I felt I needed to go, I would stop everything, turn off the stove, pause mid-conversation, and just go pee. Do not pass go. Do not collect $200. Just go pee.

Over the first few weeks, I had the increasing awareness of just how often I ignored what my body was telling me. Whenever I told friends about it, their eyes would widen with interest. Quickly, almost all would tell me they simply could not do it. They were far too needed, far too busy to do something so indulgent. They were worried about what would happen to their kids, their jobs, their what-the-fuck-ever they were concerned about. Like everything would wilt and die and the world would stop turning if they actually took care of themselves for sixty fucking seconds.

They just couldn't do it. And most didn't. The fear that any type of self-care wasn't just indulgent, it was potentially dangerous. Even with modern construction, reliable electricity, and our privileged lives, the simple truth remained. Most of us didn't feel safe unless we were putting ourselves last. I saw it everywhere and mostly I saw it in myself, taking on so much, as a means for proving my worth, and the reflexive guilt I instantly felt if I put anyone's needs behind my own. As women, we had been putting the comfort of others over our own well-being, generation after generation. We immediately felt unworthy or selfish if our needs were being met at all because that signaled that someone else may be suffering. I saw it everywhere I looked, women putting themselves last but working themselves the hardest.

Even if our partners were helping, it didn't seem to make things feel more equal. I don't know who invented the perverse scoring system, but I was certain that Manny had been awarded 100 million points by the Universe when he had buckled Jack into the car seat for the first time. I actually felt like it raised the bar for what I had to do whenever he helped around the house or took responsibility for the kids. Sometimes it really felt like more obligation to earn my keep.

And why in the world would I feel this way? I had not been given to Manny as his possession, complete with a dowry. I grew up with a mom who ran two businesses and a dad who was a great cook and who changed diapers and curled my hair before school. Everyone, regardless of gender, was expected to help with the cleaning. Was it because I had married into a more patriarchal family? Or was it deeper than that? And were other women feeling this way?

I felt like I had too many full-time jobs—mother, home-schooler, coach, wife, and now, texting girlfriend. Texting with Brad should have been an outlet, but now I was terrified of screwing it up, of making Jess feel too jealous. I was scared of losing my connection with Brad and having to go back to just Manny and me when I was completely unsure about trusting him or if he could ever give me what I needed.

I wondered if my job was even doing any good for the young women I coached. The pressure of competitive sports felt different than when I was a kid. The rhetoric about modern sports parents being crazy and only caring about winning was predominant in our culture, but I rejected it. I believed that parents really cared most about how their child was being treated and what they were learning. But often I wondered if I was being naive, if parents really did care about winning, and if the extra encouragement I was giving my athletes was appreciated at all. I wondered if my practice requirements were just making life harder for these children who were already over-scheduled.

I wondered how to be a good mom while I was working. Every time I traveled for competitions and conferences, I left the boys at home. For years, when they stayed with my in-laws, Manny continued to pick up shifts at the restaurant, long after he had switched careers. Being away from both of us was hard for the boys. When I returned home, they whined and cried and had a terrible disposition for days, usually twice as long as my trip had been. I wondered if my traveling for work was just too hard on my family. After years of this, I finally hired a nanny to stay with the boys at our house while I was away. My in-laws still helped and came to watch them during parts of the day, but the boys slept at home and saw Manny each morning and night. When I came home from competitions, the transition back to regular life was incredibly easier.

Even though I had figured out one piece of the puzzle, I still wondered if I could be a good mom and run my organization. I felt like I was failing at all of my full-time jobs. When I was working, I felt like I should be with my boys and when I was with my boys, I felt I was falling behind colleagues of mine who did not have children.

I often thought that maybe I should just finish out the upcoming season of skating and then be done, stay at home with the boys, revamp our homeschooling plan, and then things would get easier. Isn't that the way it is supposed to work? Do the right thing and everything would be easier? Work hard, try hard, and things would come together? Choose the highest level of difficulty and I would be rewarded?

I saw on Jess's face that she was experiencing her own version of the confusion and helplessness that I felt. We both had enough stress and responsibility in our lives without adding to it. Why were we doing this? Were we getting enough out of this arrangement to bear the stress of it? I asked her why she liked the lifestyle.

The attention, she told me. The way heads turned when she walked into a club. I understood. I had felt the same thing when I walked into a club, and the feeling repeated each day when Brad was dying waiting for me to text him each morning. After a day, a week, a lifetime of working so hard and being unsure of whether or not we were getting anywhere, the validation, the instant gratification, it felt like power.

And our ability to come together to try to find common ground, to try to find a solution to our predicament, that felt like power, too. In a world where we were pitted against each other more often than we were shown how to authentically collaborate, Jess could have easily decided to hate me and insist we didn't see each other anymore, but instead, she had called me there to figure out what to do about it.

But even as she opened up to me, and we tried to figure out how to support each other in this situation, I didn't dare tell her about Manny and Amber. She was already on edge because Brad's behavior in relation to me was so out of character, and I didn't want to push her over by letting her see that Manny and I were not as stable as we displayed ourselves to be. I upheld the unspoken agreement of the swing lifestyle. Everyone presented themselves as entering the subculture because their relationship was solid, and they were open-minded. They weren't there because something was missing, rather because they were open to experiencing more than what is allowed in mainstream partnerships. If you are there, you are there professing your mindset of abundance, of so much fun and sexiness to go around, not your fear of scarcity.

But Jess's eyes were wide with fear, the mix of fear and hope that I certainly recognized. I'd felt it when I had something to say but was scared to say it because I didn't want to make it come true by saying it aloud, but at the same time, held onto a sliver of hope that if I said it, then it would instantly disappear, like a monster under the bed when I turned on the light.

"I know you are going to fall in love with him," she said, waiting for the flashlight to make the words turn to dust.

I looked her in the eye and paused before replying slowly, "I am not going to fall in love with your husband."

I could tell by the look on her face that she really wanted to believe me, but she didn't.

And she was right not to because I was lying.

But, in my heart, I was genuinely making another promise, an important promise to the amazing, accomplished woman who sat across from me. A woman who was as confused as I was and who was trying so fucking hard. I might have already fallen in love with her husband, but I was never, ever going to take him.

Chapter 15

We had an alarm system installed in our new house a few weeks after we moved in. Jack and Luke were little, and I had a friend over with her son, who was the same age as Luke. When the alarm technician arrived, I answered the door and apologized for taking a while.

"Crazy house, a lot going on here," I said with a tired smile, sighing and gesturing toward the children, mumbling something about little kids.

He looked into the house, with the 3:2 ratio of child to parent and said, "Oh, I get it ... we have twelve kids."

I felt like an idiot. Hoping for praise or recognition, I was acting more overwhelmed than I actually was. Wearing my busyness as a badge of honor, hoping someone would notice. And I continued this plea for attention for years, adding, "Plus, I homeschool," if anyone commented on how I appeared to be so busy or I was managing so much—feeling foolish, yet unable not to say it.

Now I wished I could go back and relive that embarrassment. I had traded fake overwhelm for real overwhelm. I had too many balls in the air. I was trying to manage Jess's jealousy while navigating my own. I texted Brad all day and encouraged Manny to text Jess. Meanwhile, I snooped through Manny's phone every time he turned his back to see if he had any contact with Amber. And I felt annoyed that if he continued to message her from work, I'd have no way of knowing.

When we were out for dinner, I had asked Jess what I could do to help out, to make her feel more comfortable. She asked that I refrain from texting Brad early in the morning or late at night. I agreed. I had worked non-stop through high school and university, usually with two jobs at a time, but I had never had an office job or a 9-5 schedule. In that moment, being a texting girlfriend officially became my first job with regular business hours.

Generally, my conversations with my brilliant friends were worthy of recording and putting, unedited, on Super Soul Sunday. But I had not gone to any of them about this. It wasn't that I didn't want to talk to them. It was that I was scared to. Monogamy and fidelity are loaded subjects, and I was no dummy. I worried some of them would retreat from our friendship because of insecurities and paranoia that I was interested in their partners.

Unfortunately, I had previously experienced the awkward realization that most women evaluate me first as a threat before considering me as a friend. In our old neighborhood, I walked with Jack in the stroller and hung out at the playground often, as we had no yard of our own in our townhouse. More than once we met a dad with his little one, and the children had a great time playing. Then, the mom would come home from work or errands and meet her family at the playground. When she saw me there, talking to her husband, her face immediately cooled. The smartest men would then take some space and go play with the kids to give us a few minutes to get acquainted. Usually, the wife would relax and sometimes even ask for my number so we could get the kids together to play. But I kept my awareness high. Being at home with a little one is remarkably isolating, and

I did not want to jeopardize any opportunities for me to get out of the house or for Jack to have a playmate at the park.

The last thing I wanted was to trigger one of my friends around monogamy and fidelity and open another can of worms. I would then have to manage their feelings about my situation in addition to my feelings—and Brad's feelings and Jess's feelings and Manny's feelings (was he having any feelings?). I suddenly did not know where to start when talking to my sensational friends. Maintaining witty and intelligent conversations became incredibly challenging. All I could manage were pithy, sexy one-liners. I felt shallower. And dumber. It was like I had reverse evolved. I was a nympho-neanderthal.

Me Ashleigh. Me want sex.

I almost dropped my phone in the water fountain at the rock climbing gym. Arms filled with children's water bottles, I fumbled to turn off my phone before any of the little home-schoolers saw the picture Brad had just sent me, him naked right out of the shower. There was the time that I was texting and walking down the sidewalk at a shopping center and an automatic door almost ate Niko. Let me assure you, the dangers of sexting are real. And then, the moment when I got a phone call from Manny in the middle of a day I had spent mostly texting with Brad while pretending to work in my office and the realization, at that moment, that I had forgotten to pick up Luke from camp.

It's all fun and games until someone forgets to pick up their kid.

Somehow the stress of all of this had not dissipated the sexual excitement that Manny and I felt with each other. It seemed the more stressful it got, the more our sex heated up. One fateful evening, we were making out on the couch one room away from where our boys were watching a movie.

I was lying on my stomach, and Manny was kissing the back of my neck. Then he pulled up my shirt and started kissing my lower back. He pulled my leggings down just a little, and then, he paused.

"Uh, babe … "

"Yeah?" I knew this couldn't be good.

"Uh, you got something here … on your butt."

I snapped my head around to look at him. "It looks like ringworm," he continued.

I flew off the couch and into the master bathroom. I jumped up on the counter and whipped down my pants, pressing myself close to the mirror and twisting around to get the closest look possible. Manny followed me in, certain I would concur with his diagnosis.

"I don't even know." I was saying, my body contorted in an attempt to see clearly. "I don't even know what it looks like."

"I do. I had it in high school, remember? I told you. All over my neck. It was nasty."

"But this is tiny." I saw what he was talking about, a scaly circular patch, with a darker red border, about half a centimeter across. "Isn't it tiny?" I pleaded with him for agreement.

"It's very small. I am sure it will go away quickly," he assured me.

It was very small. I was sure he wouldn't even have noticed it if he hadn't had that very upsetting case in high school. I thought later that for years he had probably examined every red spot on his body and, when he became a father, our children's bodies, for evidence of ringworm without me even knowing.

I needed to figure out how to get rid of this immediately, so I turned to Google. Google, which already knew far too much about my sexual curiosities, was now getting information on my maladies. My body was healthy, and I was adept at using natural remedies, so I searched for home cures for ringworm. I also made the atrociously common mistake of first searching for "images," which almost gave me a panic attack.

Two of the first suggested remedies were apple cider vinegar and coconut oil. And like every other eco-clone, natural hippie mom, I, of course, had a gallon of each in my pantry. I alternated applying the vinegar and coconut oil every hour before bed and was confident it would be gone by morning.

It wasn't. By the next morning it had doubled in size, and another small patch had formed beside it. Manny offered to pick up Lotrimin for me, just in case. I thanked him, and I tried not to pout.

But, in reality, I felt entirely sorry for myself. When I wasn't bathing in apple cider vinegar, I was bathing in self-pity. When I wasn't slathering myself with coconut oil, I was slathering myself with permission to feel despondent. I spent hours reading everything I could about ringworm. It didn't actually have anything to do with a worm, which should have been a relief. But, when I found out I actually had mold type parasites taking up residence in the outer layers of my butt skin, I somehow didn't really feel better about myself. I learned it was called ringworm because the red, blistery sores sometimes had the shape of a worm. I also learned it was related to athletes' foot and jock itch. None of these things made me feel better.

I read about how common it was in children, especially if they had been playing in a sandbox. I also read about how commonly moms get it from their children because it is highly contagious. I kept checking my boys for signs, because they basically live as dirt children, but none appeared. Not only was I patient zero, I was the only patient.

I desperately tried to figure out where I got it. I wondered if the parasitic butt tenants were actually an unintended souvenir from our trip to New York City. But, the more I read, I realized that the timing didn't add up. I wracked my brain to remember anything I could have been doing bare-assed over the previous seven to fourteen days. And then it came to me. The only time I had had my ass out in public over the past few weeks was when I was shopping for shorts at Target. I tried on lots of pairs, and I wasn't wearing any underwear, which I know makes me a horrible human, but honestly, I always return my shopping carts, even when it's raining.

It was a constant worry to not spread it to other parts of my body or to other people in my family. It was gross. It was painfully itchy. It was threatening my sanity. And it was really messing up my plan to get it on with Brad.

I was a few days into the daily doubling of the rash when I realized that it was not going to be cleared up by the next time we were supposed to see Brad and Jess.

"Well, we'll have to cancel," Manny said, acting like he was stating the obvious.

"No," I replied, much too quickly.

He gave me the same look he always gave me when he could tell I had my mind set on something. It was a look that said he knew there was no use arguing, but also, he wondered if I knew that I was losing my mind. I wondered how in the world I was going to explain to them that we were up for hanging out but were still not willing to get naked. We were now a few dates in, which was the lifestyle equivalent of at least a year of courtship. The fact that we hadn't at least soft swapped yet was just plain nutty.

There was something about the secretive nature of the lifestyle that made a fake story unfurl in my head immediately. It was both believable and funny. I told Brad and Jess that I had gone on the zip line in Rebekah's yard and bottomed out, scraping my ass because the line height was set for kids. Jess thought the story was a hoot. She started cracking up because she thought it was so funny and was impressed that I was being honest about a story that had the potential to be so embarrassing. Yes, so honest. That was me.

The thing was, it didn't feel like a complete lie because the story was borrowed from my friend Sarah, who did actually bottom out on Rebekah's zip line the summer before. I had helped Sarah from Rebekah's backyard and into the kitchen, where I cleaned up her very injured buttocks and applied homemade calendula ointment. Because I knew it was possible and I had been there to witness it, I felt less nervous in telling the story. And it offered a fitting excuse. We could still hang out and maybe even make out (fingers crossed), but I wouldn't be getting undressed.

My swinger status intact, I turned to the issue of actually dressing myself each day. It was a problem. Anything that touched my skin was painful. I wore long dresses every day to let it air out, alternating between two dresses I didn't mind getting smeared with the treatments. When it continued to spread, even after I had started using the anti-fungal cream, I switched to anti-fungal powder because I was sure that it was spreading because it was too moist.

I spent much of my day in visualizations, trying to will it to dissipate. I combed through my natural healing books for affirmations that would help it disappear. I slept each night clutching an amethyst crystal in my right hand for protection and healing and a rose quartz in my left for self-love.

In a nonsensical act of desperation, I crushed up an entire head of raw garlic and applied compresses directly to my skin, determined to annihilate the freeloading fungal deadbeats once and for all. I was accustomed to the burning and pain of the rash, so it took me a few minutes to realize that what I was feeling was different. My skin was actually burning. As I rushed to the bathroom, I felt like a cartoon character with flames bursting out of their ears, but flames were bursting out of my ass. I shrieked and ripped off the gauze and garlic. In addition to the ringworm, my butt was now covered in blistering, weeping, second-degree burns.

I had been working and studying with a local homeopath for years, and she had been providing me with remedy ideas to complement the over the counter ringworm treatment. Now I needed her to help me treat the excruciating burns. In all the time she had known me she had always considered me to be level-headed. She was shocked to see me so out of whack. She nearly didn't recognize me. I was a wreck.

In a particularly tender moment, in that same kitchen where I had nursed Sarah after her zip-line accident, I lifted up my dress to show Rebekah the sorry state of my ass.

Through tears, I said, "See. See what I am dealing with."

"Oh … honey," was the only thing she could say in reply.

Chapter 16

I stuck to my nine-to-five schedule of texting Brad. I did not want to do anything to further upset Jess. I wanted her to like me, but I was also desperate to keep this going. Each new piece of information that suggested how much he liked me drew me to him even more—from Jess's comments in the bathroom of the club on the night when we were pretending not to know each other to her disclosing how heartbroken he had been when we took our break. When I had asked Brad how hard it had been when we weren't in contact, he divulged the precise sad country love songs he listened to in an attempt to comfort his broken heart.

One afternoon Brad called me to talk about how to ease Jess's worries. Her discomfort had peaked during a recent trip we took together down to the small club in the city. Jess wanted to dance and socialize, but Brad and I had found ourselves unable to cooperate. Instead of behaving like the adults we were, me in my mid-thirties, him in his mid-forties, we acted like teenagers, the incredibly annoying teenagers who make-out standing up for the entire party.

If it was possible to have sex standing up, without taking off your clothes, we accomplished it that night. Under my little

French Connection dress, I wore low-rise peach underwear that perfectly covered the bandages on my ass. The only time Brad and I unlocked lips was when his mouth found its way to my chest, kissing my breasts, with his hand maneuvering the keyhole opening and my matching peach bra to lick my nipples.

We would break our embrace to say hi to our spouses, who were trying to play along, who kissed a little, but then, like a magnetic pull, we were twisted up again. I felt Brad's erection hard against me, and I whispered in his ear, "I want to go down on you."

"Do it, yes, do it," he said.

Then I looked at Manny and Jess out of the corner of my eye and thought better of it. So instead, I just slipped my hand down the front of his pants, gently cupped his scrotum, and positioned his erection vertical so he would be more comfortable. And then I pressed myself against him, undulating my hips to rub up against it. It was the least I could do.

As we kissed, he traced my body with his hands. I whispered, "yes … yes," to guide him, like a game of Hot-Cold. "You are getting warmer, yes … yes." He followed my lead until he found his way up my skirt, his fingers inside me.

The last straw for Jess that night had been when she walked out of the bathroom and saw Brad and me with our bodies entangled, tongues exploring the unknown mouth, while Manny stood beside us, sipping his drink.

"It's like the two of you were in your own world. You were oblivious," she said.

Yes, guilty as charged.

So, now Brad wanted to strategize how to take this slowly, so she didn't call the whole thing off. One of his ideas was for me to stop calling him "love" in my texts. I obliged but was feeling incredibly annoyed that this arrangement had come with so many damn rules. I hated feeling like I was in trouble or out of someone's good graces, but just the fact that I existed was disconcerting to Jess. But she went along with it because she felt badly about her feelings for Cory. And Manny went along because he felt badly about kissing Amber. Brad and I went along with it because we couldn't wait to jump each other's bones. I tried to play by the rules. The next morning, at 9 a.m., I texted, "Yo, dude. How's it hanging?" He laughed and laughed and somehow found it even sexier. But I wasn't surprised. I knew he loved that I was funny. I had known it would be more of a turn on, but, technically, I wasn't breaking any rules.

Jess and Brad were scheduled to come to our house to hang out again, and I had told them that I still hadn't healed from my very unfortunate zip-line accident, even though by this point it had been several weeks.

It must have been bad.

Yes, yes, it was quite a bad accident.

I was still physically incapable of getting naked, even though getting naked with Brad had now become my top ambition in life. Since Brad had shared that Jess was feeling uneasy, we had decided that we would just hang out, no pressure of anything happening at all. We would just hang out as friends.

They showed up late. And they both looked disturbed. Brad told us that they almost canceled, but not because Jess wanted to. He wanted to. He was feeling jealous about Jess and Cory. He was specifically upset about this one time recently when he saw Cory and Jess having sex. For the record, Brad was having sex with Gina at the same time, but the image of Cory picking Jess up while having intercourse was one he couldn't get out of his mind.

Oh, my god. They are still having sex with them. The two halves of my heart twisted around each other until they snapped like twigs. Why had I not known this? Why had I assumed that they weren't? I felt the blood drain to my toes.

Manny was trying to be a good host, but he caught my eye from across the room. I knew we were both thinking the same thing. *Why in the world would someone even consider being in the life-style if they have a tendency to be this jealous?* We both felt that was a cardinal requirement for this to even sort of work. Wasn't that the main reason people got involved, because they were *not* jealous, because the idea of their partner with someone else is actually a turn on, not a source of anxiety and fear? I knew that was the case for me, that thinking about Manny with someone else was a turn-on. But, also, thinking about him kissing Amber made me want to kill him. It was more than a little confusing in my head, but Brad and Jess had been at this longer than us. I thought they would have figured this out by now or exited the lifestyle altogether.

We were open to them talking more about it. We were really there to be their friends that night. And they did. Jess explained how Brad always wanted to know all the details after she was with Cory.

"Down to every hair flip," she exclaimed.

"No." I thought she must be kidding.

"Yes," she said, emphatically, looking to Brad for confirmation. He nodded with chagrin. It was true. He wanted to know about every hair flip.

My mind was blown. But, at the same time, everything started to make sense. Brad had been the jealous one, the one making the rules, until he met me. Then rules went out the window, group texts were pushed aside for private texting and phone calls, and Jess was given a green light to text sexy photos to Manny or Cory because Brad wanted to get pictures from me. After a year of predictability in the lifestyle, I came around and Brad changed the game. Jess was left wondering what the fuck they were actually doing. And why.

All week I had been waiting for this night, desperately wanting to have just a few minutes alone with Brad, just to kiss him, to have him hold me. Our texting had been like weeks of foreplay, and I wanted nothing more than to feel his body against mine again, to whisper into his mouth, "Yes ... yes, getting warmer. He had told me this was the part he could not get out of his head after our night at the club. "You just kept saying yes," he said. My longing for him straddled the line between delicious and excruciating. But I knew that wasn't in the plan, so I kept up the conversation and tried to stay engaged.

We talked for hours, and it felt good to try to be there for them when they were having a hard time. I felt like maybe I wasn't the worst thing to ever happen to their marriage. Late in the night, a lull fell over our conversation. After just a couple moments of silence, Jess stood up and slowly walked across the living room to me. She locked her eyes on me and offered me her hand. For a second I sat, frozen. I didn't know what she meant by this gesture, but I gave her my hand, and she gently pulled me to my feet. She slowly led me over to the couch where Brad sat and put my hand in his, holding her hand over both of ours. She then went back and knelt on the couch where Manny now sat, alone, and put her hand on his face without saying a word. The three of us looked toward each other, then to her. She leaned in to kiss Manny.

My breath caught in my chest. Brad and I kept our eyes locked on Manny and Jess, trying to figure out if this was really happening. Finally, I softened and leaned in to his chest and breathed him in. I was finally there, in the place I had wanted to be every waking moment for weeks. I tilted my head up to find his lips with mine. His eyes were open, just like I remembered, but he was not looking at me. He was still looking over at Manny and Jess, who are kissing on the other couch, and somehow, incredibly, already had their shirts off, showing actual enthusiasm for each other for the first time.

I tried to pull Brad's attention back to me. I grazed his cheek with my hand. I kissed his neck.

"Do you want to go upstairs?" I offered.

He shook his head. "That would only make it worse," he said.

Make it worse? And then I realized what was wrong. It wasn't that he was distracted and off his game because we had spent the night discussing difficult topics. He couldn't handle

seeing Jess with Manny. The two of them, making out and strip-
ping each other's clothes off, not because they were suddenly
particularly interested in each other, but because they felt they
owed it to us to play along. He knew they were both doing this
for our benefit, but he couldn't shake the possibility that maybe
she would fall for him, too.

Our glorious spouses were cooperating. We finally had our
moment, and I couldn't get Brad to tear his eyes away from
them. All the stress of the past months unfurled upon me, my
dream about Amber, my feelings of maintaining a sham of a
marriage, my desire for Jess to like me, my insatiable desire for
Brad, and the fucking ringworm. I felt like I could handle it all if
I just got some connection from him, just a taste.

Desperately, not wanting this fleeting moment to be over
before it even began, I whispered to him, "Do you want to see
my panties?" I felt ridiculous and foolish, yet I couldn't stop
myself. I was determined to hold his attention, to seduce him.
Like a teenager, desperate for her crush to give her just one
fleeting kiss while playing spin the bottle, like that one piece of
attention would affirm some part of me, fill me up in the one
crucial place I was starving. I wanted it so badly. I pulled him
close and kissed his cheeks and his neck, but he was not kissing
me back. He was still looking at Manny and Jess. And they were
going above and beyond in their attempt to be good sports. The
hotter that side of the living room got, the cooler my side of the
room became.

I was still trying, running my lips up Brad's neck while
fighting back tears when he whispered loudly, "Pssst ... Jess."
Jess pulled herself back from Manny and looked over, shocked to
hear his voice. Her expression told me everything. Until that
moment she hadn't let herself look over at us because she
assumed she knew what would be happening. We would be
melting into each other's arms and taking every opportunity to
touch and kiss and laugh and press our bodies together, drinking
in all we could of each other. When she saw me, eyes frenzied

and Brad, eyes fixed on her, she looked weary, like she had finally done the thing he wanted her to do, and even that wasn't good enough for him.

"Let's go," he said.

He rested his forehead against mine. "Are we done here?" I whispered, barely audible. Then I looked up to meet his eyes.

"For tonight," he told me. I pressed my cheek against his and breathed in his scent, trying to get all I could of him into my lungs.

"I think we are really done," I whispered again, softly. I kept my movements small and my voice quiet, holding my breath, conserving energy, moving in slow motion, feeling dreamlike in an attempt to make this not real.

Jess got up from the couch, pulled on her shirt, and walked across the living room to hug me. She looked so sorry. I could tell from her eyes that she was trying.

She whispered in my ear, "We'll talk tomorrow. It's all going to be okay." She held me, and I held my breath.

Brad put his hand on my shoulder and gave me a distracted kiss on the cheek. Within a minute they were gone, out the front door and, I was certain, out of our lives.

As if I was the hostage of a sadistic demon, his Zippo lighter held tightly to the underside of my mandible, the door closing ignited the tinder box that was my throat. I began to burn. Tears pooled in the back of my throat like gasoline. I was certain the pressure would choke me.

Manny turned to me. I felt a surge of anger and grief. Manny couldn't or wouldn't give me what I needed, and now the one person who I thought could was gone.

The night after my dream about Amber, when I had told Manny that it felt like he had handed me a big golden key, a way out of my lovely-looking life, he looked devastated, but he was not surprised. It somehow all made sense, a feeling he had for years but could not put into words. He recalled how he felt when we were waiting on his tumor results years before. He remembered my mom being so upset, so scared of what would happen next. And he remembered me seeming like I was fine, like I didn't really need him, like I really didn't need anything. He thought then that if he did have cancer and if he died and left me with two little boys, I would be sad for a bit, then remarry and be just fine.

And I told him, yes, that was exactly what I thought. At first, I was terrified that it would be cancer, and I didn't know what I would do. Then I thought maybe this would be my chance to be loved by someone who really loved me. I told him that all I had ever wanted was to feel loved by him. And I didn't. I felt stuck. And I wondered constantly what it would feel like to be with someone who I knew loved me.

The more I thought about it, the more furious I became. Pissed at Manny. Pissed at myself. I felt pissed at every couple who successfully navigated non-monogamy. I felt pissed at every patriarchal culture for setting the bar so low for emotionality in men. Even though I had pushed it down so hard, I realized that when my mother-in-law told me I was lucky, I took that to mean that I didn't deserve Manny. I was so hard on myself that whenever someone told me I wasn't good enough, *it crushed me*. I had been denying the resentment I held for all these years, and now it flooded over me.

I wanted my mother-in-law to know that her perfect fucking son was not so perfect. I wanted her to know I wasn't that lucky. I wanted to burst her balloon. I wanted her to feel, for just one minute, that maybe *he* was lucky that I was choosing to keep our family together.

I felt so pissed that anyone had ever seen me as helpless as a leaf fluttering in the breeze.

Then I felt pissed because it was so fucking true. I had felt helpless getting what I wanted out of my marriage for so long. My only choices were to put up with it or leave.

I felt helpless. And I didn't want to feel helpless anymore. I had worked so hard, so fucking hard, to focus on the good in our relationship. I had worked so hard not to be a whiner, to not try to change him. And the truth this whole time was not that he couldn't offer attention and encouragement. It was that he didn't want to do it for me.

Was he too lazy? Was I not worth it to him? I worked so hard, and he was willing to do nothing to show me he appreciated it. Whenever I had a new idea, he acted like I was dragging him along. When I tried to reach a consensus, he acted like I was twisting his arm for an agreement. I felt so sick of looking on the bright side, of just feeling grateful when I was begging for his attention, and he was ignoring me.

I felt like a fucking dog, wagging my tail. *Do you see me? Do you see me?* And he would push past me. Like acknowledgment was too much, like I was not worth it. Like he could barely stand me. I felt angry and confused. I felt stupid for having sex with him for all these years when he wouldn't give me even a little attention outside the bedroom.

I felt gaslit. I felt like he saw me as a fucking solar-powered Stepford Wife. *Sure, I'll push out the babies and raise the chickens and can forty quarts of tomatoes and run my business and hum to the kids all day. And then we can have sex. Sure. I'm good. Nothing needed here.*

Manny had not cried at our wedding. He had not cried at the births of our boys. The only time I had seen him cry was the day the doctors told us they had found the tumor in his spine. On that night after my dream, we both held each other and wept, unsure how to move forward.

After he shut the door and I heard Brad and Jess leave our driveway, I was so overtaken by the grief and despair that had built up over our decade together that I couldn't even make it out of our front hallway. Sobs overtook me, and I stayed there and cried for hours. Never uttering a word, Manny sat with me as I burned.

Chapter 17

The morning after Brad and Jess left our house, we drove to the beach for a family vacation. The trip was agony. We had Manny's parents with us, and I was crammed into the back of the car with the boys. During our vacation I felt numb. Every time I looked at our beautiful boys, I felt terrible for not feeling content with my perfect looking life. I wondered if I even deserved to feel happy if I couldn't appreciate the things I already had. I felt like a fake.

I went through the motions, desperately tried to find something to cling to for hope, something I could relate to. I wished just one cheesy t-shirt on the boardwalk was something that would give me solace. The best I could come up with was "Fries before guys."

I recalled Jess's eyes just before she left our house, exhausted and trying so hard. I also remembered my promise to her. I would not steal her husband. I was done. I couldn't handle the stress of this any longer. We messaged Brad and Jess and told them we wouldn't see them anymore. I deleted every message and photo Brad had sent me, then deleted them both as contacts in my phone.

When we got home from vacation, we had a note on the door

from a neighbor. They thought one of our chickens was in their driveway. A stationary chicken is not a healthy chicken, so I braced myself for what I would find.

It was decapitated.

I went back over with a shovel to pick it up off the pavement.

I had thought things couldn't get worse, but they had. Now our pets' heads were falling off.

More than anything, I felt stupid.

And I had spent my life feeling smart. Feeling smart and feeling powerful. I grew up in a home where girls were not limited because they were girls. I grew up with teachers who had no issue letting me know I was as smart as or smarter than the boys. I grew up believing I had influence and agency over my own life, and now I started to question all of it.

And suddenly, it was as if a veil had been lifted. Fast and furious, all my current and past misogynistic experiences hit me at once. I was bombarded with the retroactive clarity of all the times I had been the butt of a joke that I didn't know existed and had been patronized without even realizing it. I was shocked by how I had been able to misinterpret situations based on my preconceived notion that women had already achieved equality.

I recalled the time, very recently, that I gave up an entire summer, unpaid, to sit on a committee to hire a new employee at the rink. I felt grateful to be welcomed into the fold as the only figure skating member and the only woman on the committee. During each interview, they gave me space to ask my questions to gauge the candidate's knowledge of skating technique, and I felt honored that my opinion was valued. Although I was confused when we received applications from experienced candidates that were ignored, I held onto the belief that I was appreciated as a skating authority and I was being included because of my lifetime of experience in this field and the value I held as a longtime fixture at the rink.

I didn't realize until the end that I was just a pawn, put on the committee under the guise of representation. Weeks before interviews had started, the men on the committee had met with the applicant who would become our top pick. They had agreed that they would hire him and even negotiated the terms. His new salary was double mine, even though I had been there for ten years.

As I sat at the board room table, two demon arms reached up from my pelvis, high into my chest, through my throat, and into my skull. They each grasped a temporal lobe of my brain and snapped them off like thighs off a turkey. Windmill style, first the left, then the right, the lobes of my brain were thrown against the wall and fell to the floor.

Smack, tumble, tumble, flop.

Smack, tumble, tumble, flop.

I looked at the men at the table. "Thank you," I smiled. "Thank you for including me."

Be grateful, only ever grateful. That was what they banked on during that hiring process. They were certain that I would just play along and be considerate enough to only ask the right questions, feeling so incredibly appreciative to even have a seat at the table. And I had. Now I was pissed. I left the room with my brain still lying on the floor, warm and throbbing.

I had spent three and a half decades believing I was smart and strong and influential. And in a matter of months I had realized that I did not have enough leverage to keep my husband faithful. I did not have enough leverage to persuade another man to want to connect with me more than he wanted to control his own wife. And our new hire at the rink? After only a few months I could no longer get him to answer a single fucking email.

Any power I thought I possessed started to crumble until it completely vanished. I realized the attention I received had more to do with my appearance and the fortunate geography of my birth than with actual equality.

Even the promise of pretty seemed like such a sham.

I felt witless that I had thought my attractiveness gave me

any power. In addition to believing that gender equality was a box that had already been checked, I had always received favor for my appearance, so much so that I truly believed life was easier being a woman. "Pretty" was the first thing I remember being told about myself. It was part of my identity, and I quickly learned that it was something people liked about me. It became apparent that people were happier when I looked prettier. They liked me better when I looked nice. Unconsciously, rapidly, I began to believe I owed it to them. It was my rent for existing on planet Earth. *Look nice for us, would ya?*

But don't look too pretty, okay? The awkwardness, the need to try to charm other girls and women after they had looked me up and down and had decided that my appearance did not make them feel happier. As many women do, I walked the tightrope of trying to look nice enough for the people who wanted me to look nice, yet not too pretty for the people who were on edge.

Before my parents were married, my mom was a talented radio broadcaster. She dreamt of being one of the biggest names in news radio. When I was growing up, I recall her critiquing every interviewer she saw on TV, telling me the things they could be doing better. What she said made sense. I knew she wasn't wrong. I also knew she wasn't running interviews with anyone. Despite still being news savvy and having an exceptional voice, she was running our household, and her skating teams, and my parents' business. She had quit radio when she became pregnant with me.

I understood why she told me what she did, why she told me there was nothing I could not do—because she wanted it to be true. She wanted me to have my big dreams and have the support I needed to make them come true, even if I chose to become a mother. And I understand why it seemed like a good idea to tell little girls that there is nothing a boy can do that they can't do, but I think it's possible that we have an entire generation of women who have been raised to believe we are equal— who have now taken their eye off the ball. Maybe we have actually made things worse. Maybe we have backslid. Suddenly, I wondered if I had been too confident with promises of equality and received enough favor for my whiteness and my cuteness that I had actually made things worse for other women. Sickly, I saw that my naiveté was neither adorable nor harmless. It made me complicit.

Months passed. Each time we got to a holiday I realized how incredibly sad I had felt on holidays for years, and I wondered if this would be the last set we would spend together as a family. I didn't know how long our marriage could last.

We kicked off the New Year with a bang. To be clear, I was asleep before midnight, but Manny and I had a blowout on New Year's Day. This was notable because even though we were facing challenge after challenge, through all the stress, we almost never fought.

We were discussing our recent hosting experience on Christmas Day (which went wonderfully), and I brought up the Mary-Martha Bible story to illustrate the difference in our hosting styles. Martha slaves away in the kitchen (him) while Mary sits and enjoys her guests— (me).

When it comes to Jesus, I will never stop having a loving reverence for his teachings and the vastness of his material, especially when I can pull from that material to help me prove that I am right.

This never went over well with Manny. He disliked my selective Jesus-quoting almost as much as my assumption that he needed a football analogy to understand anything I was saying. It drove him crazy. And I always forgot.

He was annoyed. He misinterpreted my story to mean he was wrong, and I was right. Honestly, I was just trying to build on some common ground we had gained. He muttered something about not hosting dinner again. And I lost it.

I told Manny that I was so sick of him cleaning and acting like a martyr rather than actually interacting with me and the boys.

He exploded with, "I clean because *I have to.*"

Finally, he offered the truth behind all the doing, all the seemingly selfless doing. He thought he was picking up my slack. He thought that it was actually my job and that he was doing me a favor by pitching in. I felt like I was on fire. And the words flowed out like lava.

"Excuse me?" My corneas had been replaced by flame throwers. "Are you saying that cleaning the house is my responsibility, and if you do it you are doing me a favor?" He said nothing, and I assumed that to be an affirmative response. "Don't you *dare*. Don't you fucking *dare*. Everything I do is expected and everything you do deserves a fucking parade. *Fuck* off. Fuck *right off.*"

I felt like I was drowning. Still, everything he did was being awarded bonus points, and everything I did was barely letting me measure up. We were both keeping score, and I didn't know how to terminate this harmful habit. We had both been conditioned to keep score. Any time a dad spends with the kids is glorified. Any time a mom spends with the kids is expected. And she is expected to love it. He felt he was picking up my slack.

Why is it that even if our partners are helping, we somehow still feel like we are the ones who are not measuring up? Is it just the deep knowing in our bones that the way to keep yourself safe and loved as a woman is to just be more helpful, more agreeable, and quieter? To take care of everyone else and put yourself last? Why did I feel like the only two options were to make myself subhuman or superhuman?

I could never measure up, not under that system. That was the racket. That was the hustle. Every little thing done for everyone else essentially counted for nothing, and any time I took for myself was considered a huge deduction. Women could never reach the bar that had been set for them. But it was beneficial to the archaic paradigms of society to keep us trying.

Try to work more hours, try to spend more time with the kids. Keep the house cleaner, brighter, kids looking cuter, your face smoother, hair longer, eyelashes fuller, your portfolio at work more robust, the promotion sooner. Buy some more products to try to make life easier. Buy even more still in an attempt to make yourself prettier and happier.

Gandhi said that Western women will save the world. But almost every Western woman I saw was almost killing herself trying to measure up with a photoshopped and filtered Instagram model or to make a toddler's snack worthy of being photographed for Pinterest and monitoring the shape of her ass in the mirror.

I hated all of this, and I could also see the sick brilliance in keeping women distracted like this. Well played, capitalist patriarchy, well played.

At least four days of the week I was certain I was going to tell Manny to leave when he came home from work. I thought my boys spending time with anyone would be more beneficial than them being around me. I felt like a failure and a fraud at work. My life was a train wreck and no one even noticed because I kept doing what I always did. I did it all and tried to make it look effortless and beautiful.

My period was all out of whack, and after several short cycles in a row I realized I was menstruating on the full moon. I'd had my period during the new moon for as long as I had paid attention. I recalled a friend saying that it was considered healthier, but not to get caught up in it. Well, I Googled it, because it had been a while since I updated Google on the shit storm that was now my life. I was caught up in everything and what would be just one more thing? I read that menstruating with the New Moon is traditionally thought to reflect the "archetype of the mother," while bleeding during the full moon is consistent with the "archetype of the seductress."

And in that moment, I realized that the moon thought I was a slut.

That was not a word I had used or thought about for years, but suddenly it echoed through my head. What did that even mean?

I know I was in eighth grade the first time I was called a slut. I was at the rink watching a hockey game, and during the intermission an older girl stormed toward me in the hallway under the stands. She pointed her finger in my face as I backed up against a wall, "You better watch out when you come to high school, you slut."

The second time was when I had freshly arrived at high school. Older girls, two this time, took my school planner from my locker and ripped it into pieces, posting the pages around the school, each page with the note, "This is from Ashleigh's Bear Book. Slut."

The third time I was at a graduation party in another town with my best friend. I was dancing in a group of people in the middle of the dance floor when a newly graduated Senior broke through the mob. "You slut! You *slut!*" I don't recall what words came next, but she kept yelling in my face and the crowd parted to watch. She yelled and yelled and yelled. I didn't say a word. I just stood there, shaking, reddening, tears wetting my face. When she was done, I ran to the bathroom and hid in a stall, silently sobbing, my body convulsing without making a sound. Outside I heard my friend laughing with her about what had just happened. And then I understood the reason for the tirade. Her ex-boyfriend was in the group of people I was dancing with.

The next public slut announcement I can remember was at a campground where I was staying with my family. This time from a different older girl, shouted from fifty yards away so that everyone around could clearly hear. "*Slut!* Ashleigh Renard, you are a *Slut!*" Cue the cascade of laughter. I quickened my pace as I continued walking to the snack bar to get an ice cream sandwich.

I had sex for the first time two days later.

We could feel bad for me at this point if it weren't for the fact that the word was in my lexicon for years before it was ever used on me. I remember the first time I tried it out to a family friend who was visiting from out of town. I told her that another girl was the "town slut." This was of course absurd, but that is what

I told her. The friend told her mom what I said and asked what that word meant. Word got back to my mom, and she was mortified. More than anything she was embarrassed that I would go down in history as the girl who taught her friend's daughter that awful word.

Afterwards, I wondered what did I mean when I called her that? What was I trying to convey to my friend about that girl? I was trying to say that other girl liked boys, and it was likely she would try to steal my boyfriend. She couldn't be trusted. That's what I meant. I had already internalized the message that approval from boys alchemically translated to power, prestige, and worth. There was not enough attention to go around, and we must wage a silent battle against each other to acquire it. We weren't allies. We were single-woman armies, trying to garner the approval for ourselves. Any other girl who tried to entice the favor toward herself was a threat to the amount of recognition available to me.

I was eleven years old.

Chapter 18

I am seven, and I am back on the stairs. The patch of carpet to my left is still being warmed by the sun. I examine the dust particles more closely. They drift carelessly up and down the sunbeam. And this annoys me. Why can they just glide through existence when it feels so hard for me? I feel my familiar ache. I have always thought this ache was one of impatience. *I cannot wait to grow up.* But now I feel something else. Aside from the ache, my body burns. It burns from exhaustion and a rage that threatens to light my thin bones like matchsticks and let my fascia plunk to a pile on the floor. I'm seven, and I'm tired—tired of enslavement to the two rules of perfectionism. Be everything. Need nothing.

Why are the rules of life so dangerously easy to break? Any misstep or uncertainty or even asking for help results in both being broken. Broken in tandem. Double the embarrassment. Double the shame. Double the burning sensation, the exhaustion I carry in my little belly like a hot coal.

I am fifteen, and the water in the shower is so hot that the vomit running down my arm feels cool. Grey sludge pools beneath me, and I try to push it down the drain with one foot and then the other. It is New Year's Eve, and I am puking in the shower. I ate a bowl of mushroom soup with a sleeve of Nabisco crackers, and I feel too full. I go to the party with an empty stomach and get far too drunk, far too quickly. But I am there with friends, and they are taking care of me when I am vomiting for the second time that day. They hold my hair back. In between retches, I cry and tell them I have been purging for six months. I tell them my New Year's resolution is to stop. And then I pass out.

And I do stop. It was like I flipped a switch. I never put my fingers down my throat again. But, after that night, I don't ask for help again. I have already broken rule one by not being able to control my hunger. I will not break rule two by admitting it to anyone else. My friends and I never talk about it after we leave that bathroom floor.

And no one guessed. I always seemed confident, even as I lived with dysmorphia and an obsession with food. For a year before the purging and for seven years after, every day I compulsively counted and recounted the calories in what I had eaten and what I planned to eat, hundreds of times a day. Then one day Manny and I were at a restaurant with a beautiful view, newly in love. But I wasn't enjoying any of it. I was in the middle of a standoff with a sushi roll.

Finally, the fear of breaking my rules: be everything, need nothing, became less than my fear of never, ever being at peace. I blurted out, "I can't even enjoy this. This whole night should be amazing, and I can't focus on any of it. I can't stop calculating how much of this fucking sushi roll I should actually eat."

In our few months together, he had come to know me as a persistent optimist. Never had he met anyone happier, except when it came to food. In that moment he confessed, "You hate your body more than anyone I know." He had a look of exasperation and confusion, a look I would come to know well over the next two decades, not because I saw it often, but because of its intensity, a look saved only for moments of desperation. "It makes no sense to me."

Until that moment I had operated under the silent assumption that everyone hated their bodies in a manner that directly correlated to their weight. The only people who hated their bodies less than me were certainly women who were thinner, fitter, perfect-er. My cerebral cortex did a backflip. Were some women happy with their bodies *no matter what*? Was this really a choice? Could I just decide right now to stop? To stop living my life half-paralyzed, always distracted? Never content?

I decided to believe him.

I flipped a switch, stopping the only way I knew how to stop anything, cold turkey. I threw out my scale. I blacked out the nutrition information on every food container in my house with permanent marker. After eight years of chronic calorie counting, I knew the nutritional content of everything, but I hoped this would help me forget the old and remember the new. *We are not doing this anymore.*

I was awake for less than a minute the next morning before my brain started at it: *this many calories, this many carbs.*

Plugging my ears only made the voice in my head louder. I started silently saying the alphabet backwards, in a panicked attempt to drown out my internal calorie counter. The backwards alphabet took just enough of my focus to keep me away from the food thoughts until another thought drifted into my consciousness. Countless times that day, I repeated it, Z, Y, X ... For as long as it took for another thought to take hold. And the next day, and the next day. And every day since. I had learned how to mind over matter just about anything.

My pregnancies were easy, and my labors were long, eighty hours total for the three. During each contraction I looked deep into the discomfort, like an explorer, diving, drilling deeper into the core of the pain, with a curious mind. Every intense training session I had ever done as an athlete was essentially a meditation and preparation for labor. Over and over I had shown myself that I could tolerate any measure of physical pain if I knew it was bringing me closer to a goal. I knew the key was to let go of resistance, to not spend the whole time condemning the pain. In between contractions, I was vomiting and looking the opposite of Zen, but during every contraction I would relax my body and go deeper. I could manage this until the very end with Jack and with Luke, then I would tense up, not able to handle the intensity of transition before pushing.

But, when in labor with Niko, I was finally able to lie still and completely relaxed during the hardest of the contractions. Manny lay in bed beside me, sleeping, as I lay silent and still for each contraction. It was in these last hours of my last birth that I realized for the first time that each contraction started at the top of my uterus and worked its way down. During every contraction, I lay limp as I had the sensation that the top of my head was opening, and the entire Universe was ripping through my body. And then it would stop. And I would touch my body with amazement, that I was in one piece and that I was actually still alive. It was in that moment that I realized we can handle excruciating pain, pain that we are certain will kill us, and come out whole.

The key was not trying to rush it. The key was not to resist. To not diagnose the reason and the meaning and then push the feeling aside. If things were moving more slowly than I would like, I needed to trust it was because there was more for me to learn. More information for me to seek out and bring back.

I knew curiosity could save me when it felt like pain and impatience were trying to slaughter me. Curiosity could turn my pain into purpose.

And I tried so hard to just bring curiosity to my current situation, my current hurt, my darkness. I didn't know if I had ever felt so sad and alone. Part of me really wished I could go back. I really wished I could go back with the intention to be content with how my life used to be. What was my problem, exactly, with my previous lovely-looking life? Trying to remember and rationalize why I was not happy when I had the kind of life people longed for was agony. I watched the news coverage of the international refugee crisis and thought, *These women are carrying their babies for miles, through WAR ZONES, and you don't feel fulfilled? With your first world problems? You're awful. Just awful.*

That did not make me feel better.

And I could not go back. I couldn't go back and un-dream about Manny and Amber. I couldn't go back and deny the dizzying rush when my hand touched Brad's at the bar. I had to move forward. I had to figure out how to keep moving. I knew part of it would be giving up the hope of seeing Brad again. I knew part of it was to stop fantasizing about him. I knew part of it was to stop feeding the idea that I had somehow missed out on the love of my life. By all measures, I knew these fantasies were irrational. But I couldn't figure out why Brad's attention had such an effect on me. Had I just been completely shut off, completely starved for that kind of attention for years? Or was it that I had rushed into my relationship with Manny, that I was too focused on the next mature step. Had I just married the first nice guy I met after college? Maybe I had overemphasized the importance of stability and would always be unsatisfied emotionally because of it.

One of my biggest regrets was that I didn't have sex with Brad. I felt like if I had, even just once, been with someone who wanted me, who needed me that badly, then this agony would be worth it. And I knew in the back of my head that if I contacted him and asked him to meet me, he would do it. I craved it so badly. I had the urge to pull back up his number and call him sometimes when I drove by a hotel, and every time I saw a car that looked like his—but I didn't do it. I remembered the look on Jess's face when the two of us were out for dinner, after I assured her that I was not going to fall in love with her husband. She loved him, and she was scared they were not going to be able to keep their marriage together. And, even though I was hurting, I didn't want to hurt her. I knew I needed to leave them alone.

But I also needed to stop obsessing about him. I knew that

would be smart, logical, safe, and responsible. I knew that. I knew all of that. I also knew how I could do that. I knew how to break bad habits. I knew how to flip the switch. I coached people on how to break bad habits. Half of my coaching was teaching mental training techniques to help my athletes manage their self-talk. I had been meditating for ten years. I knew how to do this. But part of me didn't want to. Part of me didn't want to forget him.

Something had been born or reawakened through my connection with him. The desire had uncovered a raw, sizzling awareness. It was excruciating and exhilarating and humbling at the same time. And I didn't want to lose it.

I found the Hindu myth of the god Krishna and the goddess Radha. He was married and an avatar for sexiness and power and desire. He played his flute, and all the women in the village dropped what they were doing to go to him. They put down their babies. They let their dinner burn on the fire. They let automatic doors eat their toddlers. They forget to pick up their kid at camp. And they flocked to him. In the woods. In the wild, sexy woods.

There he danced a hypnotic dance with all the women. And all the ladies loved him. But he loved Radha best. And he snuck away with her into the woods. They made love in the woods for eons, and then Radha went back to her burned dinner and her abandoned family. This happened again and again. Each time the women dropped everything and went to Krishna. Each time, of all the beautiful, adoring women, he chose Radha. And then it was over. He left the village and went back to his wife and his family and his kingdom. And Radha could not have him. Never again. She knew this. And yet, she did not want to forget him. In her pain and longing, she saw him everywhere. To her, every flower, every rock, every morsel of food, seemed to pulse with Krishna's divine energy.

And I got it. There was a part of me that would not go back and undo what we had done, even if I could. There was an aliveness in my ache. That ache that felt like it could crush me. When we feel like we may die, but we don't actually die, we are reminded that we are still very much alive. I had felt this way before. I had felt a certainty that I was going to die from pain, and when I didn't, I felt the wonder of enduring what seemed to be unendurable. After Niko's birth I had felt the wonder of still being alive, maybe more alive than ever.

So, I tried to be curious about what was on the other side. I trusted that I would not feel this dark forever. I knew there would be an end to this confusion and this sadness. I knew there must be something big and different waiting for me. I knew this upheaval would cause a metamorphosis. I knew I was no longer the same person.

Becoming a different version of myself felt treacherous. In my old version, I knew what people disliked and liked. I knew who wanted me to be different and why. I knew who in my life would prefer me to be less spiritual and those who wished I would finally become religious. I knew who desperately wanted me to gain five pounds and who wished I would quit my job. I think all women know these things about the people in their lives. And I think we all calculate, constantly, how far from our real self we are willing to stray in order to make other people feel more comfortable.

I worried if I could still trust myself to know what was best for my family. That theory that I had tested over and over, with big decisions and little decisions. Should I really spend the money on the organic apple sauce? *Yes.* Should we really move? *Yes.* Will it really make our lives better? *Yes.*

Every time, my gut feeling was right. When I ignored it, things were rocky and didn't smooth out until I did what I knew in the first place was the thing I was supposed to do. But that was before Brad and before Amber. I thought I knew what was best for my family. And suddenly, I was no longer so sure. I thought I was solid in the feeling of the Divine caring for me, having my back. Maybe I only cared about myself, and it was my ego telling me what I wanted to hear. Maybe I could not trust myself. Maybe I could not trust that there was any life force connecting us and supporting us. I felt so uncertain. When I finally got the impulse of the next right step, I feared I would not have the courage to take it.

I feared my intuition would tell me to do something that I did not want to do. Something that I would never have considered in my past life. Something that may render me completely unlovable to everyone around me. Something that might render me completely unacceptable to myself.

So, I sat in the musty darkness, and I was terrified to look toward the light.

I worried most that my gut would tell me to leave Manny.

I had no sense of normalized divorce. My in-laws were still married. My parents were still married, and all of their friends were still married to their high school sweethearts. I remembered my mother-in-law telling me what Manny said as a child when he heard that his aunt and uncle were getting divorced. He was astounded and disgusted that they would separate. He told his mom right there that if she and his dad ever did that, he would be too angry to live with either of them. He felt it was a betrayal to the family. I worried that divorce would break my boys' hearts.

And then I wondered if I was doing them a disservice by not exposing them to a man who was in touch with his feelings. They were sensitive boys. I thought Jack was sensitive until I had Luke, and I thought Luke was sensitive until I had Niko. They were soft-hearted boys and they needed a role model for how to deal with their emotions. They didn't copy me, but they wanted so badly to be like their dad. I had seen it over and over. Anything that Manny did, they would mimic in a second, especially Jack. I could suggest or demand something for months. The second Manny did it they would imitate him and adopt it. I had told him this, begged for him to help me out with teaching them to express their feelings. I had begged for a blessing at dinners, a sharing of our favorite thing of the day, and he always resisted or participated apathetically. The latter was more infuriating. Then the boys would copy him and roll their eyes, knowing that Dad thought this was some dumb thing that only Mom wanted to do.

And being alone? Oh, how could I be alone? I knew I couldn't be alone. Eventually, I would want to meet someone. Oh, my god, how would I date? Dating apps seemed like certain insanity. If my experience texting Brad was any indication, I would be a wreck. I would drive off a cliff, or my kids would put themselves up for adoption. It would be a mess.

There was a stigma around divorce, but also so much stigma around how people did marriage. Traditional, patriarchal rules for marriage felt too stifling, too small, too constricting. But I felt a little jealous that we did not have a set of rules on which to base our marriage. I felt overwhelmed trying to figure out how to do marriage without a road map.

Was all this upheaval because I needed a religious awakening? I was cool with spiritual awakening. I would have welcomed that, but organized religion? Each one had way too many rules that sounded like they were written by scared, possessive, egotistical men, men who had recreated God in their image. Religions were too often last to promote the safety of children, last to speak out about racism, last to take a stand against sexual assault.

Then I wondered if the difficulty in our marriage was God's way of punishing us for not following a Christian view of partnership from the beginning. Around this time, we attended an Antiochian Orthodox wedding, where I got to hear our marriage ceremony in English for the first time. I sat there, soaking up every word (repeated in triplicate), and I wondered if there was something we had been missing.

I asked Manny what he thought about the priest's words. He said, "Huh? Oh, I wasn't really listening."

So, I examined it myself for a few months. I was still not sure what I deserved, what I could demand, what I could insist upon in our marriage, and what I had to tend to myself. I wondered if we were missing out on something crucial by not being more possessive of each other. Was that a mark of real love? And did I have the right to feel angry with Manny for not protecting me? For not protecting my heart? I wondered. And I felt confused. The thing I loved best about Manny was the freedom I had being with him. No controlling, no micromanaging. He let me be me. I didn't know if I wanted him to protect me, if he owed me that, or if I even wanted it.

And I thought moving backwards did not feel right.Before all of this mess, God and I had been good. Now, when I sat in meditation, I heard nothing. For months, not a single peep from my intuition or my greater knowing or my Inner Self. Silence.

My ringworm, perhaps comforted by the damp, dark conditions of my soul, continued to linger. I called my homeopath for another remedy, and she gave me the number for a therapist.

Chapter 19

The first day I walked the leaf-covered path to Jacki's studio, I was shaking and nervous. I trusted my homeopath to recommend someone sensational, but I knew I had to open up as much as possible if I really wanted her to be able to help me. I was terrified of condemnation because half of me already believed that I had brought this all on myself as a result of my dismal decisions and all-around, self-serving character.

As soon as I saw Jacki's face, I felt comforted. She looked just like the mom of my childhood best friend, Tricia. Tricia's family lived down the street, and the two of us (and our tag-along younger siblings) had been inseparable for years. Even though they never had good chocolate at their house, only carob bars, I loved hanging out there. Her mom, Lori, searched out natural health treatments for her own medical ailments, and she practiced her muscle testing and reflexology on us when she was getting each new certification. Over the years, she became the most well-known natural healer for miles, and I had even visited her for help getting pregnant with Jack. I was still a registered skeptic at that time, but I really wanted a baby, and we had been trying for eight months, so I gave her the green light to try whatever she thought would help. Ten days later, I was pregnant.

Because Jacki had been recommended by my homeopath, I knew it was unlikely that her methods would mirror mainstream talk therapy, and I was glad for that. After a decade in home birthing, homeschooling, hippie mama circles, rather than being skeptical of woo-woo, it made me feel right at home.

I visited two other energetic healers before her, and Jacki told me the same thing they had. I was having a crisis of creativity. Except, healers don't say things like "crisis." They use words such as "opportunity" and "expansion" and "energetic potential." I imagine in their notes they write things like, "client's aura is the size of thimble … spirit guides appear to be snoozing due to client ignoring them … low frequency of counterclockwise rotation in second chakra." But they were all saying the same thing. My second chakra was fucked. And not in the way I had hoped it would be. I was glad we had a consensus, but what the hell did that mean? I had a creative job, which was funny to me. I grew up believing I wasn't creative or athletic (too many people telling me figure skating wasn't a sport), so to be a coach and choreographer of an artistic sport (because it is, of course, a sport) was rather absurd. Or my beliefs were absurd, rather— which got me to thinking about everything else I had assumed to be true, that maybe was not. And I felt scared again.

But every time I sat down with Jacki, I felt supported. She was kind, smart, extremely open-minded, and so funny. Early on there were plenty of sessions where I just sat and cried, but quickly we made progress that made everything feel much lighter.

One of the first things Jacki showed me was a set of breathing exercises to help with the stress and emotion I held in my body. Oftentimes I had such a build-up of stress that I felt I could not get a good breath. It felt like my lungs were closed off at the bottom. The harder I tried to breathe deeply, the worse it felt, and the more frustrated I became. I remembered the first time I experienced this sensation. It had been in the movie theater in my hometown when I was eleven years old. The sensation came and went during my life. For the first time, I realized that the feelings in my body that led to the discomfort in breathing were what people were probably talking about when they used the word anxiety. I had always called it "stress" and thought that was just something busy people had in their lives.

I am a good student, so I used the exercises consistently. They made a huge difference, and I was able to start to detect when the stress would build up again in my body and work to diffuse it.

Often, I woke up anxious. I woke up feeling that I had already fallen behind in completing tasks for the day, feeling like I would never be able to accomplish what I had set out to accomplish. I remembered the first time I noticed this tendency. When I was in university and was still competing, I would get up early to work out or skate before classes each morning. On my drive to campus, I would take notice of whether the traffic lights were blinking or had switched to their regular pattern of green, yellow, red. If the lights were still blinking, I felt like I had a chance to have a productive day. If they had already switched to their regular pattern, I felt that I had already started too late to get anything done. That meant it was already 6:30 a.m.

Even though I hadn't played the race against the stop-light game in years, my incessant self-judgment had taken other forms. When I chose to put laundry in the dryer instead of hanging it on the clothesline, I felt terrible. I knew it was ridiculous to feel terrible. Finally, I was able to catch myself on the bullshit self-talk. The little troll inside my head was chiding, *Oh, you really care about the environment? Really? Then why are you so lazy putting the clothes in the dryer?*

I had also started walking for relaxation, completely by accident. My friend Rebekah and I live close, and there is a beautiful lake a few minutes away. We had planned to meet for a walk one day, and she canceled at the last minute. I was already pulling up and was about to turn around but decided to walk alone. As I walked silently on the path, around the lake, and through the woods, I realized that I had never walked just for the sake of walking. I had pushed my boys in the stroller when they were really little or met a friend at a park for a playdate. I ran a lot in university and even trained for a marathon, but I was on the first walk of my life.

I started walking a few days a week, and I saw Jacki on a regular schedule. The increased calmness in my body made it possible for the activeness of my brain to slow down. My meditations became more focused. I felt much more grounded.

Jacki helped me reframe my idea of responsibility. Instead of trying to do everything and do it perfectly and anticipate the needs of everyone around me, she told me that it was really my *ability to respond*. She encouraged me to look at every situation as an opportunity for learning and growth. There was no need to instantly label my actions as right or wrong. Every situation was a new opportunity. We often talked about my confusion in my marriage and my continued pining for Brad, but often we did not. Every session I brought to Jacki what was at the front of my mind, whether it was stress with the boys or a difficult situation at work.

I knew that many of my reactions in present-day were a result of conditioning and patterning over the years. With Jacki I was able to recognize and release many of these. Many childhood memories came up, things I hadn't thought about in years. On one day, I thought of a friend who got in trouble in sixth grade. He passed a note with a dirty poem on it and was instantly labeled a bad kid by the teachers and many parents. I was so confused because I knew him to be one of the kindest hearted kids I had ever met. As a sixth-grader I had subconsciously internalized a belief that haunted me ever since. *What people think of you is more important than what is true.*

It was this kind of thing, uncovering old beliefs and catching myself on the bullshit that I let fly through my brain every day, believing it was true, that helped me know I was making such good progress with Jacki. After every session I had a new view of something that I had long held as true or unchanging.

And it started to completely rewire the way I dealt with stress. If anything went wrong, previously, I instantly tried to determine who to blame and almost always blamed myself. Instead of looking at challenges as mistakes I began to embrace the idea of them as opportunities.

As I dropped the self-shaming and blame throwing, I realized the thoughts that were coming into my mind were much more productive and interesting. When I stopped giving myself a hard time about everything and looked for the opportunity, the lessons from each situation came through like messages, like ideas. Like things I needed to write down.

When I was little, I loved school. But, one of my favorite times of the year was the end of the school year. I would gather my notebooks and turn to the empty pages at the back. On these empty pages, I wrote and drew. I never bought a notebook exclusively for these activities, and I didn't write and draw during the school year. It was only after the work was done that I let my creativity spill out onto these last few "extra" pages.

Quite often this happened at Clear Lake at my Grandpa Jack and Grandma Betty's cabin. When school was finished in June, we headed up to visit them in Riding Mountain National Park. We called it Clear Lake, after the lake nearby. I packed up my notebooks and brought them along, knowing that I would get the perfect opportunity to fill them on the large, screened-in porch off the back of the cabin.

Their cabin backed up to four others, and the resulting shared back-yard was filled with spruce trees, thick and old, towering over the tiny cabins. My favorite thing about that porch was the cool, damp, sprucy smell that hung through it for most of the summer. I sat facing the corner, looking out into the trees, and filled my notebooks with pictures, drawings, poems, and song lyrics. After they were full, I felt satisfied and was content to wait until the next year, when I would get to do the same thing again.

When I was eleven, we moved from our big, old two-story farmhouse-style home, to a newer, split-level, across town. I was devastated. There was magic in that old house. I was sure of it. I had yet to find them, but I knew there had to be secret passageways. I knew that the unfinished basement with the creaky staircase and uneven stone walls held mysteries that I just needed more time to discover.

I staged a revolt. I was not moving. Interestingly, and somewhat out of character, my parents did not engage. Despite my vehement opposition to moving, I don't even recall an argument about it. They mostly just shrugged, and I recall a comment about, "When you're a grown-up, maybe you'll love living in an old house, but we are ready for a new one."

We had to be out of our old house before we could take possession of the new, surely horrendous one, so my parents found us a temporary rental. It was in a part of town that I had never explored and was very close to my junior high school. To my delight, it was old and huge, with high ceilings and crooked floors and a living room so big that my little brother and sister rode their tricycles inside. During the Spring that we lived there we had a huge hailstorm on Easter, and I recall hunting for eggs outside in the snow. I had my own room, with drafty old windows and hardwood floors. I was in (temporary) heaven. I loved that the hallway sloped down towards the bathroom and the ceiling in the bathroom sloped to match the hallway. It was like the house had stories to tell me, but I was the one who left stories behind.

I had kept a diary during grades four and five, pouring my little heart out onto the tiny pages of the three-by-five book. I was delighted that this bedroom had a secret cupboard hidden up high in the wall, so I hid my diary there. *I bet new homes don't have any good hiding places*, I thought, smugly. It was such a good hiding place that I forgot I had put it there. When the day came to move to the new house, I left my diary in the cupboard.

And there it stayed. I forgot about it, distracted with the excitement of painting and decorating a room that was all my own for the first time, and in organizing the medicine cabinet in my own bathroom, knowing my younger siblings would not touch a thing.

I felt very grown up in that new house, and I had forgotten about my diary, about my childlike stories. That was until I heard, from my cousin, Kirk, who was connected with all the older kids, that two older boys had found it and were carrying it around, sharing it with everyone. I am certain he said everyone. I envisioned reading parties, where, standing room only, my whole town showed up to find out the inner workings of my nine and ten-year-old mind. And I was horrified.

"Oh my God, I think I wrote about holding hands with Brant at the movie theatre and how it was so romantic," I groaned.

"Yup. Yup, that was in there." Kirk nodded.

It was clear. It was not safe. It was not safe to *ever* write your thoughts down on paper.

For most of high school, I kept a diary, but I was too embarrassed about what I had written to even look back and read it myself. And after each book was full, I shredded it, pulling out page by page and tearing it into pieces, careful not to catch too many words, as the sight of them, strung together, would make my stomach flip. *How embarrassing that you wrote that, that you thought that.* I even criticized my own writing *as* I was writing. One journal began, *What if there was nothing? Universal nonexistence?* And on the next line, *Oh my god, I can't believe you even wrote that. That is so stupid.*

It was as if I was filling the role of harshest critic so no one else could be that for me. If I always wrote alongside my words how terrible my words were, then essentially no one could offer harsher criticism.

So, I ripped up my journals or kept my stories in my head,

only sharing the ones I thought were the funniest or most interesting with friends. And, for years, this is how I nurtured my
stories, going over and over them in my head, finding the words
that felt clever and suiting, then sharing them aloud with friends
and my skaters, and tucking them back into my heart.

One day I was grocery shopping with the boys, and a display
of journals caught my eye: one, in particular. I took it in my
hands and felt a sense of peace in my heart, like my world had
just become a little lighter. On the cover was a self-portrait of
artist Laurel Burch. I didn't know anything about her. I just
knew I must have this journal with the blonde woman crying
tears of gold.

I sat every day to write in it. And it felt good. It felt like I was
moving forward or seeing more clearly, slowly, slowly. I told
Manny that I was writing. He told me that the first thing he
remembered me telling him about myself was that I was a writer,
and I was going to publish my first book by the time I was thirty.
And I remembered the first time I told anyone I was a writer,
when I was nine, and filling my first diary. I told a teacher that
the reason I read so many books was because someday I was
going to write my own. My eyes filled with tears.

"Maybe I meant forty." I smiled a sad and hopeful smile. I
wiped away the tears and looked down at the face of the blonde
woman with her tears of gold, and I wrote. It wasn't long before
I had filled the journal, then another, then another. Soon, I had
seven journals filled.

And then, one morning in meditation I had the urge to
register my name as a domain. The next day I learned how to set
up a WordPress site. I wrote my first piece to share. As I was
preparing to hit publish, I felt terrified. I felt scared that I would
say the wrong, stupid thing. I feared that this would prove I was
different from everyone else, and they would all gang up and
laugh at me, or worse, talk behind my back like I was certain the
whole town did when my nine-year-old writing was shared.
"Poor, stupid, Ashleigh. Such a shame she doesn't just keep her

mouth shut. She should stick to math, not ideas." I published it, anyway, and I shared it on Facebook. And I waited for the bad things to start happening, for the text from my brother, the public heckling.

I waited for the sky to fall.

These things didn't happen. People liked it and commented on it and shared it. People sent me private messages and thanked me for writing it.

I felt emboldened to try again. And again. And again. I got to a point where I knew if I was writing something good by how close I came to vomiting before I hit publish. And if it was a piece that was especially terrifying and nauseating to share, then the messages I got back were the most touching. Some came from acquaintances and people I had known most of my life. Some came from strangers, strangers who now felt they knew me, who felt they weren't alone.

Thank you. I thought I was the only one.

I didn't know we were so similar until I started reading your writing. I always thought we were so different.

I feel like I know you better now than ever.

When I started following you, I didn't expect to learn from you, but I do, every day.

I don't feel as scared sharing my story now that I read yours. Sorry to dump it on you, but here it is …

Sharing my words didn't become less scary. It just became more familiar. I realized that the rush of having people connect with my writing was filling that need for connection I craved so deeply. I realized the satisfaction of writing a well-thought-out post was much deeper than the momentary thrill of composing a sexy text message. I realized that one of my favorite things in the world is having someone dump their story on me.

I got into a routine. I had a new idea. It percolated in my heart and mind for days or weeks or months. And then one morning in meditation, it would start bubbling out of me. And I tried to sit and focus on my breath and stay still until the timer went off, but sometimes I had to jump right up to my desk to get it out. And then I shared it, the moment it was finished. Because if I waited I would talk myself out of it for this reason or for that. I would want to try to make it perfect, so instead I would just share it. And often, I went back and my finger hovered over the delete button, sometimes more than once. But, I resisted the urge to destroy my writing. After it was posted, I let myself re-read it over and over again. I let myself feel all the feelings of reading words laid down by me that were already being read by people all over the world.

I'd edit a typo if I saw it, or just as often after my mom sent me a screenshot of it, but I wouldn't change what I had written. And sometimes I thought that I should hold onto my ideas and let them grow bigger or better before I shared them because I didn't know if another idea would come to me after I let one come forth. But, new ideas always came. After one piece was shared a new idea bubbled up, seemingly out of nowhere, like it had been waiting, just waiting for me to have space for it. So, I made an agreement with inspiration. I would put the words down and share them, as long as it kept feeding me new ideas.

I hung on the funny parts because I got a thrill out of the idea of making people laugh with my stories. I stayed for a moment on a sentence that I knew could be misunderstood, and I felt it. I knew I couldn't jump out of anyone's computer or phone and explain exactly what I meant by every word, so I surrendered to it. To share my writing was to risk being terribly misunderstood. And after the piece was shared, it didn't feel like it belonged to me anymore. I knew people were connecting their own dots and filling in the story with their own experiences. I knew that they saw each one of my stories through a filter of their own experience, the same way I do. And I think this is the reason humans love to read and why we rarely enjoy a movie as much as the book, because each one of us saw the story unfold differently in our heads.

And I realized the vulnerability I hid from, the fear of writing down my thoughts, lest they be misunderstood or thought fool-ish, now didn't make me feel afraid. Sharing my thoughts publicly felt remarkably similar to the rush I experienced when I danced in my lingerie at the club.

I felt exposed and exhilarated.

I felt I was tapping into a deep, true part of myself.

I felt alive.

Chapter 20

I had been meditating for years, but the addition of my writing brought a whole new awareness to my thoughts and the stories I would spin on the threshold of my subconscious. And with the support of Jacki, I was able to shine a light on it with a little self-compassion and tenderness for the first time. I could hear my most awful-sounding thoughts and think, *whoa, now that's interesting*. I fell in love with catching myself on my own bullshit. I wanted to uncover all the places that my big, beautiful human brain, trickster that it was, had fooled me into believing something that was untrue.

Rebekah and I were hanging out on a picnic blanket at the park, when she told me that our friend Stephanie was doing a new experiment that involved doing the thing she most judged other women for doing. Stephanie had started by letting her kids watch TV all day, one whole day without limits on screen time. The premise of the experiment was to get honest with herself about why she was triggered by other people making that same choice.

I immediately understood the purpose of this experiment. I had seen, over and over, if something really annoyed me about someone else, it was because that tendency also lived inside me.

One memorable revelation came to me at a Waldorf playgroup on a day when my boys were behaving particularly badly. One of the main facets of Waldorf education is slowing down to teach children reverence. On that day, my boys were wild and unruly, the definition of irreverent. They were creating a mess I couldn't hum my way out of and I felt very judged by one of my mama friends. Even though we had hung out a couple of times a week for six years, I didn't like this particular friend that much. I mean, she was funny and smart, capable and thoughtful. If she ever picked up a water bottle that my boys forgot, she would return it to me, washed and filled with cold, filtered water, *because what good is an empty water bottle?* Despite her great qualities, she always gave advice that felt judgmental and condescending. Not only did I feel rotten in the playgroup, wondering if I possibly had the worst children in the world, but I obsessed about it until the next day, sobbing over my kitchen sink as I tried to do dishes.

Somehow, in my dismay, I realized that this couldn't possibly be about my boys misbehaving around my lovely friends. I was just too upset for that to make sense.

What was it?

I asked myself over and over, *Why are you so upset?*

Why?

And then the answer.

Because you're a know-it-all, too, and people hate it.

True. Whenever friends or acquaintances, hell, even a virtual stranger, shared with me a challenge they were having, I shared with them the book, the TED talk, and the homeopathic remedy that would certainly fix their life. I did that *all the time.* And then I secretly worried that people *hated me for it.*

I wasn't so upset about feeling judged by my friend. I was so triggered by it because very often I judged other people, tried to help, but worried that people thought it was condescending.

I started to laugh. And laugh.

I started to recall encounters with this friend that had filled me with resentment. I remembered advice on laundry, and bedtime, and table manners, and how to prevent children from walking on furniture, and how to get out the door without rushing. *And it was brilliant.* And my heart filled with gratitude and love, so much love that I had to tell her.

Hands still wet from the dishes, my cheeks still wet from tears, I picked up the phone. And because I understood now that she was actually one of the raddest humans I knew, I wasn't surprised when she picked up on the first ring, and that she listened, with sick babies on her lap, as I awkwardly recounted my realization, starting with, "I have really good news. It's not going to sound good at first but stick with me. It gets better."

I asked her if she had ever picked up on the awkwardness of our friendship. *Yes,* she said. *It is like a dance.* Day to day, she never really knew where she and I stood.

"Okay, this is why," I told her. "Nearly every single thing you say rubs me the wrong way, like big time. And, wait for it … this is the good part. Your advice annoys me because I worry that my advice secretly annoys other people." I continued quickly, wanting to get to the best part. "It's not about you. It's about me. It's *all* about me. And I am sorry, and I love you. I really love you."

She got it. She really got it. And we have had a genuine friendship ever since.

I'd always felt scared of my words. I worried that I must keep them to myself because they had the power to hurt beyond repair. I wished that I would only think lovely thoughts. On that day I realized that if I spoke my truth from a genuine place, and if I was speaking to a person who was more concerned with listening and understanding than being right, the deep digging, the uncovering, made it possible for something new, beautiful, and authentic to arise. Just as new life emerged when soil was overturned, the same could be true with relationships. Something that had remained stagnant for years had the potential to suddenly flourish in an unexpected way. It was as if this new and beautiful thing had been dormant, just waiting for the space and light to grow.

So, when I heard about Stephanie's experiment of doing the thing she judged other people for doing, I knew what I resented other women for. I resented the "luxury" of working outside the house without children crawling all over them. I resented that some women left their house every day to work and let someone else look after their children like it was no big deal.

I knew this wasn't rational. I knew it was a gross, nasty over-simplification. I knew the ridiculous amount of mom guilt that almost every woman carried. I knew no one made decisions about their family like it was "no big deal." And I knew that a huge percentage of women would choose to stay home if they could. It wasn't a luxury. I knew that was bullshit, and I also knew that it wasn't even true for me. I left the house almost every day for practices, and I traveled out of state a couple of times a month. I had other people watch my children often. But, during the day, when I was doing choreography, or practice planning, or administration, I was trying to do it at home, with no office, with no set hours, and with no boundaries.

If I was answering emails or on a conference call, I felt terrible for not playing with my boys. If I was playing with my boys, I felt terrible for not devoting the amount of time that I thought was given by my childless colleagues. I realized that I had been working non-stop my whole life, I had still not yet given myself permission to be a working mom.

I realized that my resentments and fear of doing the things I judged other women for doing weren't really about the "thing" at all. The perfectionist nature that served me well in skating and exceptionally well in school had become treacherous in mother-hood. I had approached adult life like it was a competition, like I was striving for the 6.0. Comparing myself to the imaginary gold standard, my autopilot setting was to identify the highest level of difficulty, to go for it, and allow myself zero slack.

I had lived so long by the rule of training in sport—you are not really trying if you're not truly exhausted. You're not getting better unless you push yourself to your limit every day. And it had manifested into other impossible standards I had set for myself. You're not a good mom unless you have a heroic number of children. You're not working hard enough unless you feel almost dead. And you should be able to do it all. And you should be able to make it look effortless and beautiful.

But even though I tried to make it look effortless, I held a deep longing to have my efforts recognized. But even that is too weak of a word to describe it. If I was being honest, and honesty was becoming a little addictive, I would have to say I craved for my effort to be commemorated, exalted. I wished for it to be memorialized in some way. It was like I was aiming to be a martyr. I had fallen prey to the special type of martyrdom that was held exclusively for mothers. I had embraced the Martyr-mom. And although, in the moment, martyrs may think they are really helping someone, I was certain this type of martyr did no one any favors. Over and over I saw people, mostly women, overwork and over-do, in an attempt to help, to care for, to show consideration for the people around them. It was always presented as an act of self-sacrifice, as a gift.

When I witnessed it in other people, I noticed that the martyrdom often had so little to do with the cause they were "fighting" for and so very much to do with the spectacle they created out of their own suffering. It seemed that they were trying to figure out how to gain the most recognition and appreciation for their self-sacrifice. It seemed to me to be selfishness masking itself as selflessness. I had felt this truth firsthand. I knew the root was not selflessness. It came from a part of my psyche that could best be described as Narcissistic She-Wolf.

There were the loud declarations I favored, like when I would plead with my boys to notice all I did for them when they were asking for the tiniest thing from me. There was the wearing of my busyness like a badge of honor. And I witnessed the quieter, less in-your-face, why-won't-you-thank-me-for-doing-all-I-do type of martyrdom displayed by others, which involved silent suffering, mysterious aches and pains, and the unwillingness to drink a glass of water or go pee when they needed to go pee. I saw the pleading within the suffering. *Can't you see how much I love you by how much suffering I am willing to endure? Can't you feel it, all this sweet love?* I felt it. And it didn't feel like love. It felt sticky, like resentment, and not being fucking honest.

And then I found a quote from Stephen Chbosky that put into words my distaste for martyrdom and my irate frustration that this tendency lived so deeply in me: "You can't just sit there and put everyone's lives ahead of yours and think that counts as love."

If it doesn't feel like love it doesn't count as love. Plain and simple. I didn't care if what I was doing was supposedly out of love. I was ready to get my head out of my ass and ask myself if it actually made the people around me feel loved. If not, it was not love. It was self-serving, and it did not count as love.

And more deeply, I realized that most martyrdom started as an attempt to ignore my own suffering. If I regurgitated this suffering with my newly earned exhaustion, I could spew it all over the world and call it a gift. A selfless gift that desperately begged for recognition. No one wanted this gift. They didn't ask for it, and this is not a special occasion. No thanks. Zero stars. Do not recommend.

I saw it being glorified constantly. I saw women doing most of the work to enforce it in other women. Veiled as camaraderie, I saw women perpetuating the idea every day that it was okay for us to survive only on coffee and wine. Never mind the fact that it was glamorizing chemical addiction as a method for surviving motherhood. That it was okay to be an extension of the SUV, as full-time chauffeurs, ensuring their family members were able to spend countless hours a week on their passions. I saw women working tirelessly in real life, but I saw the joking about it online. Women sharing jokes about "mommy juice" with a wine glass and sarcastic memes. I felt that most women were unhappy with the workload and expectations on them, but joking about it felt safer than working to bring awareness to their conditioning and considering what was at the root of their incessant doing.

I wanted to notice all the ways I perpetuated this Martyrmom culture. I did not want to do it anymore. And I certainly did not want to model it for the young women I worked with. What if I told the looming 6.0 to fuck right off? Maybe it was time, because really, even that judging system had outlived its usefulness in skating. What if I took Stephanie's advice and did the thing I most judged other people for doing?

So, I hired a nanny, four days a week, five hours a day. I set up a lovely office overlooking my gardens. I set hours and closed myself in there. And it was bliss. The boys were happier, and I was happier, and we were able to welcome a wonderful new helper into our family. I would come down after my five hours of work, and the house would be tidy, the laundry put away, and the kids played out. Sometimes dinner would even be started.

The new space and boundaries around my work brought forth new freedom for creativity to flourish. After years of bringing in outside choreographers, I decided to resume doing the choreography myself. It used to be one of my favorite parts of the job, and I could not recall why I started outsourcing it. I also became invigorated to add value to my program that stretched beyond technical instruction and work ethic to encompass self-awareness and empowerment training. I wanted to stop playing the fear-based competitive game and focus on building our culture intentionally. My goal became that any parent in my program, no matter what the time commitment, would say, "The things my daughter learns here she learns nowhere else."

The narrative about parents only caring about winning was predominant in our culture. I decided to ignore it. I committed to the idea that if we prioritized the right things, parents would be supportive, and the competitive success would be a welcomed by-product. Almost without exception, my athletes had parents who were devoted to them. They were loved and cared for and given the remarkable privilege of participating in a very expensive sport.

At the end of one practice, I sat with twenty preteen girls. I asked them to share the one personal accomplishment that made them feel the proudest that season. The first athlete shared that she was so proud that she had become so much faster. The second athlete shared that she was so proud that the team had worked so well together that season. The remaining eighteen athletes also shared lovely things about the team, great improvements they had made as a group.

As we went around the circle, I thought I must not have been very clear with my directions. I really wanted to hear about the personal improvements they had made over the past year. The things they shared were heartfelt and meaningful, so I did not stop them during the exercise or dwell much on it. At the end they all handed me their papers. And when I read them, I was amazed. I saw that *every single girl* had written an amazing personal accomplishment she had made that year.

I have become so much more confident in groups of people I do not know.

I have learned how to take responsibility instead of blaming others when things don't go well.

I am a great performer.

I am a good listener.

I was blown away by how well these young women were getting to know themselves. They had assessed their weaknesses. They could identify their strengths. And yet, it only took one athlete complimenting the whole team to make them feel uncomfortable giving voice to their personal accomplishments.

When I saw them the next week, I told them how much I loved reading their notes. I told them I noticed something funny about what was written and what they had shared in the group. They laughed a little, and many of them nodded.

"Why would that be?" I asked. I pressed, and they had

already become accustomed to the fact that I wasn't moving on from something like this until we got to the root of the issue. They started raising their hands to tell me why they had changed their mind about what they wanted to share.

They didn't want to be seen as bragging, and they worried that someone may not agree that they had improved in the area they mentioned. They nodded and continued to share, all having the same concerns. I told them that so much of the great work we do in this world is done when no one is watching. I wanted them to know that it was okay to tell themselves or the people close to them when they did something fantastic. So, we made a new team rule that day. Each of us was now mandated to share our strengths and accomplishments without adding a qualifier, deflecting, or diminishing.

We practiced like this: "I feel so proud that I improved my strength this season." If they felt uncomfortable, like they needed to add a disclaimer like, "Oh, but I still know I have so far to go. I am not the strongest on the team," I encouraged them to add just one word, "Period."

"I feel so proud that I improved my strength this season. Period."

The girls blushed and laughed a little, but it felt good for all of us.

The athletes quickly became much more comfortable giving themselves credit for good work and much better at recognizing the strengths in others. They developed the habit of giving their teammates credit for improvements. When they heard a teammate diminishing their own accomplishments, they spoke up, they encouraged, and they empowered each other to own their own strengths.

With my new understanding and the chaos of the 2016 US Presidential Election, memories that had been dormant for years started to resurface. News of predatory men going after vulnerable people started to pop up in every news outlet. Pedophile physician Larry Nassar, Catholic priests assaulting children and then being protected by the powerful church leadership, prominent politicians and titans of industry who had gotten away with years of heinous acts were now forced to the forefront for a reckoning. For the first time I looked at the ties between my experiences in the past and the issues at the forefront of the national discussion.

I was eleven when my friend told me about her sexual assault. I marched dutifully to our teacher, then to my parents, and then when requested, to the police station to make a report. I was certain that justice would be served. I visited her house a few months later and saw the man still working on her family farm. Apparently supporting their daughter was more inconvenient for her parents than hiring a new employee.

Later that year Murphy Brown—well, the fictional character played by Candice Bergen—had a baby. Murphy Brown was my favorite TV show, and even though I was not yet twelve, I was cognizant enough to realize that some people had a problem with it. Dan Quayle, for one. He made a big, hairy deal about the show glorifying single motherhood. Quayle gave his ignorant and off-base speech after the riots that followed the Rodney King verdicts. My mom was a news junkie, so I had been following that coverage as well.

The speech was racist and elitist, but all of that was ignored because at the end he said, "It doesn't help matters when primetime TV has Murphy Brown, a character who supposedly epitomizes today's intelligent, highly paid professional woman, mocking the importance of fathers by bearing a child alone and calling it just another lifestyle choice."

This comment stuck in my head for years. What in the world had he been talking about, and why had so many people jumped up to agree?

This memory and the debate rolled over and over in my head.

Just another lifestyle choice.

Just another ... choice.

Choice.

I was seventeen when a high school teacher from another town firmly grabbed my ass in front of half a dozen other grown men, declaring that my ass was the first thing he had noticed about me when he saw me years before, and "wasn't it a nice one?" The men all smiled and laughed. As I looked at each one of them—teachers, husbands, fathers, and community leaders—

not one of them stood up to protect me. I was suddenly struck by the eerie realization that maybe we weren't on the same team. Later that night the ass grabber cornered me, pushed me against a wall, and forcibly tried to kiss me. I still don't know how I got him off of me. My parents were incensed, but I was certain that I did not want to tell anyone else about the incident. They supported me, but it took months to shake the feeling of his drunk, heavy body off of mine.

I heard someone say the name Justice Clarence Thomas, and I froze. I was suddenly taken back to the day, as a ten-year-old, when I walked away from my mom watching Anita Hill's testimony on TV to grab my dictionary and look up the word "bestiality." I slammed the book in disgust, certain that the bad man on TV was not getting that big job. Then, for over two decades, I lived within that belief, right and wrong crystal clear to ten-year-old me, completely unaware that he had actually been confirmed.

Seething, I watched the news stories unfold while treading to keep my head above the surface of my old memories. I already knew when something really bothered me it was because it lived in me. It was often not pretty, but figuring it out felt like a relief. So, I asked myself, why? What can I do? Why do these things make me feel so upset?

And then I realized why I was so bothered: I had begun the slow process of realizing and meeting my own basic human needs. I had denied them for so long, even hating myself for nearly a decade for feeling hungry. I had begun my own re-humanization. The common denominator in all of these events was a consensus, a prevailing opinion that someone did not deserve basic human rights. The right to feel safe in their own home. The right to make their own choices about their life. The right for a child to be protected rather than protecting the people in power.

And I knew that if I was able to treat myself as subhuman or ask myself to be superhuman, then I could be convinced at some point that maybe other people were not worthy of being truly, fully human. Maybe the reason why mass numbers of people have not defended the rights of others over and over in history is because we all practice the subtle dehumanization of ourselves and others every single day. When I was desensitized to it, I was willing to turn a blind eye. I needed to learn how to no longer be complicit.

Chapter 21

The ringworm had finally left town, but I continued to experience other weird health issues. I never missed an annual exam with my midwife, but I had not been to a doctor who specialized in anything but vaginas in a decade. That next year I visited doctors and specialists often enough to make up for ten years of no contact.

Things were coming up that I couldn't handle myself, things that were terribly persistent. One was a scaly patch of skin on my forehead. It was itchy and wouldn't heal, so I visited a dermatologist for the first time in my life.

I was expecting the biopsy results on the same day that Manny was planning to attend Amber's birthday party. I dreaded that he was going, but when he had brought it up, I had said, "Yes, go ahead," because I didn't want to feel like a whiner. I felt sad and worried, but also so fucking jealous that he was going to see Amber while I still had no contact with Brad.

But then I got the call from the doctor, and I had an excuse to ask Manny to skip the party.

"Please come home babe. I have cancer."

A fire ignited in my chest, fueled by my worry that I would need to get my face cut open and the blunt absurdity of needing to hear "basal cell carcinoma" in order to feel justified in asking Manny to consider my feelings over Amber's feelings. It all felt fucking insane.

The doctor recommended I get surgery, and I scheduled it for a few months out, after I was done traveling for the season. But there was something deeper going on. I felt sad and frustrated, and more than anything, I wanted to know what I needed to do to get better. *What is wrong? How do I get better?*

And one day in meditation, it came to me:

You need someone who loves you better.

Uh, okay. So what does that mean? Does that mean I tell Manny to leave today? Does that mean I leave today? Does that mean I need another boyfriend on the side? What does that mean?

Silence.

How could leaving my marriage possibly be the best for my family, best for me? The stress and heartache of divorce and dating, how could that bring me greater fulfillment? How? It couldn't be. But, why was my intuition telling me I needed to seek a truer, madder, deeper love?

I begged for the answer, and for months following, I got nothing more than silence. Every morning I would sit, and every morning I would get no closer to the answer. I had never experienced silence in meditation for so long. I felt confused, but I tried to hold onto a sliver of hope that I had not lost all connection with a greater guidance and my ability to rely on my intuition.

Every day I would ask for the next step, listen, and feel for the answer. But nothing came. I felt broken and confused. Beautiful-looking life, continuous mystery ailments, doctor after doctor. What do I do?

You need someone who loves you better.

Do I ask him to move out?

Silence.

Does this mean I should get a divorce?

Silence.

I felt sadder, and I felt angrier. And I felt stupid. And I felt helpless. Was this a cop-out, or was not having someone who loved me enough really the root of all my challenges? Was this why it was so hard for me not to yell at my kids? Was this why it was a struggle for me to do the housework with joy? Was this why I felt pulled in two different directions with work and family? Was the truth that if I had someone who loved me better this would all be easier?

I had never bought into the "you complete me" phenomenon. I had railed against it since high school. I was probably the only person who disliked the movie *Jerry Maguire*. As a fifteen-year-old I was like, *You had me at hello? Blech. Woman, stand on your own two feet. Please.*

However, I *had* 100 percent bought into the promise of perfection. I had begun to realize that I had believed if I controlled everything and lived with enough discipline that life would unfold before me like a yellow brick road. If anything went wrong, someone was surely to blame. Obstacles were a sign that someone had screwed up. But I was unpacking those beliefs with Jacki.

Why would this be coming up? I wanted to be making progress, to be repairing our marriage. I wanted to feel healthy again.

Did I really need someone who loved me better? Maybe I needed more in order to be a whole, healthy person.

I continued to sit—for another six months.

One day I sat in meditation, not thinking this day would be any different from the string of others that had come before. And I heard it again:

You need someone who loves you better.

Yup, I heard you the first hundred times.

It's you.

Huh?

It's you.

Oh. It's me.

It was me.

All this time it had been me.

After months of feeling broken and confused, hopeless and helpless, struggling to see any future vision of my family that was connected and happy, I finally had some guidance. I had my next right step. I had my answer.

And I laughed.

I laughed out loud.

And I cursed the Divine a little through my laughter. Why hadn't I received the message clearly in the first place? I had been listening, after all. Why did it have to take so long and be so confusing? *Next time, would you please make it clearer? And faster? Please?*

Finally I *had* heard it, and few things excite me more than a new project. And this project was pretty straightforward. I needed to love myself. I needed to love myself better. I needed to love myself, maybe, for the first time.

I knew immediately how I would do it. I would start with words.

I started writing love letters to myself every day.

At first, they were to me, from me. And some days I wrote several in a row. I offered myself what I felt I needed at that moment: encouragement, love, forgiveness for losing my patience with the boys. I gave myself credit for trying, permission to rest. Sometimes I told myself that I just looked really pretty. I told myself that my outfit was cute. I assured myself that the intention behind my work with my boys and with my skaters was evident. That my actions were definitely coming from my heart.

Immediately, I felt relief. I felt comfort.

Whenever I had asked Manny for more encouragement or recognition, he had begrudgingly complied for a few days or, more often and more hurtfully, looked at me in a way that I interpreted to be the way one looks at a seven-year-old who has a sundae and is crying for a cherry on top, after she has already been given *five* cherries.

Honey, you don't really need what you think you need.

I would feel like I just needed to grow up and stop being so needy.

But through the letters I realized I really did need this kind of support. I wasn't asking for a cherry or even a sundae. It was the equivalent of asking for a cracker. I was asking to be fed.

At the beginning, I made a list of the things I thought would change in our family if I continued the letters to myself, if I continued demanding that we set the bar high for the love expressed in our home. I conservatively predicted that everything would change. I had already seen through my work with Jacki that when I changed my way of thinking and relating to others, everything and everyone around me started to change. Even if a situation became heated, my responses seemed to flow peacefully and de-escalate the situation. I left confrontations feeling much more grounded than I ever would have in the past, the stress no longer following me around like an aftershock.

I wrote about my wishes for Manny, for each of the boys, and for me. I imagined us happier, more secure, more comfortable in our own skin, more joyful, and more connected. I imagined Manny less stressed with work. I imagined the tumor in his back causing him less pain. I imagined him talking to me about his day. I imagined the boys cuddling with us more. I imagined us cuddling as a family. I imagined myself healthy. I imagined myself confident in my marriage. I decided to pretend, even if I did not believe it completely, that I was worthy of this kind of family, this kind of love. That we all were.

Why was it for all these years I did not feel worthy of this love? I felt I needed to be better before I loved myself. I felt I needed to accomplish more, complete more, achieve more. If I let up on the pressure, I feared I would stop doing everything. I feared that I was lazy at my core, and the only reason I took on all I did was to prove my worth. I needed to start exploring just how much love and encouragement I needed. I had been so hard on myself. For years I had restricted food and enjoyment. And when I kicked that, I focused on restricting affirmation and rest.

Was it that I thought marriage and parenting and professional life were all even higher degrees of difficulty without love and affection, even validation from myself? Did I think that made me even tougher, even more accomplished?

I had desperately hoped that each new accomplishment, the next project around the house, the next garden harvest, would yield some sort of affirmation from Manny. I fished for compliments, for confirmation that I was doing a good job. He could smell the fishing from a mile away, but often he would not indulge me. Why? Did that feel like some sort of control? Did he want these things, too, but also felt unworthy or tougher because he didn't "need" them? He got praise from his mom, in loads, but never from his dad. Did he just feel that women encourage people, and men sit silent? To engage in affection or encouragement was a sign of weakness? Of neediness?

And there we were with our three kiddos, soft, love-searching, encouragement-needing kiddos. How were we to support them? Was it enough for me to shower them with these things while they gazed longingly at their father, who seemed to have a very limited quota of affection that he could allot each day? The boys had started to brush off my attention like it was patronizing. For, if that was really something for boys, wouldn't they be getting it from Manny, too? Why would they have to beg for it? If you have to beg, is it really worth it?

When I had the dream about Amber, I felt I had been handed a great golden key, a way out of my marriage. But if I chose to stay, I had also been gifted leverage. And I knew I needed it. I knew I needed leverage in order to feel justified in receiving love. Was it that being needy made me feel unlovable? Was it that doing marriage and motherhood without love and validation was the highest level of difficulty? Had Manny's cultural conditioning really trained him to ignore the sound of a woman's voice? Was he too shut down emotionally to ever offer me the support I needed? Would I always have to start our conversations with an update on my current proximity to divorce in order for him to listen?

I didn't know for sure. But I knew that I would take the upper hand. As I wrote the letters to myself, the fear of being too needy, of pushing for what I wanted in our family, dissipated. I felt braver. I realized that every time I took on a new project, a new goal, a new venture, I hoped to receive admiration. And often I did.

But admiration is not the same as love. Admiration comes and goes. What I wanted was a love that stayed. And I knew that in order to give it to anyone else or receive it from anyone else, I had to know that I deserved it. I had to love myself unconditionally. I worried less about what would happen if I made myself more vulnerable. After feeling so lost, I decided I didn't have anything left to lose.

As any self-deprecating perfectionist does, I had carried a list in my head of the dumbest things I had ever said over the course of my entire life. I started writing letters to heal these parts of myself, the memories I had carried with me for so long.

I was four years old the first time I felt stupid for saying the wrong thing. We were visiting my parents' friends after the birth of their baby. The mom was nursing, and my brother, then two years old, asked me what she was doing. I whispered to him that she was, "Feeding the baby from her booby." The nursing mom heard and wailed with laughter. She then repeated it to everyone who came over that afternoon. Shamed, I felt like the stupidest thing to ever walk the earth. I should just stop talking. That was the only way to prevent myself from saying something so humiliating again.

Of course, as I got older, I realized that my mom's friend had just thought what I said to be immensely cute, and that is why she repeated it. But whenever I caught myself saying something stupid, I again felt like that humiliated four-year-old. So I wrote myself a letter from that woman.

I wrote a letter from the boys who found and shared my diary. I apologized from them and told myself that they didn't actually think that I was the dumbest person in the world. That they were sorry that what they thought was a funny game had upset me so much and for so long.

My biggest fear in coaching was that if I did not give a kid enough chances, I would ruin their confidence and their life. And skating parents, gotta love them, had often told me exactly this. But in truth, I regularly gave skaters far too many chances, to the detriment of the team. Aware of this, I became more confident in my coaching and started making braver decisions. A skating mom came after me immediately. Upset, she thought I should have given her daughter more chances to skate in competitions. Truthfully, I should not have placed her daughter on that team level to begin with. I had repeated my old mistake of placing athletes based on potential rather than on track record. I had apologized for that. The mom was still very angry, and it gnawed at me. So I wrote a letter to myself from her, with expanded perspective, letting me know that she reacted because her daughter was upset. She knew that I wasn't actually trying to crush the souls of children.

I wrote a letter from a coworker who I felt showed me no respect or consideration.

I wrote letters from other colleagues, thanking me for supporting them.

I wrote letters to me from Manny, saying all the things I wished he would say.

I wrote letters from my boys, forgiving me for losing my temper.

Every single day, more letters. Every single day, more love.

Several times I felt the need to reach out to someone I had not spoken to in years, to offer an apology or a reconciliation after I examined our relationship in my letters to myself. I grew inspired to make self-awareness a significant part of our mental training program at the rink. One week I introduced the love letter exercise to my skaters. They always gave me good feedback after a writing exercise, but this one made an impression unlike any other. I instructed them to write a love letter to themselves from themselves or from someone who had hurt them. Eyes gaping, they asked, *Like, anyone? Yes, like, anyone.* Immediately they started scribbling on their papers. When the time limit was up, several of them asked for more time. When we were finished, hardly any of them had dry eyes.

Teenage girls are my favorite demographic of humans. The cocktail of bravado and naiveté is impossible to resist. I also find them so darn funny. The rink was a safe place for most of them to be themselves, but they often shared about places where they did not feel as supported. One of their common complaints was how some of their female classmates were so mean, "because they think they are so great."

I had the opportunity, over and over, to let them know that people are not often nasty because they think they are so great. That mean girl does not wake up in the morning, look in the mirror, love what she sees, and on a whim decides to leave a path of tears and destruction in her wake. Hurt people hurt people.

If she is mean to you, imagine how mean she is to herself. They always nodded, trying to make sense of it. But after the letter-writing exercise, I could see that a new tap of compassion had been opened, for themselves and for others.

I was seeing proof of a belief I had held for a long time. People can only be as loving to others as they are to themselves. And they can only be as mean to others as they are to themselves.

When my boys were giving each other a hard time, a harder time than usual, more than what I considered the requisite amount of sibling torture, I knew it was because they were not feeling good on the inside.

One day when they were fighting, instead of sending them to

their rooms, I sent them to get pieces of paper. They were each going to write themselves a letter, a love letter from themselves.

They looked at me like they would rather be grounded.

I knew I had to shake loose a little self-compassion in order to establish more harmony between them, but they looked utterly baffled. They each got a case of unmovable writer's block. So, I shifted it. *Write a love letter to yourself from me or daddy.* Still nothing. And then some tears started to well up. I could feel their frustration. I was making this worse. I wracked my brain. I started to panic, begging myself to think of one instance of unconditional love that my sweet boys could connect with without embarrassment. Just one.

And then I found it. We had just gotten a puppy.

"Cosmo," I said. "Write a letter to yourself from Cosmo. Can you think of any things he loves about you?"

And then their faces changed.

Chapter 22

I continued to write love letters to myself every single day. I felt better. Manny had not become much more affectionate, but overall, he seemed more at ease. When I was more relaxed, the boys were more cooperative. And when they weren't cooperative, I was able to navigate it with more patience. But just like every other change we had made for the better in the past year, the ease only lasted for a while. I could feel more changes on the horizon.

Jack and I were having an especially hard time getting along. We seemed to be fighting about everything. The least of the worries was schoolwork. The fights were about putting his socks on or eating breakfast, things that frustrated me intensely because they should have been so simple.

I was talking on the phone to my cousin Jordelle. She was the one who had 0 percent of her children shitting their pants years before on vacation at my parents' lake house. Of all my cousins, we are the closest in age. She lived on the west coast of Canada with her husband and two children, similar in age to Jack and Luke. She told me that the school system was experimenting with new classroom structures that she worried were not serving the needs of her oldest. Also, they had been having a really hard time getting out the door each morning. Her husband was a teacher, and she had to get the two kids and herself ready for work.

"I just keep thinking," she said, "when we are rushing out the door, that you guys are likely knitting together and singing songs while breakfast rolls bake in the oven." For the first time, she wondered if she was doing the wrong thing for her family by doing the mainstream school thing.

And then I told her what had actually happened in our house that day: I had called Jack an asshole seven times before breakfast.

"You are being an asshole!"

"I'm so sorry I called you an asshole."

"But you're acting like an asshole!"

"But I should stop saying asshole."

"Maybe if you would stop being an asshole!"

"I'm still saying asshole."

Then quietly, "Would you please stop being an asshole?"

He just stared at me.

I knew my next step was to figure out how to ease the tension between us, how to find a little more harmony in our days. He was grumpy and uncooperative. I tried to think back to the times over the past few years when he had seemed really happy. Our schedule was the same, year after year. The skating season dictated my working hours, my travel, and our time together as a family, so I had an impeccable hold on what things happened when, the events, and the resulting emotions of my skaters, their parents, and my boys. The demands at work were intense, so when things were not copacetic at home it really stressed me out. Jack had always been cooperative, until right before Niko was born. Since then, even the simplest of things had been a fight.

After that, the only time we had ease was when Jack was in summer camp. He loved being busy. He loved being around big groups of kids. I had started many homeschool classes in order to keep up with his preferred pace, but still, the only time he had been consistently happy was when he was in camp, specifically theater camp. It was the most intense. They auditioned, cast, learned, and performed a whole play in five days. There wasn't much downtime during the day, and each night he practiced his lines until it was time for bed.

If only there was a camp that ran all fall and winter, where he got to be with a lot of other kids and they were busy learning and working together all day and he had to work on his projects at night, too. I wondered if I should try to start a camp like that. I considered what would be involved, renting a space, hiring facilitators, running registration ...

And then I realized something like that already existed.

It was called school.

I visited local private schools, and even though I loved them, I didn't get the feeling that Jack would enjoy himself. I spoke about it with Rebekah, and she reminded me of what I already knew, that Jack would prefer the busiest, most competitive place I could find for him. He would love public school.

The next week I visited our local elementary school. I told the principal I was looking into homeschool retirement and asked if he could help me out with that. He stared at me, trying to decipher whether or not I was joking. "I'm serious," I told him.

He laughed, "Yes, I think I could."

It was mid-December, and I enrolled Jack to start January 3rd, halfway through third grade. With joy, I realized I was continuing with Stephanie's experiment of doing the thing that I secretly judged other people for doing. I was going to send my child to public school like it was no big deal.

I downloaded the supply list and got all of it through Amazon. I didn't want to bother with school supply shopping in the midst of the Christmas crowds. The weeks flew by. We celebrated Christmas and the New Year. Then it was time to drop my sweet Jack, my first baby, off for his first day of school ever.

As I walked him through the hallways, I wanted to shout, "We've got a first-timer over here!"

See this kid? He's never been to school before. This is his first day ever. Please be nice. Please be kind. Please give him some care.

I felt scared and excited for him. I wondered if we were doing the right thing. I wondered if all these years of homeschooling were the wrong thing. I wondered if the teachers would think I was an incompetent homeschooling mom. I wondered if I would be an incompetent public school mom.

My choice to homeschool had served us in nurturing ways for years. We had complete control over our schedules, and it had afforded us much time together that we would not have had if they had been in school all day, and I had been at the rink every evening and weekend. Now I was ready to grant myself permission to change my fucking mind. To change my mind a million times, if I wanted to.

After I dropped him off, I had to go to my own scary first day. I drove to the dentist to get cavities filled for the first time in my life. I often found times in normal conversation to brag about my perfect record of dental health, to point out that I had never had a cavity, despite the fact that I got cleanings every five to ten years and never flossed.

Well, my luck had run out. I had *seven* cavities.

As I walked into the office, freshly emotional from my first school drop off, I raised my hand meekly and said, "We've got a first-timer over here."

I've never done this before. These are my first cavities ever. Please be nice. Please be kind. Please show me some care.

Then I proceeded to weep and weep in the dentist's chair.

The dentist and his assistant were a little caught off guard, but they were so incredibly supportive. They listened to my first day of school story. They assured me that the fillings would be no big deal, and they handed me more tissues. After they determined I was emotionally stable, they got started.

As I lay there with my face half frozen and my make-up surely a little runny, I thought about how lucky I was to have these two professionals who had chosen a vocation that allowed them to help crying, dental misfits like me get on the road to dental rehabilitation. I thought about what Jack might be doing at that moment. I remembered that morning how I had seen so many smiling, loving teachers as we walked the halls. I felt so grateful that there were teaching professionals who had chosen to dedicate their lives to nurturing children. How lucky were we that we had all these other people to help us? How lucky were we that there were these good people, so we didn't have to do everything by ourselves?

I felt incredibly cared for. And then I thought again about Jack and wondered what of the hundred new-things-you-experience-at-school-that-you-experience-nowhere-else-in-life I forgot to tell him about.

Pledge of Allegiance, shit. I forgot to tell him about the Pledge of Allegiance.

And again, I felt so scared for him.

Then I remembered something important I taught my athletes about fear: fear doesn't mean we are doing the wrong thing. It doesn't mean we are not ready. We can be scared and still be really, really ready.

Countless times a year my athletes looked at me with wide, frightened eyes and said, "I am so scared" or "I am so nervous."

I told them the same kind of thing every single time. *That's okay. I feel nervous, too. We feel nervous, and we are still okay. It's all gonna be okay. If you didn't feel nervous, I would have to check you for a pulse. Congratulations, dear. You are human.*

So, my day went on. Jack's day went on. I knew soon I would know how parts of his day went. I knew soon that many parts of his day would not be shared with me.

Within a few weeks it was evident that Jack loved it. I felt so proud that he was comfortable being tossed in with a new group of kids halfway through the school year. But I also knew that it was the perfect situation for him. He felt special because he was new, and this extra attention made the transition even easier. I felt grateful that the faculty at the school was so caring. His teacher had never had a brand-new student in third grade, and she was excited for the opportunity. She had a sister-in-law who had homeschooled, so she called her whenever she had questions. She had no concerns about Jack being beyond grade level in some areas and behind in others. She assured me that he was fitting in and keeping up just fine.

We liked it so much I decided to send Luke to the same school the next fall and to enroll Niko in full-day pre-K. I had wrongly judged other people for sending their children to public school and acting like it was no big deal. It was not "no big deal." It was the best deal ever.

It had the same hours as summer camp, but free, already paid for through our property taxes. Plus, I didn't have to drive them. Instead they were picked up by the school chauffeur, in a big yellow stretch limousine, right from our driveway. I didn't even need to go outside. And for $2.40 they could buy a crappy lunch that truly made their day. A surefire way to make Luke smile? Tell him he gets to eat walking tacos.

I felt excited to increase the quality of time we spent together as we decreased the quantity. We had been spending an enormous amount of crappy time together. Crappy in all the ways: crappy because we were all tired of each other's faces and tendencies and annoyances, and crappy because we could all just let it fall apart around each other all day, every day. We needed a greater duration of time each week where we were required to keep it together. We could just let it all out with each other, which was a gift, but it got too sloppy and messy after a while. We needed to have more time being on our best behavior instead of our worst, practicing patience when things didn't go our way. We needed more time apart so we could appreciate our time together.

I had worried that without the tether of homeschooling, I would not spend enough time with my boys, that I needed to schedule and mandate in order for me to connect with them. But just a few weeks after I sent them all to school, I realized I was reading them bedtime stories for the first time in years. With the pressure and time demands of homeschooling and the stress of work, I had stopped sharing the thing I loved the most in the world with the people I loved the most in the world.

Each time I did the thing I secretly judged other people for doing, I realized that I dropped a part of my persona, a part of myself that I thought I needed in order to be admired. I was getting closer to finding my real self, and it showed me how skilled I had become at building facades of achievement in every area of my life. I didn't know what it was like to just be me, independent of what I thought people would think of me. As I started to drop these roles, drop these goals and drop the striving, I realized how incredibly tiring and taxing it had been to hold them up in the first place.

When I abandoned an attachment to a certain ideal or way of being, it was an act of loyalty to myself, my true self. It was as if I was testing a theory that I could be innately me and innately good without a title or badge of honor to prove my worthiness.

Through my letters to myself, I realized that I was a lot needier than I ever knew. I needed encouragement. I needed admiration. I needed to be noticed. I needed to be loved. I saw this overarching neediness and tended to it in my athletes, but long ago discarded it as unsavory and childish in myself. Even as a child, I abhorred the idea of seeming childish. Had I thought that children were too needy, and that neediness was a turnoff? Did my neediness render me unlovable? Was complete self-sufficiency going to make me lovable? Did I have to meet all of my own needs or discard them entirely? In pushing down, pushing away my emotionality and neediness, I wasn't, as I thought, discarding the parts of myself that were childlike. I was discarding the parts of myself that were human.

I wondered, if I had pushed away my needs, if I had also at some point, pushed away my dreams as well. At one point I had considered quitting my job and pouring more of myself into the boys. Instead, I concluded that maybe the best way to teach my

boys to reach for their dreams was to reach relentlessly for
my own.

And since I had begun to outsource some of my work and
drop some of my roles, I had some space to ask myself what was
next. What was it that I really wanted to do instead of trying to
do it all and trying to make it look effortless and beautiful? I
wondered what dreams I had pushed away that I once held
close. I felt a pull to share my gifts in a larger way with the
world, but I didn't know yet what that would look like. I knew I
wanted to broaden my reach and take it beyond my skaters and
their families.

I found freedom in questioning everything. I also saw more
clearly my tendency to want to redouble my efforts in one area
of my life if I eased up the pressure on myself in another. I
thought about the work ethic woven so tightly into the double
helix of my DNA. I credit my ancestors on the Prairies for
passing down this subconscious fear: if I relax, if I take it easy …
Everyone. Will. Die.

Yup. Immediate and certain death for me and all my kin. I
knew this wasn't a reasonable fear for me. For my ancestors, this
had been true. If they didn't finish their sod house before winter
came, GAME OVER. Even for my grandparents, in houses made
of stone, if the family didn't gather enough wood for the winter
or collect enough ice off the frozen pond to keep their food cold
and safe all summer, serious shit could go down. From what I've
heard, some serious shit *did* go down when my Great Grandpa
Cecil realized that my Grandma's older brothers had put her
down the ice well they'd dug off the side of their kitchen.

Sure, I grew up in a climate where I could get a brain freeze
from breathing through my nose, but shouldn't I be able to shake
off the fear that my temporary lack of labor or incessant pushing
would cause my family's demise? Especially with modern insu-
lation and a backup generator and a fully stocked pantry? Yes, I
should have, but it wasn't that easy. Also, I had to shake off the

fear that emotionality, neediness, was not unsavory, it was not childlike. It was not a distasteful weakness. It was human.

But, as a Manitoba Woman, I was not only willing to work at the things that were easy. It was in my bones to work at the things that were necessary.

And looking closely at what was underneath: my attachments, my facades, my need for admiration, my repulse for weakness, this was my most necessary work.

I knew it wouldn't be easy.

And I felt scared.

And I knew it was okay.

And I whispered to myself. *Congratulations, dear. You are human.*

Chapter 23

I had a high school romance that could have been plucked from a movie script. Him a hockey player, me a figure skater —we were perfectly cast as the Canadian version of the football player and cheerleader who fall head-over-heels in love and coast through high school in a sweet, sparkly embrace, the relationship equivalent of soda pop. The morning after I first set eyes on him, I told a friend that watching him walk down the stairs to that basement house party was like watching an angel descend from heaven.

Under his well-worn baseball cap, his head was shaved, as is sometimes the case during hockey season when a team decides on a superstition to which all players adhere. He was laughing, holding the hand of a girl whose pixie cut juxtaposed the serious look she carried on her face. Despite her sternness, he was lit with a constant smile, narrowing his eyes into little half-moons. He only relaxed his smile to speak, showing me his full, pouty lips (oh, the lips! I've always been a sucker for great lips) and the grey-blue eyes that matched my own. He wasn't the only one attached. When I got the urge to look toward the stairs, I was sitting with my boyfriend, who I had dated on and off since elementary school. He was one of the boys I often kissed when the teacher turned her back in kindergarten. I tried to appear innocent as I arranged an introduction. He and I struck up a conversation that had both of us bent over laughing while pixie-cut and current boyfriend certainly wished they could dismiss us both to separate realms through foot pedal-controlled trap doors. I knew I should look away, but I couldn't. He was beautiful.

By Tuesday he held my phone number in his hand, passed to him at his next hockey practice on a tiny slip of paper that had been carried through towns by acquaintances with my instructions for delivery. Days later he showed up at the rink where I worked, serendipitously located at the mid-point between our two towns. A week after that I stood inside the front door of his parents' house, bidding him farewell after a secret meeting. He touched my hair, and he touched my face. When he couldn't keep his hands from shaking, I held them both in mine as we shared our first kiss.

From that point we were inseparable. Despite living in different towns, managing school schedules, jobs, his hockey, and my skating, we spoke every day and spent every weekend together. He wrote me poems, drew me pictures, and taught me how to drive a stick shift on his tractor. At parties we would not leave the dance floor. On clear Manitoba nights we sat out on his farm, short-horn cattle lowing in the distance, and chose a star that would be for the two of us, forever.

Despite any messages I had picked up regarding girls and sex, I had no qualms about enjoying it. We both came to the relationship with a little experience, but together we learned quickly what we liked and how to ask for it. He was sweet and tender, and we were both adventurous. On road trips we would take turns reading each other erotica, trying to see how long we could keep our hands off each other.

Almost entirely, it was a magical youthful romance. Even now, when I hear "Time After Time" by Cyndi Lauper, I am transported back to his high-school bedroom. We roll around under the covers, cuddling and laughing. Everything is bright, like a camera with the exposure cranked way up. Sunlight streams in and illuminates the room in a rosy glow. I smile. And I realize this image must be more fantasy than memory. I know light can barely squeeze in through a basement window, and no one in their right mind would give a teenage boy white linens.

Maybe foolishly, and in my insatiable need to grow up, I broke up with him the summer after high school graduation. I had met another guy who seemed more mature, and I established a regrettable pattern of having boyfriends who overlapped. In actuality, the new guy wanted nothing of the type of commitment I was looking for and broke up with me a few weeks after I arrived at university. Later that school year, my high school boyfriend came to visit friends in Winnipeg and ended up in my dorm and in my bed. We moved with ease, our bodies fitting together as if they had never parted. My mouth found the place he liked to be kissed behind his ear, and his fingers found their familiar spot inside me. We had forgotten none of the secrets of pleasure that we had helped each other unlock. The bodies we had when we entered our relationship were not the bodies we had when we parted. I remembered the first time he had made me come with his mouth. We were in his parents' basement. It was late at night, the lights were off, and we were experimenting with our first sex toy. He slipped a short, wide dildo inside me and gently licked my clit. I arched up onto my elbows, fists clenched, the pleasure so extreme it bordered on too much.

"You okay?" he asked, quickly sliding off the couch and bringing his face up to mine.

"Yes," I exhaled. "Just … go slow." He brushed a hair from my forehead, cupped my cheek in his hand, and kissed me softly on the mouth.

"I promise," he whispered into my mouth and kissed me again.

It hadn't been my first orgasm. It wasn't even my hundredth.

But, something about the intensity, his careful, tender stimulation that brought me closer, closer, then back, then closer again,
over the course of that hour cracked something open within me.
When I climaxed, I clamped hard on the unyielding firmness
inside me. He kept his mouth on me, even as my back arched
and my body writhed beneath him. I saw an explosion of color,
orange and red, a veritable firework of radiance, reaching
beyond the room, beyond the house, piercing the black prairie
sky.

Afterwards, legs weak, I steadied my hands on the bathroom
counter, examining my reflection in the mirror. My eyes glittered
wildly. My hair reflected the moonlight in impossible patterns
and laid like a silk sheet halfway down my back. In the front, it
rested over my breasts, my nipples peeking out through the
waves, pale pink and hard. When the sky had been sliced open,
something new had rushed down, infusing me from above. For
days my skin glowed golden, my whole body filled with light.

That night in my college dorm, I laid on top of him, effort-
lessly finding orgasm after orgasm. He left in the night, neither
of us suggesting he stay until morning. A year later we found
our way to each other again, this time on a dance floor at a party
near our hometowns. This time there was no sex. Instead, we
danced, sweaty and wild, all night long. The next morning, I
went to his house to talk about getting back together, but our
hearts weren't really in it. It was if we knew, even at our tender
age, that getting our bodies to fit together was easy, but the
stretch of life where our paths merged was short and in the past.
By that point I had even forgotten which star we had chosen.

When I met Manny, I was completely smitten by his maturity.
We had just graduated college, the uber-clear threshold of adult
life. From the start I could see our paths stretching far out before
us, merging with ease. When our bodies fit together, too, it was a
no-brainer. We were good partners. We never fought. We agreed
on how to handle our money. Even when we felt more like busi-

ness partners than lovers, we still had great sex—partly because I knew sex was a surefire way to get connection. Our attraction had never included the weak-in-the-knees, let-me-tell-you-everyday-how-beautiful-you-are kind of love. And if it had, I likely wouldn't have trusted it. To me, that kind of love was the red flag that a relationship had an expiration date. That kind of love was for fairytales. That kind of love was for teenagers.

The lust, the passion, the affection, these things had been my lifeblood when I was in high school. I'd sworn them off for over fifteen years, dismissing them as fantasy, and then Brad had given me a taste. And it made me doubt the story I had spun for myself. Maybe there actually was this adult version of my teenage love story being lived out by couples all over the globe, and in my haste to be taken seriously, I had jumped in too deep with the first nice guy I met.

I had been making great progress with Jacki. I had already considerably rewired the ways in which I dealt with stress. Life with my boys had become easier. Through our sessions I got clarity about so many next right steps for my teams and my coaching staff, and my organization was thriving. My athletes were growing, and their teamwork was deeper, more committed and genuine than I had ever experienced. Jacki's joy and enthusiasm at my progress was one of the things I loved so much about working with her. She loved hearing about the ripple effect of my own transformation: everything and everyone around me was transforming as well.

I loved the forward momentum in my own personal development, but progress in my marriage was slow. Things had gotten a little better since I found out about Amber and after we broke things off with Brad and Jess. Manny usually gave me a kiss hello and goodbye. He would say *"I love you, too"* if I said it first. But, still, I felt that we had the bar set so low. Sometimes I felt angry that I had to do all the emotional upkeep. I was the only one tending to our emotional lives. I resented that I had to remind Manny and the boys to step up. I wanted to be able to slip and know that Manny would keep the emotional momentum going. But we were not there yet. Things were slowly getting better, but sometimes I felt very frustrated. And I still thought a lot about Brad.

He and I had no contact, but somehow, I knew he also was thinking about me. When we cut off contact, the connection didn't dissipate. Instead, it felt like the connection had grown stronger, like we knew what we had in real life was over and the only way to let it live on was to keep it alive in our imaginations.

I still had told no one about Brad. I assumed that if I had, they would say it was a good thing our relationship had not progressed physically, but I wondered if that was true at all. I didn't have a physical affair to compare it to, but I had concluded that an emotional affair, a period of sexually charged communication, could be just as powerful and difficult to quit.

The whole relationship existed on the fantasy plane. We were protected from the awkwardness of being real and naked (figuratively and literally) with each other. My connection with Brad had been built on sweet, sexy texts, read and edited before they were sent. Every photo we sent had been with good lighting and from the right angle. Each interaction had been carefully curated.

My suspicions about him thinking about me were soon confirmed. I set up a Twitter account to share links to my writing. The next day I got a notification that Brad was one of my first followers. I blocked him, but now I knew he was thinking about me, too. This didn't make it harder or easier. It just assured me that I was not crazy, even though I often felt it.

Digging deep, I first doubted marriage itself. I wondered if our modern expectations of monogamy were too much to ask. Authors like Esther Perel supported my apprehension. In the past marriage had been more of a business arrangement, to protect assets, to keep races and religions segregated, and class structures intact. Only recently have we asserted the ideal that a spouse would be a best friend, a confidant, a soul mate, an unwavering source of support, a responsible money manager, and a hot lover for the entirety of our lives together. Was I just setting myself up for disappointment by expecting so much from Manny? Would it be wiser to just lower the bar? Paradoxically, removing the past shame and stigma of divorce paved the way for the idea that it was now considered self-debasing to stay in a marriage that did not meet all these needs and expectations. Cultural expectations had painted me into a corner.

I still wondered if there was wisdom in polyamory, in not expecting one partner to meet all of our needs. And then I remembered how intoxicated I felt when I was communicating with Brad. I was like a junkie. I knew that if things got stressful in regular life and one of my options was to start a new romantic relationship rather than dealing with my problems, I would reach for the new fling every single time. Just like other people could use drugs, shopping, or food, I knew attention could become my ultimate vice and could destroy the life I had worked so diligently to build.

To say I still thought a lot about Brad would be an understatement. I fantasized about him constantly, imagining I had taken him to my bed that night we had made a steam room of desire out of our hallway. I imagined I had kneeled beside the bed that I shared with my husband and unzipped Brad's pants, taking his penis in my mouth. I imagined he showed up at the rink and bent me over the desk in the coaches' room. Every time I traveled, I imagined that I ran into him at the airport and we had sex in a tiny bathroom stall.

Mentally, I bounced back and forth between the idea that if Brad kept coming relentlessly to mind, we were destined to be together or I was simply insane. My other hypotheses were that I was selfish or self-indulgent or impossible to please. Every possibility was worse than the one before. I desperately wanted to land on an explanation that was more accurate and authentic, so

I started paying closer attention to *when* thoughts of him rushed to mind. When I started seeing his car make and model everywhere. When I had the urge to unblock him and check his or Jess's social media to see what they were doing or to send him a message to check in.

I watched for months, trying to find the common denominator. And I found it. I realized thoughts of him came up the most strongly when I was on the verge of something big, creative, or daring. With more time to devote to my self-development, my writing, and the expansion of my business, new ideas came forward at lightning speed. It was exciting and uplifting. Oftentimes when I was buoyed by the thrill of a new project, I would suddenly be sidetracked by constant thoughts of Brad.

My friend Jeanette, a world-class triathlete and adventurer-racer, shared about a relay race she had completed through the woods, around the clock. On this particular race, she and a team were running 120 miles. Each runner had to do their leg of the race on trails, alone, much of it through the night. She shared about the thick woods and the almost total absence of moonlight. All of them had traveled across the country to meet for the race, so the trails were unfamiliar to each of them.

She wore a headlamp that illuminated the space immediately in front of her. For the first few miles, every time she heard a sound in the woods she turned her head and lost her footing. After tripping a couple of times, she realized that the only way she was going to make progress and safely get through her section of the race was to stay completely in the moment. She quickly figured out that the only way to get to the end of the dark, unknown trail was to keep looking straight ahead. It was when she was focused only on the trail in front of her that she could take each secure step. It was only when she looked straight ahead that she wouldn't stumble.

I kept thinking about her story. I had figured out that trying to live a perfect life, a life worthy of a 6.0, had not provided me with a clear path that resembled a yellow brick road.

Living a brave life was more like trail running at night. The darkness was unavoidable. It was easy to slip into panic when I felt certain I was truly lost. I recognized my cultural conditioning to look everywhere else except within, except straight ahead, for the direction of my next step.

I realized how easy it was to listen to fear. Fear rose up to say, *Look here, look here, what if there is something you are missing?* The fear that taunted me to take my eyes off the path, that tried to convince me that I didn't already have everything I needed to be happy.

That was the answer I was looking for. Anything that was good for me would feel good in the moment *and* give me more energy and enthusiasm for the important things in my life. A truly good thing would not pull me away from a project that I felt passionate about. It would not give me an exhilarating high, later leaving me drained, distracted, or guilty. A truly good thing would not dull the shine of the rest of my life.

I later listened to a podcast with Elizabeth Gilbert as she told a writer the thing artists are really looking for when they comb through reviews and feedback: it is not the best review. Like everyone else, creative people look to find information about themselves and their choices. All of us do this. We think that when we look outside ourselves for answers, we are looking for that missing puzzle piece, the golden ticket, the thing that will make us believe in ourselves and show us the way. We think that we are looking for confirmation of our goodness, our worthiness, our talent, our power. However, Liz really thinks that we are looking for the opposite. We are actually searching for confirmation of our deepest, darkest fear. We are looking for a voice that specifically, precisely echoes what we worst fear about ourselves to be true. We are looking for information to confirm our self-loathing. Then when we find it, the criticisms dig so deep because it is what we have secretly feared all along to be true. *We are not good. We are not worthy. We are not capable of amazing things. That thing I feared is true!*

To have this realization was an incredible gift. I realized why criticisms from others sometimes hurt so badly. They stung the most when they echoed what I feared about myself to be true. *You are lazy. You are selfish. You are too soft to be a competitive coach. You are just a small-town girl. You are not going to do big things.*

I realized exactly why I had been so heartbroken about my period being out of sync with the new moon. I skipped past all the articles that said being in time with the full moon was no big deal. I even skipped past the articles that said menstruating with the full moon had traditionally been associated with wise women, healers, teachers, and high priestesses. It was a sign that these women were not in a phase of their lives where they focused on pregnancy, on growing new human life. Instead, they were in a phase where they had the capacity to focus on self-growth, mentorship, and creating a new way of life for themselves and others.

I could have read it to confirm what I knew in my heart to be true. Anne Lamott asserted that writers need to make a commitment to forge ahead, to pay attention, to dig deep, and to shine light on truths to help others. I ignored all of that. Instead, I jumped right to the part that confirmed what I worried deep down inside to be true. I jumped to the part that confirmed that I was bad and dirty, and even the moon was judging me.

Now I understood why it was human nature to focus so intently on the negative and why it affected me so strongly. For years I had wondered how just one angry skating parent could throw me off-kilter so severely. Even if I had a hundred families, totaling almost 200 parents who seemed to appreciate the work I was doing with their child and be in support of my decisions, knowing that one person was upset with me was unbearable. When I understood this, I could identify my most hidden fears simply by paying attention to what criticisms hurt the most. I was able to observe them objectively instead of having them fester deep inside me as I continued to subconsciously feed them.

I wanted to keep looking deeper within. I wanted to stop looking outside myself for the confirmation of the good or the bad. I had figured out that thoughts of Brad came up in order to clarify a deep fear in me: I would never be happy with what I already had.

Thoughts of Brad were my sounds in the dark woods.

Chapter 24

W hile nature slept, I hustled.

From September to March, I felt like I was strapped to a treadmill.

This had been my rhythm since before I could remember. Fall and winter were my busiest times. The earth lie dormant and I was flying, across the ice, across the country, across the globe, across my kitchen to grab a snack to eat in my car on the way to the rink.

Every single year spring astonished me. I was alarmed that the earth was coming back to life. I assumed it had retired. I don't know if this was because of generations of ancestors living on the Canadian Prairies or if the responsibility could be granted to my three-and-a-half decades on the ice, but when things started to thaw, I was stupefied. In my mind, ice was solid. It was permanent. It was the thing I walked on, worked on, the thing that made so many parts of my life possible. The oddity of it turning to *water*, unencumbered, baffled me. When ice melted at the rink it signaled a problem, and everyone leapt into action to prevent it from happening. *The water must stay frozen.* But outside, when the ice melted, it signaled magic beginning.

Nature had not retired. It had *rested*. And it was ready to put on an incredible show, including the part of spring that strikes me as the most subtle and exquisite, when the patterns of light and shadow change every day as the buds rapidly unfurl.

Even though I had worked all winter, when the earth awoke from its rest, I did not take mine. I kicked my planning into high gear for my next fall and winter marathon.

With this pace, time flew by. I had two years under my belt since recommitting myself to my work. I was coming off my most successful season of coaching and had no skaters leaving. I felt like everyone was happy and proud to be a part of my organization. For the first time, I felt like a good, responsible leader. I had broken all ties with the skating club, and after a decade of running my organization like my own business, it truly was my own business. After years of being underpaid, I had given myself a raise. I was working on one of my favorite parts of the planning, costume design, and music selection. The dress for my highest-level team was more exquisite than anything we had ever planned. It was a luscious magenta with a silk skirt and over 1000 gold Swarovski crystals. Finding the perfect music to go with such a costume had proven challenging, but finally, after a suggestion from my mom, I had cracked the code. I was listening to the rough cut of what was certain to be the most dynamic program I had ever choreographed. Then I got a text. From Brad.

The space from my chin to my sacroiliac joint was suddenly hollow. A cold wind barreled through, icing every inch of my empty torso.

He was checking in to report that he and Jess had broken up nine months earlier. He had wanted to leave me alone, but he was going to start dating, and first he needed to know, was I happy?

Was I happy?

In his texts to me, Brad said Jess had told him it was over.

And she had stuck to her guns, even though he tried to change her mind. I wondered, had I not done enough to keep my promise to her? I had tried to make myself vanish. Had I been the reason that their marriage had ended? I unblocked both of them on Facebook to try to find answers. I had blocked them not because I thought they would be bothering me but because I knew I couldn't be tempted to look and see how they were doing. But now I needed to know. I searched back in photos, scanning for Jess's wedding ring. When did she stop wearing it? Was he telling me the truth? And I found my answers in the creepy and brilliant way that our lives are laid out in public. The timelines matched.

I saw something else in her posts. It was subtle. There was overreaching, glossing over, there was stretching to make things look just a little happier. I had the uneasy sensation that each post had been constructed to convince herself that things were better than they actually were. I knew because her posts felt like mine.

I texted Manny to let him know.

"Brad just texted me. He and Jess broke up."

Manny's response:

"Not surprised. BTW stopping at Home Depot on my way home."

After years of struggle. After consistent reminders that Brad was still on my mind. After everything. That was his response.

I was shocked. Not because it was out of character—it was 100 percent classic Manny. It was the Manny who told me once that he loved me, and unless he told me otherwise, I should assume that he continued to love me. It was the Manny who didn't mind if I shared a bed with another man on a work trip. It was the Manny who wasn't interested in seeing my texts with Brad.

I was shocked because I had thought we had made some actual progress in our connection, in his understanding that I needed way more than I felt comfortable letting on. Was he so egotistical to think that I wouldn't act on this? Or was it that he didn't care? The improvements in our relationship had been slow. It had felt like two steps forward, one step back, but I wondered if I had imagined that we had made any progress at all. Maybe my increased happiness was just a result of my own work. Maybe I felt more joyful because my passion for my job had been elevated. Maybe my fulfillment was a result of making space for my creativity.

I had moved myself into a new place, but our marriage was right where I had left it.

It ate at me, the years of frustration and effort and looking on the bright side. A few days later, as I was putting dinner on the table, I realized I was picking up my phone. And I realized I was texting Brad. It felt completely out of body. There was one part of me that was typing a message, while another part of me was watching, astounded. *Oh my God, she's TEXTING HIM.*

"Can I see you tonight?"

My phone screen signaled that he was responding. The kitchen floor swayed beneath me.

And then, "Yes." A second later, "Private or public?"

"Private," I replied. Then quickly, "I mean, public."

"Are you okay?" He asked.

"I'm nervous." I replied.

Jack had a baseball game. Manny was already at the ballfield with him, and I was scheduled to drop Luke and Niko off because I had Moon Circle, a monthly get together with my closest friends. I didn't need to create an alibi. I had the night to myself.

I hadn't showered, but I brushed my hair and pulled on a sweater and jeans. I looked myself squarely in the mirror and was surprised when a single chuckle erupted from deep in my belly. I felt like a psychopath. Or maybe this is how it felt to be a woman who was doing exactly what she wanted to do. Psycho or free, regardless, I felt incredible and delirious.

I pulled into the parking lot at the ballfield. Manny saw me coming and walked to the parking lot to meet us. The boys jumped out, and I rolled down the passenger side window. He leaned into the car.

"You'll be late, right?" he knew what to expect when I hung out with my friends.

"Mm-hmm," I nodded. I waved, and he walked the boys toward Jack's game.

He has no clue, I thought.

And I was nervous, but I was also certain. I didn't know what was going to happen, but I knew I needed to take this next step to find out. I felt so sick of spinning the old story in my head. Maybe if I saw him, I would realize that I was already over him. Maybe I would realize that I was in love with him and that I should leave Manny so we could start a life together.

I felt terrified and resolute. I had tried to figure a way out of this fantasy a hundred different ways, and I had remained stuck —stuck on the same chapter for years. I needed to see what came next in this story.

I parked at the restaurant and waited, using every mental training tool I had ever taught my skaters to keep myself calm. A few seconds later I saw him. He was taller than I remembered and better looking. Shit.

When he heard my car door close, he looked in my direction and watched me walk toward him. I could tell by the way that he was breathing that he was nervous, too.

"Hi." I leaned into the awkward and exhilarating rush that made me feel completely alive and also like I may fall over dead all at the same time.

He reached toward me for a hug. I stretched up on my toes and reached for him. As we embraced, I couldn't believe my hands didn't pass right through him like a hologram. After existing for so long only in my imagination, he was actually there, in the flesh.

We got a table and turned down the server's offer of menus. We each ordered a beer, and we started to talk.

He recounted the unraveling of his marriage with Jess. I was straight up in telling him how I thought about him every day, but I had spent time trying to piece it apart.

"We are not for real life," I asserted. "Really, it's so easy to believe what we had was special, but that's because it is totally a fantasy. We've never had to do real life together." I told him that I had realized he came up in my mind when I was on the verge of something new and brave, as a distraction from playing bigger, from doing the things I was really here to do. I told him that I knew my mind brought up the fantasy of him to serve as a distraction, to trick me into believing I did not already have everything I needed to be happy.

He suggested that maybe he had been on my mind because we were meant to be together. "Maybe you are overthinking this." He smiled.

"I'll have to think about that," I took a sip of my warm beer.

In homeopathy, the fundamental principle is that like cures like. The cure for an ailment shares an energetic signature with the ailment itself. Taking it in small doses triggers the body to alleviate the symptoms. Through every word, every feeling, every lowering of his eyes, and the look of hope that would return when he raised them, I could see Brad needed someone to love him incredibly, fully, perfectly in order to feel like he was actually worthy of love. I knew that feeling. That energetic signature also lived in me.

I needed to be getting home. We left our half-full glasses on the table and stood up to leave. I stepped down from my barstool and looked up at him.

He smiled at me, amused. "I'm taller than you remember, aren't I?"

"No." I shook my head as I fumbled for my purse.

I checked my phone to see if I had missed any messages. There was one from Jacki. She usually did not text me unless she was confirming an appointment. The message said, "You're on my mind. Is everything okay?" My stomach dropped, and I tossed my phone back in my purse.

"Walk me to my car?" I asked as we walked outside.

"Why did you park way over here?" he teased with a smile. He knew exactly why. He hadn't known me for long before he went without seeing me for years, but he remembered enough to know I wouldn't pass up this opportunity to be alone with him.

Private or public?

He got in the passenger's side, and I sat in the driver's seat. I made a comment about a Ford Flex being the sexiest type of car. We both laughed and he paused.

"Do you know the first thing I noticed about you?" he asked, eyes shining bright in the darkness.

"Uh-uh," I shook my head, softening my eyes.

"This," he said, putting his hand softly on my cheek. "This dimple."

I put my hand over his as I sucked in a breath and held it. No one had ever mentioned to me before that I had a dimple.

"Really?" My eyes reached for his.

"Yes," he assured me, "it was the first thing I noticed." And with that he leaned in to kiss me. We kissed the kiss I had imagined we would kiss on my couch years before, when instead he was looking over at Jess and Manny. But here, he looked only at me. And his eyes were open, smiling at me and studying my face the whole time.

We kissed, and we kissed, and I realized I was leaning across my center console to the passenger's side of the car. He touched my hair and my face, and we just kept kissing. My hand found its way to his thigh, and I squeezed up and down his leg, wanting so badly to squeeze even higher but stopping myself.

I pulled away, breathless, leaning back against the driver's seat with my eyes closed. "I need to get going." He leaned in to kiss me one more time.

I drove home, feeling absolutely drunk from his attention,

and I realized I had not found any answers by seeing him. I had only found more questions.

I came through the front door to find Manny eating chips and watching TV. I kissed him quickly and told him I was going to bed. I lay in bed, wondering what the fuck I was doing. I had hoped that seeing Brad would verify what I had discovered, that he was just a distraction. I thought I would know from our conversation that there was nothing about this connection that was substantial enough for real life. Instead, I was more confused than ever. I considered that maybe I just needed to have sex with him, and then this fantasy would be over. I scribbled a fake women's circle on the calendar for the next week and planned to see him again.

The next morning, I woke up with a raging yeast infection. It was beyond ridiculous. I had experienced yeast infections before, and they had been a little itchy, but I had never experienced any discharge. There I was with cottage cheese leaking out of my crotch and it was like my body was saying, in an eerie ghost-like, taunting voice, *Aaaaashleeeeeigh, you will learn everything you need to learn about this situation with your clooooothes oooooon.* And I just wanted to tell my bodily wisdom to fuck right off.

In fairness, my body had taken incredible care of me throughout this whole experience, but I was still pissed. After the skin cancer diagnosis, I kept pushing off the surgery to get it removed. I just had a gut feeling that I could wait a little longer. And then the spot started to fade. Soon it had vanished. I went to the dermatologist to confirm, and they agreed; yup, it went away. So, all at once I felt so very grateful for the wisdom of my body and so fucking annoyed. *Seriously, thanks for healing the cancer and everything, but I am just trying to have a little affair here. Won't you give me a break? I mean, like another break? Just one more? I mean, it seems like a smaller favor than healing the cancer, doesn't it? It's just a tiny favor. It's just a little affair. And affairlette, really. Tiny.*

But, nope. No dice. My vagina made it clear that it was closed to visitors.

Brad and I spent the next week talking and texting (well, actually, after my secret date with him, I cleared the text messages and started messaging him through Instagram). We were carrying on our love affair again, but this time there were no gatekeepers, no one to tell me that I shouldn't call him love, no one to monitor our communications. Still, my yeast infection showed no signs of departing. I was irate, but I decided to see Brad again, anyway.

As one would do when they actually have advanced notice of a secret date, I showered. My make-up was fresh. I wore my favorite shirt, a lacy lavender off-the-shoulder, flowy top from Anthropologie. As I was leaving, Manny did a double-take. "You are glowing." That was the first time he had ever said that to me. I smiled nervously and ducked out of the house quickly.

As I was driving, nerves and guilt began to overtake me. I wondered if I left Instagram open on my laptop and if Manny would see our private messages. I wondered if it was even possible to see Instagram messages on a laptop. I wondered what I was actually doing. I arrived first again and saw Brad head toward the restaurant.

When we had been talking during the week, we had tried to figure out where we were going with this. We tried to have conversations about normal life. He had a litany of very practical but at the same time *absurd* questions about moving forward. Would any of our vehicles fit all the kids? *No.* Did we have a place where Manny could move to if Brad moved in with me? *Yes.* He talked about money and combining our finances. My head was spinning, and then he would send me a screenshot of a sappy country love song that made him think of me, and I would be pulled right under again.

There were the practical signs I could have heeded, forgetting Luke at camp, Niko getting assaulted by an automatic door, the rampant ringworm, and the seething yeast infection. There was the fact that if I began dating Brad I would have to deal with the stress and scrutiny of two ex-wives and would definitely end up crying in a corner at every family function. All of these things should have been clear, but it wasn't until we were out for dinner that Brad insisted on talking politics (in an effort to prove to me that he and I were really made for real life), and I became certain that our relationship would never be consummated.

He started by telling me he was more of a "moderate" than anything else. I knew this was a red flag, common practice when a conservative spoke to a liberal, trying from the start to pass off their right-wing ideas as mainstream. Then he mentioned that he had read an article about how it wasn't advisable to let highly educated foreigners immigrate to the US because, this was the kicker, it was bad for the developing countries.

Fuck, he read that on Breitbart.

Then he told me his son (he had told his twins about me) was upset that I was Canadian.

"What? What does he mean by that?" I was so confused.

"Oh, like you're not American," he said, as if xenophobia was a great explanation. The Young White Nationalists Association will clearly not be wanting for leadership.

And then he told me, in an attempt to prove that we had common ground, that he didn't really have a problem with Hilary, but Bernie Sanders terrified him.

Okay, it was clear. We were never having sex. Check, please.

I have recounted this story to friends and told them this was an unforgivable mistake of not knowing your audience. You do not insult Socialism when trying to establish a unified world-view with a Canadian. Who doesn't know that?

But, truly in that moment, I realized something that should have been obvious this whole time. I didn't even know him. I mean, I knew some of his preferences in bed. I knew he liked it when I said, "Yes … yes." I knew what sad country love song he liked to listen to when he thought we could never be together. I knew the happy country love song he listened to when he thought we would be together. Basically, everything I knew about him could be summed up with what Jess told me in the bathroom years before. He was really into me.

And that was it.

That one thing that had meant so much when we first met now seemed ridiculous.

Brad paid the bill and went to the bathroom. I thought about Manny at home with the boys, and suddenly I missed them so much. I thought of Manny putting them to bed and grabbing his snack and watching TV and just being okay with himself and okay with life and okay with me.

Even though I thought I was aware of my tricky human brain, the tendency for my ego to be activated and my confirmation bias to take over, I did not realize how alarmingly easy it was for me to draw conclusions that made me feel safe and right. I wondered how often I saw things the way I wanted to see them instead of realizing the truth right in front of me. A week before, in my car, I had clung to the fact that Brad was the first person in my life to point out that I had a dimple. I had tried to forget that in the next moment he touched the lines between my eyebrows and said, "Stop frowning. It's giving you wrinkles." And I realized the gift I had in being loved by someone who didn't need me to change. Who didn't need me to love him a certain way in order to feel loved. Who didn't need my love in order to love himself.

Brad and I walked to my car.

"I think we are done here," I started.

"Just for tonight?" I don't think he realized those were the same words I asked him when he told me he had to leave our house. But the look on his face told me he knew where this was going.

"No, we are really done here. We are not for real life." I shook my head and offered him a hug. He held me close. I pulled away, and he tried to hold me longer. He was trying to figure out how to make this end differently—to not end—just as I did at our house so long ago. I thought about the energetic signature we shared. I realized that he didn't just need someone to love him well enough to actually feel loved. If his desire for attention was as strong as mine, he probably needed the love of two or three adult women at once in order to feel loved. And I was just me.

It was time for me to go.

Chapter 25

After my boys were done nursing, I always put them to bed the same way. I cuddled them and whispered to them a list of all the people who loved them. "Mommy loves you. And Daddy loves you. And Yiayia loves you. And Papou loves you. And Grandma loves you. And Grandpa loves you..." I would go through all our family members, our friends, and our pets. I repeated it over and over until they fell asleep or I fell asleep. Jack and Luke had always lay silently, just listening.

Niko enjoyed the list so much that he often responded with enthusiasm, "Oh, yes. I *know* they love me."

He was certain, so perfectly certain. And I loved that he was certain. And I also wondered what it would feel like to feel that certain that I was loved. Manny had fallen back into his old habits of being disconnected from me and the boys. I knew that I wanted better for our family. I wondered if the next thing on my list of things to do that I judged other women for doing was to leave my husband.

And the thought of divorce now felt less scary. It had nothing to do with Brad. That chapter was closed. One day I felt clear and calm, and I wanted to tell Manny how I was feeling.

"Babe," I offered.

"Uh, yeah." He looked up from the kitchen sink.

"I want you to know I am not mad," I started, "and things aren't really bad…"

He tilted his head, looking like a perplexed puppy.

"But I wonder if we should really stay together. I want the boys to have more than we have, and I am getting tired of wanting that from you if you don't want it, too." I told him that I was still unhappy in our marriage. If I left him now, it would be for the boys, not in spite of them. I wanted a family that demonstrated love and connection. I was determined to show them that affection and appreciation were not something only girls and women offered. Our sons deserved more love and affection from him, but he also deserved to feel how good it felt to offer it. It was essential for our boys and the people they would love in the future that they were comfortable expressing their emotions. I did not want to be the only parent to model this. And even if I never found a partner who could show them, at least they would remember that I wanted to set the bar higher for them and for their future relationships. I wanted them to always be certain they were loved.

I didn't yell. I didn't cry. I didn't stomp my foot. I told him calmly.

And he heard me.

I think for the first time, he heard me.

I don't know if it was my certainty, my resolve, or the fact that I had grown myself into a new version of me, but after a lifetime of being trained to ignore the sound of a woman's voice, he finally heard me. I had been unmuted.

"Babe," he looked at me with eyes filled with tears, "all I want is to be with you and the boys, forever." He wiped his cheeks. "I'll do anything."

Manny and I had never fallen head over heels in love with each other, but at some point, we had both fallen madly in love with the family we had grown. Finally, the fear of being vulnerable had become less scary than the fear of losing his family. He agreed he wanted to make things better than ever. He even agreed to start seeing Jacki.

I resisted the urge to ask much about their sessions, but he did volunteer one of her assignments. He was to begin giving me twelve hugs a day. I also hoped that Jacki was in the process of giving him an energy extreme makeover, an affection boot camp, a list of 72 things a day he should do to help him open up emotionally. I hoped there were plans to balance his chakras, cleanse his aura, and reflect on past lives. I hadn't even done all these things, but I was certain he would require them. But I didn't ask about any other details, and we focused on a family hug project, ensuring each of our boys each got twelve hugs a day, too.

The hugs often stretched out, turning into chats or cuddles. The boys began to use the hugs as an opportunity to ask us questions or tell us how they were doing. These small acts of affection became our touchstones, our guaranteed times of connection, even on the busiest or most stressful of days. Almost immediately, the boys seemed happier. They were more affectionate, and their manners improved.

I began to understand the intent behind the assignment. Romantic, demonstrative love was something that Manny and I had subconsciously struck from our agreement at the very beginning. Affection was for children and (in the Greek custom) only to be offered by women. We didn't need that. We were already confident enough, grown-up enough. We had love. We had love like people have an antique vase, up high on a shelf. Or like a couple would check their apartment for appliances before making a wedding registry. Yes, we had that already.

Check that box.

But somewhere along the road I had decided I wanted more. I wanted to *feel* love. I wanted love to swirl through our house, to wrap around each one of us, to give us a feeling of warmth and buoyancy, to be more alive and electric than was possible for an old vase on a high shelf. I didn't want love, the noun. I wanted love, the verb. It was love the verb that I felt when cuddling Niko to sleep, when he told me he was certain that all those people loved him. Love was not a box he had checked. It was assurance in action, in the way faces lit up when he walked into the room. The way people glowed back at him, mirroring his light when they were with him.

Day by day, hug by hug, love became no longer something we *had*. It became something we *did*. We all became people who were now tended to.

I thought about the difference between the work of gardening and the tending of gardening. The work was strenuous. It was tiring and sometimes mindless. It could be hired out. It was essentially the checking of boxes. *Raised beds built?* Check. *Compost ordered and delivered?* Check. *Seeds planted?* Check

Tending a garden was different. It involved the gentle guiding of a vine over a trellis. It required watching the forecast and carefully planning when to water. It called for attention, protection, concern. It took multiple visits to the plant to see if our actions were helping it thrive. In the tending of gardening, we saw our care mirrored back to us. Work can build a garden, but tending makes it grow.

Manny and I had both signed on to do the work of building our life together, but we hadn't known about the tending. We liked checking boxes. We liked moving along in life like it was a road, one signpost after another, showing us that we were making progress, proving to the people around us that they needn't worry about us because we were on the right track.

But it's not a road. It was never a road.

It's a garden.

Our new chapter of tending to the life we built had begun. We were caring for each other, and we were growing. And I mostly remained unmuted. I was finally being heard. So, when I told Manny that it was really time for us to go to Greece with his parents, he listened, although not without a little pushback. My mother-in-law wanted nothing more than to visit Greece with her grandchildren. I was not resistant. I had been hankering to visit Greece since we met, but Manny and his dad always rejected the idea, armed with excuses about the distance and the cost and the consequences of being away from work for two whole weeks.

I don't know why Manny and his dad pushed back for so long, but I would guess there is something to the idea about dismissing the emotional needs of others in an effort to protect yourself from emotional needs coming up in yourself. I had greater confidence in pushing and not taking no for an answer. There was no rational reason for not going. His parents were still in good health, and our boys were excellent travelers. So, I insisted.

The beaches on their home island of Chios were the most beautiful I had ever seen. It was a traditional, non-touristy island and there were no crowds, even though we visited in the middle of summer. The water was calm and shallow, easily heated by the sun. Niko learned to swim in the Aegean Sea, and for the first time in over twenty years, I got my hair wet at the beach. As I floated on my back in the salty, warm water, staring up at the cloudless sky, I felt so at home. Even though I used ice as a platform almost every day, it was in the water that I felt truly held.

I had spent months worrying on and off if my mother-in-law would approve of my wardrobe for Greece. On the first day there, I found out that she had spent months worrying on and off if I would approve of Greece. I knew this truth but appreciated the reminder that most of the time, humans are too busy judging themselves to judge other people.

She and I spent most of the vacation hatching a plan to spend July in Greece every year. It was the best bonding we have ever had. I realized how spoiled I had been all these years with my father-in-law's tzatziki. On the trip I concluded that his recipe was the best on planet Earth. The family members in Greece had never met our boys, some had never met me, and most had not seen Manny in twenty years. Still, their love for us was intensely felt.

When visiting my in-laws' village, I was invited into many homes and was struck by the similarity of the kitchens to my mother-in-law's kitchen in America. They were all nearly identical. Each china cabinet, the same. Each dining room table, the same. The pictures on every wall and every side table, the same in size and style and arrangement. The tray that offered the ouzo and candied lemon rind—the same. I saw it so clearly, the narrow parameters of what it meant to be an acceptable woman in their culture. They had to each fit into a tiny little box. Seeing the impossible weight of the expectations on her from her culture helped me to see my mother-in-law with more love and tenderness than ever before.

Years before, when Manny and I had moved into our new house, she had been helping me unpack boxes in my kitchen. She opened a cupboard and jumped back, gasping. Then she paused.

She turned around to look at me. "I don't know if I should say anything, honey. But if you were my daughter, I would tell you. So, I'm not trying to tell you what to do, but ... you can't have your cupboards like this."

I stayed quiet, trying to figure out if she was joking. She wasn't. She went on to hurriedly explain what she meant. The top shelf of each cupboard had an array of random items. She told me that when a guest comes to your house and helps themselves to a water glass, they should not be able to see any junk in the cupboard. It was okay to have junk, she said, but it had to be all together, in a cupboard out of the way. The water glass cupboard should have some of the prettiest glasses, wine or martini glasses displayed up at the top, so when someone opens it, they will see all the nice things you have.

And in Greece, I finally understood it. Manny's mom knew the exact guidelines by which I would be judged by women in her culture. And she wanted me to know. She wanted to help me avoid the embarrassment. She did not want me to get a reputation as someone who didn't know how to keep a house clean and orderly. She also knew that then this would reflect on Manny, *poor Manny, a wife who doesn't know how to keep a house.* And it would also reflect on her. *Didn't she even tell her daughter-in-law?* But, mostly, it was for me. The currency with which women made themselves valuable was so distinct that she could not let me be in the culture without informing me of the rules by which I would be judged.

When we had first met, my mother-in-law had told me I was lucky. And I thought it meant I didn't deserve Manny. But now, realizing my privilege and the wide expanse of opportunities I had been afforded, I felt so, fucking lucky. I had been granted great freedom over my life, but I had spent most of it living inside a tiny little box, too.

I had built it myself.

Chapter 26

I hadn't told Manny about Brad, about seeing him in secret, about realizing that the real-life version of him did not live up to the fantasy I had created in my head. I had always intended to tell him, but I was waiting for the right time. I wanted to tell him at a time that things were good, so he didn't feel I was bringing it up as a threat. I also didn't want to tell him when things were too good because finding out your wife was set to have an affair and you had no idea is definitely a buzzkill. And then it came, by surprise, the perfect time to get it off my chest.

I had just arrived home from my first competition of a new season. It was late at night, and Manny was still up. I was hopped up on caffeine from the drive, so I initiated sex, even though it was past my usual bedtime. We were fooling around, and Manny offered to just go down on me. That was a little unusual, and when he moved to the end of the bed I saw that he wasn't hard. I didn't want to make a big deal out of it, so I accepted the offer of oral sex, had a great orgasm, and was ready to move on. Afterwards, Manny came up and sat beside me on the bed. His eyes were lowered, his face tense.

"Are you okay?" I asked. Him not getting an erection was a

very rare occurrence, but I felt like the upset on his face was something bigger.

"I need to tell you something," he said, his eyes filling with tears.

Shit. He cheated on me. "Yeah? You can tell me. It's okay," I assured, trying to appear calmer than I felt.

"Ian called me to see if I wanted to hang out with him on Saturday. He was going to a strip club. And I went with him."

"Okay ..." I offered, not impressed by this choice of outing with his work friend, but also not understanding why he was so upset. When we had committed to monogamy, I had clearly stated our rules since we had possessed no set rules at any point in our relationship. Strip clubs were on the no list. But, still, I didn't know why he would be tearing up about it.

"And I got a lap dance." He started crying. "And I am so sorry. I knew you would be upset, but Ian was getting one, and I felt bad saying no," he rambled quickly, adding, "I am so sorry. I hate to disappoint you."

"Okay, whoa," I said, taking his hand. "First off, I'm okay. We are okay. You got it?" He exhaled, and his shoulders dropped. "But, babe, you hate to disappoint me?" He tried to object. I held up my hand, indicating that I needed to finish. "You'd rather hold the guilt and worry for days than say no to Ian and deal with his disappointment for five seconds. That's crazy." I stared at him hard. He tilted his head back and forth, considering the validity of my point. "Okay, also, can we just admit that monogamy is maybe not the easiest thing for either of us?"

"Babe, what are you talking about? I'm the one that fucked up." He shook his head, confused why I was not madder at him.

"Hmm, I have something I need to tell you." His confusion intensified, all his rehearsals of how this would go thrown out the window. He had braced himself for a difficult conversation, but this is not the way he saw it playing out.

"I saw Brad last Spring." I let it sink in. "Twice."

Manny's hands flew to his head, certainly trying to prevent his brain from exploding. "What?"

I continued, "Yup, do you remember when he texted me telling me he and Jess were broken up?"

"Uh, yeah." His tone of voice added an unspoken "duh" to the end of his sentence. I found it fitting because his response to this information the first time around was possibly his largest *duh* moment ever.

"And do you remember how I told you for two years before how often I thought about him? How I was *this close* to divorce? How I was *this close* to adultery? How I wasn't over him?" Manny nodded slowly, eyes widening in the realization that words were perhaps something to heed. "Well, I decided to see him. I knew I hadn't been able to get over him in my head, so I thought seeing him in person would give me the answers I needed."

"Oh my God." Manny groaned, laying back on the bed and covering his eyes with his forearm. "Did you have sex with him?" He shot a look at me. "Ugh, you had sex with him, didn't you?" He leaned back again, this time staring at the ceiling. "Just tell me."

"Actually," I brightened, incredibly proud of this plot twist, "I didn't. I wanted to, but I didn't."

"Seriously?" he rose up, looking at me skeptically.

"Seriously!" I smiled, so pleased that I was actually telling the truth.

He scratched his head. He looked relieved, relieved that he felt he could almost believe me, and relieved that I wasn't threatening to divorce him over his lap dance. He also looked confused by this relief, coming so quickly on the heels of his confession and his realization that he had picked up no clues that I had seen Brad behind his back. "Well ..." he started, not knowing how to end that sentence.

"Well," I made my best attempt, "clearly neither of us is

perfect." He nodded. The facts laid out were indisputable in that regard. "And clearly, we both want to be in this marriage, right?"

"I do," he insisted. "Do you?" he looked at me searchingly.

"I really do." I meant it.

It was nearly a year later when Brad messaged me again. This time, instead of basking in the attention for even a little while, I told Manny that Brad was back. This time he didn't reply by telling me he had a Home Depot stop to make. He asked for Brad's number and texted him himself. I never asked what he said because it really didn't matter. After a lifetime of attempted self-sufficiency, I was just relieved that I didn't have to deal with it myself.

A few months later I was in Sweden with my co-director, Kati. We were there to watch the world championships and had extended our trip, coming a few days early to explore Stockholm and make it a little vacation after just finishing our own skating season. When I traveled to Europe, I always prepared by learning at least a dozen words in the native tongue, even though I knew I would struggle to carry on a full conversation in most places. My best bet was France, having studied French for nine years as a standard part of Canadian education. When Manny and I visited Paris for New Year's Eve when we were dating, my wallet was snatched in a metro station on New Year's Day. I felt the hand slip into my purse and screamed. As soon as Manny was in pursuit of the man, I relaxed. Manny was very fast. He had run the forty-yard dash in 4.4 seconds at his peak and even though a few years had passed, I correctly assumed that no half-drunk French pickpocket would be able to outrun him. Manny caught him and said, which I am sure is the customary give-back-my-wallet-greeting in every country, "Man, give it back. I'm not playin'," and within seconds the metro police had swarmed the corridor and had *le voleur* roughly pressed to the ground. I kept a copy of my police report, given all in French, to remind myself that I had retained more than a little of that Canadian public school education.

In Sweden all I could manage were a few words, then, graciously, the Swedes would break into the most exquisite English. They sounded like fancy native English speakers, like the Brits or the Aussies. Kati and I had spent the day walking most of Stockholm. I leaned back against the bench on the ferry, relieved that it would drop us at the door of our hotel, perched right on the edge of the Saltsjön Bay. I closed my eyes and let myself be lulled by the water and the lyrical flow of Swedish spoken in low voices all around me.

I was shaken out of my Nordic daze by the recognition of Greek words mingling with the smattering of Swedish. I perked up and looked toward the back end of the ferry. I saw two couples and four children, all chit-chattering back and forth in what I now certainly recognized as Greek. I leaned towards them, *"Signomi ... mila Eleenika?* Excuse me ... speak Greek?"

They froze, intimating that hearing a blonde woman speak Greek in Stockholm was probably more shocking than being spoken to by a pigeon. Then they quickly broke out in smiles. *"Ne!* Yes!" followed by a very fast and detailed Greek question that I could not understand.

"Ohi," I replied quickly, *"Milau, leeho Eleenika. Them enea Elineetha.* No. I speak a little Greek. I am not Greek." And then, to solve the mystery, in English, I added, "My husband is Greek."

"Oh! *Yasou!* So nice to meet you." One of the Greek women slid close to me. She asked about my husband and my in-laws. I told her they were from Chios (she was from Thessaloniki), and we had visited just the year before with our three boys. She and her husband were both doctors and had moved to Stockholm just the year before with their two children. Her sister and husband were visiting with their son and daughter for Greek Easter. I had been so engrossed in my Swedish experience that I had briefly forgotten that it was Greek Easter back home, too. She wanted to know everything. *How old were my boys? What was I here for? Where can I see that kind of team skating? And you are away over Easter?* And then, her eyes widened with realization.

"You are away from your family during all of Holy Week?" With each word she tilted her head down a degree until the irises of her eyes were only half visible. Her mouth hung open. My heart dropped to my toes and my face paled. I braced myself for her admonishment. She lowered her voice and said slowly, "You are so lucky." Her breath caught in her chest like a sob, but she didn't cry. And then I saw it, the exhaustion in her face. She looked toward her family. The children whispered and giggled, playing an imaginary game. Her sister sat, spine straight, legs crossed at the knee and arms crossed at the forearm, body tight, lips pursed, jowls hanging slightly, the skin under her eyes a pale purple, as she looked blankly out the window of the ferry, seemingly not noticing the thousand lights glittering on the water and the outline of Gamla Stan in the distance. She looked as if she was the hostess, the one baking the Easter bread and the countless hand-formed cookies, cleaning, cooking, serving. The men were laughing jovially, both leaning back with legs spread, arms wide, relaxed. I could not determine which was the host and which one was the brother-in-law. They both exhibited the carefree demeanor of vacationers. I had been living alongside the culture for fifteen years, but it was in that moment that I realized the reason the men looked so relaxed. In a traditional Greek family, a man was treated like a guest in his own home.

The look in her eyes followed me home. Her honesty, her reflexive reaction to realizing I was married into a Greek family but had not saddled myself with the expectations put on her. The lack of desire to impress upon me that her culture was superior, and I should assimilate. The eyes of a woman who felt the freedom, maybe for the first time, to show how she really felt, tired and envious.

I was home a week before Jack looked into my eyes, searchingly. "Hey, Mom?"

"Yeah, bud?" I leaned in, guessing he was going to make a case for getting a new video game.

"Did you know Dad took us to church when you were in Sweden?" His eyes were clear. He looked calm and grown-up.

I heard my heart in my ears, and my eyes clouded. I pressed my tongue to the back of my bottom teeth to focus. I blinked and took a long exhale. "Uh, no. I didn't know that."

"Yeah. I didn't think so." He gave me a sympathetic nod and turned around.

A fire sprang up from within my belly. I fumed. I raged. I was indignant. Years before, when I had decided I could no longer be complicit in the shit storm that was modern life, I told Manny that it was time to stop taking the boys to church.

"I can't," I told him, "I can't let them go anymore. Just like we wouldn't let them watch a racist or homophobic movie, I can't endorse it."

He was upset and worried what his mom would say, but he heard me. I was unmuted, after all. We began church shopping together and found a place the boys and I loved. We wanted to go every week, but Manny did not. He admitted that he really had been taking the boys to Greek church just to appease his mom, and he had no desire to go as a family and did not want to sacrifice our weekend schedule with a regular church visit, so we stopped going after a few weeks. Instead, our Sunday mornings were spent with coffee and cuddles. The dog begged for sausages, and the boys begged for new mods on their video games. So, we let the church issue be, but I threw the gag order out the window and began speaking openly with the boys about God and about my beliefs in front of Manny. Previously, all discussions of a spiritual nature occurred when he was not home. Manny even joined in and adjusted some of his terminology to match mine. We were beginning to find our way forward together.

But, now, this. After all this time, all this growth in our marriage, after the years and the tears and the final agreement that we would make our own decisions for our family, he had gone behind my back as soon as I left town. At this point I knew I didn't want to leave my marriage. For the first time in years, I saw our paths stretching out far in front of us, merged, walking side by side, but I was furious and sad.

"I hate disappointing you," Manny professed when I confronted him, his eyes reaching for mine.

My gaze was icy. "No. You don't." The ice turned to fire as my eyes blazed. And then I softened, saddened, "I am your favorite person to disappoint."

"What?" Manny began to protest.

"I'm your favorite, your favorite person in the whole world to disappoint, because you know I'll get over it. You know I won't make a stink. You know I'll go upstairs and meditate and journal and figure out what the fuck I need to do to make it better. And you just keep going behind my back."

He didn't respond, but his face showed his emotions—hopeless, stuck, confused, certain he was tasked with pleasing me and his mother, and certain it was impossible.

I didn't bring it up again for months. I had nothing else to say. I meditated, and I journaled, and I prayed, begging the Divine for an answer. But nothing came until months later, when I was cleaning out closets. I separated stacks of photos into individual memory boxes for the boys, copying a tactic my mom had employed my whole life. After stacks and stacks, I was nearly done for the day when I came across a birth announcement and froze. It was printed on glossy paper with a pale blue background. The photos were of Jack, taken just a few days after he was born by Manny's friend Chris. I remembered the photoshoot. I remembered ordering and mailing the birth announcements. I remembered sticking one to the fridge with a magnet. But there had been one thing I hadn't remembered.

The photo I held in my hands was of Jack, but text on the card announced the birth of Yanni Emanouel.

We had ordered a fake set of birth announcements for the Greek family.

Manny had been so terrified to tell his parents that we weren't naming the baby after his dad that he couldn't stomach sending them the birth announcements. He avoided even saying the baby's name around his parents and they never asked what he had been named, just assuming he was named Yanni, consistent with the Greek tradition.

Over the next decade they had figured out at some point that Jack's real name was Jack. I guess on some level Manny had always known that would happen, but he needed them to find out gradually, accidentally, without him ever having to take responsibility for the naming, like he wasn't quite sure how the baby had ended up with that name, either. As if, at some point he would have to say, "But the kid answers to 'Jack,' so we can't really change it now." The birth announcement ploy was clearly not a long-term solution, but it was all Manny could muster when faced with the prospect of mailing out a printed confirmation of his departure from tradition. And I had gone along with it.

I sat back, the room spinning. My body became a hollow cavern of fascia, rapidly drying out from an internal howling wind. The gust swirled in my head, plugging my ears, crisscrossing inside my empty skull until it became a deafening ring.

It was true. In his mid-twenties, as the first man of his generation to get married, he wasn't willing to overtly break with tradition. When he did, he pushed it under the rug and hoped no one would notice. It wasn't just that he wasn't willing to have an honest conversation with his parents about how the needs of our family sometimes ran counter to their desires for tradition. After a decade and a half of wishing, pleading, crying for him to set boundaries for our family, I realized he couldn't.

But, I could.

The deafening, ringing wind stopped in my head. It was

silent. I was clear. I knew what I had to do. I needed to be the
one who spoke to my mother-in-law.

And then I felt frozen in terror.

I could think of nothing less desirable than speaking to her
about this. Well, actually, one thing. The one thing that I wanted
less than confronting my mother-in-law was to continue living in
the fear of her expectations. I wanted it for me. I wanted it for
Manny. I wanted it for our boys. Together, Manny and I had
already logged so many good years of reinforcing this with our
kids. They knew their purpose here on planet earth was not to
make us feel happy or safe or comfortable. We had not planted
the seeds that they need to be married, or be straight, or give us
grandchildren, or live close by, or go to college, or have a certain
type of job in order to make us feel okay. But we were not
walking the walk. I wanted to show the boys that this is where
unhealthy obligation would end. In our family we each live the
life we want to live.

I knew what I needed to do, but it took me nearly a year to
work up the courage. The catalyst came when the next Easter
rolled around, and Manny was pushing her off when she asked
when he would be taking the boys to church. Greeks are loud,
and I could make out her words as she berated Manny through
the phone. I had picked up enough Greek to get the gist of her
complaints to him. *You are letting Ashleigh tell you what to do. You
need to stand up and be a man. You need to stop letting your wife make
the decisions.*

This was the lowest of blows. She made every decision for
her family, and she was trying to shame Manny for making a
decision along with me. I heard the panic in her voice. I knew I
needed to put an end to this, not just for us but for her.

I called and told her everything, all the history of our conversations around religion, the falsity in the "Ashleigh is keeping
the kids from God" narrative. I knew it had been hard for her to
know nothing of our conversations about religion, to be kept in
the dark. I didn't want her to be in the dark anymore.

I told her that we had both been involved with other people, that our marriage was not as perfect or as easy as it looked. I told her that I resented not being able to decide back when we got married how we wanted to build our life together. I told her we were taking space to do that now. That our marriage was better than ever because we had recommitted to each other and the boys. We had missed out on years of strengthening our partnership because we had lived for so long with disjointed priorities, but now we were coming together.

After the phone call, I called Manny, and he braced himself for the worst, that maybe my words had made her heart stop, and I had hung up and called 911 when I heard her collapse on the floor.

"It went well," I told him. He held his breath, disbelieving me completely. "Really, it did. I stayed calm. I was able to say everything I wanted to say. I told her about Amber. I told her about Brad. I told her we are making our marriage better than ever, but we are not taking outside opinions. We are going to make decisions for our family."

"Whoa. Okay," he attempted to reply. "And what did she say?"

"Well, she hung up on me," I admitted.

"Ooh, should I go over there and talk to her?" he asked, starting to panic.

"No, just wait," I asserted.

"Okay." His voice was tinged with worry, but underneath it I could hear a layer of relief.

Neither of us knew what would come next, but after over fifteen years of silent resentment and the feeling that our hands were tied, I had thrust us into a new dynamic. I felt terrified but also giddy from the reprieve. He waited until the next day to go over to the house. As he was leaving, I stopped him. "Hey, babe."

"Yeah," he looked back to me, eyes heavy with apprehension.

"That conversation was hard for me. It was scary. But I did it for both of us. For the boys. I even did it for your mom. I did it for all of us."

He nodded and sighed. He understood. He just wished it was easier.

"I just took a huge step forward for us. Do not go backwards."

He nodded again and turned toward the door.

"Babe," I repeated, firmer this time. He turned back to face me. "I am serious. You have never stuck up for me with your mom." He raised his hand to object. "No, never. And I don't know if you are going to be able to do it today." I looked at him intently as tears covered my eyes like a curtain. "But I hope you do. I hope you choose me, and I hope you choose the boys. I hope you choose us." I motioned to him and put my hand on my chest, the pressure building. He nodded solemnly and walked out the door. I turned and braced myself on the corner of the couch as sobs thundered through me.

I putzed around the house for an hour, cleaning, but not actually getting anything cleaner, incessantly checking my phone. Finally, a simple text from Manny: "All good, on my way home."

He walked in the same door he had left through just over an hour before, and I stood in the same position, eager to know everything.

"I told her she shouldn't have hung up on you." Tears sprung to my eyes again. "And she told me she just loves the boys so much and loves us so much. She just doesn't want to lose us." He hugged me tightly, feeling heavy and light all at the same time.

Later that afternoon she called. Manny spoke with her briefly and then came to me, poking his head into my office. "Um, I know this is quick, but she wants us to come for dinner tomorrow." I nodded tensely. "And, um, it sounds like she's making all of your favorites."

"At once?" I asked quizzically.

"Uh, yeah." A grin stretched across his face as he nodded.

The next day we entered through the garage and the kitchen door, as always. The air smelled of food, as always. And my mother-in-law hugged me, as always. But this time it was tighter, longer, and she whispered, "I love you."

"I love you, too." I leaned down and buried my head in her shoulder.

And then we turned and made our way to the table, already set, and already covered with every one of my favorite Greek foods, the stuffed peppers, the lima beans and artichokes. Manny looked different to me, the way he held his shoulders, the way he scanned the room with ease. I had seen him at that table countless times over the last eighteen years, and for the first time he didn't look like a child in his mother's kitchen. A few months later I would continue this conversation with her, letting her know that I knew I wasn't the daughter-in-law she wanted, but I am the daughter-in-law she got. And she's the mother-in-law I got. And we don't need to agree on everything. Agreeing is not a prerequisite for love. And she would tell me that she doesn't understand many of my decisions, but she would try. She could only promise that she would try.

But, that night, I didn't bring up our conversation. I simply ate the food that was offered to me, accepting it for what it was —an olive branch.

Chapter 27

"Five, six, seven, eight ..."

The rink was silent, save for my cue and the twenty sets of blades making a crisp t-push on the ice. In unison, they executed their counter turns, then stopped. They each squatted down close to the ice to wipe away the snow on their tracing with the cuff of their warm-up jacket. I unzipped the bottom half of the zipper on my long parka, so I could crouch with them.

We were looking for flats.

I was pushing them harder that season than ever before. After a few years of placing skaters at the appropriate team levels, I had fallen back into my habit of seeing potential over performance. I was starting to think I would never shake it. Whenever I looked at a skater, especially one of my sweet skaters, with their quirks and their wittiness, and their heart, their potential shone bright, blinding me to their actual capability.

So, there I was, kneeling on the ice at 6:30 a.m., trying to make up the difference.

After so many years of the stress of coaching feeling easier, it was feeling harder again. Every season the competitiveness ramped up. There was a bigger push to have synchronized skating included in the Winter Olympic Games. Parents were willing to pick up their kid and drive farther each day toward a more competitive organization. The reason I moved to this country, the reason there had been job opportunities for me to begin with was because Americans were willing to spend so much time and money on their children's athletics. It was starting to work against me, and my nerves were fried.

At a recent team meeting a parent had been drilling me about my alternate policy. I stated it over and over. It had been the same for years. They just kept pushing, insisting that there had to be some other motive, some other reason for me to sit kids. As they ceased to relent, I became increasingly more upset. The children in the room were all eleven and twelve years old, and I could see the stress building in their little faces, and I couldn't contain myself. For the first time in a parent meeting, I burst into tears.

A few nights later I lay in bed under the New Moon. As I drifted off to sleep, I thought that I should be getting my period the next day. I hoped that I would get my period the next day. I really hoped I did. Manny and I had concluded a long time before that we were done having babies.

Then, as I relaxed further, a thought occurred to me. If I was pregnant, I could quit my job, and no one would be mad at me. Yes, no one could be mad. My body relaxed as my mind started to wander. *If I get my period tomorrow, maybe I should try to get pregnant next month so I can quit my job. So no one will be mad at me.*

I sat straight up in bed, scaring myself out of sleep. What the fuck had I just been plotting? What the actual fuck?

That had been the scariest ten seconds of my life.

The thing was, we did not want a fourth baby, but we could have handled a fourth baby. Manny was a legit baby whisperer, and our boys were at a great age to start babysitting. Even though I was nearing forty, I would likely still approach labor like BMX riders approached the X-Games. *Bring it.* The terrifying part was how I had heard clearly that I really wanted to make a change and was manufacturing a grand excuse—in this case, growing a new freaking human—to give myself permission to make that change.

I was ignoring the lesson I had learned the most painfully and repeatedly over my career as a coach. My gut always told me the right thing to do. And sometimes people hated it and even acted like they hated me. But, when I ignored it, the situation intensified until I eventually did what I had known was right all along.

This was the teaching I had communicated to my athletes more than any other. As I counseled them during upsets with friends, conflicts with their parents, and when choosing colleges, they all knew that I fiercely believed that they would always know what was right for them. If they got quiet and listened, they would always know what to do. Everyone around them would have an opinion, but they would have the answer. And they needed to find the courage to act on their wisdom, even in the face of disappointing people who cared about them.

Even though in a hundred different ways having another baby would have actually been easier than finding the courage to tell my skaters that I was moving on, I couldn't do it.

I had to quit.

And I had to show them how to walk through it. How to do the thing no one wants you to do and to do it with grace and honesty. I wanted to show them how to love something so much and still walk away. I want to show them that the only person they could ever really abandon was themselves. And I wanted them to truly believe that I never, ever wanted them to do that.

What followed was the longest transition I had ever choreographed.

During a synchronized skating program, the team changes shape as they flow across the ice. Each change of configuration from one shape to another is called a transition. Transitions were fun to choreograph but notoriously challenging for skaters to perform. They knew they were going from one point-getting element to another, and often they let their brains and their performance rest.

"Ladies," I pleaded, "you need to keep your expression through that transition." I paused the video and zoomed in to show the blank eyes and hanging mouths. A giggle pulsed through the team.

"See this?" I begged. "All of you have it. It's like you think we have a choreographed Resting Transition Face. I didn't choreograph that face." I threw my hands in the air. "Seriously, you all have a bad case of RTF." I looked at them with wide, serious eyes. They tried hard to contain themselves, but their shoulders shook with suppressed laughter. I kept my face flat. "You know what your expression is supposed to be. Don't zone out." The giggles were building inside me, but I kept my expression extra serious as I looked to them for confirmation that they understood. They nodded, eyes clear, but mouths twisted, trying not to laugh. "Do it again, and no freaking RTF," I said as I waved them toward their starting positions. They turned away, and I rested my head on the boards, chuckles erupting from my belly as they made their way to their spots.

So, in the months that followed, I often reminded them that we were all—in life, in our sport—in a period of transition. And we could let ourselves zone out, or we could accept it for what it was. Life was really more transition than anything else. We always thought we would feel different when we arrived at a new place, a new accomplishment, but more often than not, it was an imaginary finish line. Wherever you go, there you are.

We had talked a lot about how we all had our own imaginary finish lines. I used to think I would feel accomplished when I had two teams in my organization, then three, then ten. Or when I got a team to nationals, when I got three teams to nationals. Or when we were on the podium more often than we were not.

For the skaters, it was when they got to that team level, when they passed that test, when that boy or girl liked them.

All imaginary finish lines. If we couldn't love ourselves

before we reached them, we wouldn't be able to love ourselves when we did. We had to stay in the moment, even when we were certain we were in-between the important parts. I told them later, on one of our last nights together, "Life is almost all transition. The last six months have proven that to all of us. And you know what you did? You didn't zone out. You weren't just waiting for the next thing. You focused in with me, with this team." My eyes filled with tears as I smiled. "You didn't have RTF."

Every day I tried to keep pushing them while I tried to fall deeper in love with this sport that had been so dear to me for so long.

Newton's Third Law - every action has an equal and opposite reaction. I repeated it all the time in my instruction. The harder you push back into the ice, the harder it will push you forward. It was science. It was true. But every time I said it during that last season, I had a feeling deep in my belly that I was missing something. I pushed down further and kept pushing the skaters, desperate to make them as strong as possible before I left.

And then, I remembered what I had been forgetting, that whisper, that nag low in my belly. The ice doesn't just push back. That's part of it, but the pressure of the blade actually changes the ice's melting point.

We bend. We stretch. We flex. We push. And the ice?

It yields.

It surrenders.

It melts.

We were in our last week of practices, preparing for Nationals, our last competition together, when I needed to stop and spend some time with them to improve their circle spacing. Figures had long ago gone the way of the dodo bird, and my athletes, having never trained them, often struggled to understand the true shape of a circle.

I pulled my thick black marker from the pocket of my coaching parka. I waved my skaters out of my way with a motion of my arm and a nod of my head. They cleared tight to the boards, giving me the space I needed. I removed the lid from my marker, and I took three pushes to work up my speed. Going fast, I bent over and placed the tip of the marker onto the surface of the ice. Head down, I sailed around in a huge loop. Within seconds I joined my tracing to where the marker had first touched down.

I stood to give the skaters my next instruction. They were still and quiet. I paused as I looked at them searchingly. One girl spoke up, eyes gleaming, "Watching you do that may be the thing that I miss the most," she said. The skaters all looked longingly at the tracing on the ice, a perfect circle, at least forty feet wide.

It had been the preciseness and the calculation that attracted me to the sport in the first place, figuring out how to place all those bodies on the ice in a pattern that was beautiful. It had been the symmetry.

We all knew the standard definitions of symmetry—mirror image, matched parts facing each other around an axis, but my favorite was this: *Symmetry is the similarity or exact correspondence between different things.*

Within a coach-athlete relationship, many may assume that the athlete is the one who learns the most in any given season. But, looking at those wide, bright eyes, the bravado, and potential of those adolescent girls, I knew that I had been the one who had learned the most. When I had started, I had barely been older than my oldest skater. Then I became closer in age to their parents. And at that very point there were girls in my organization whose parents were younger than me. Over those years I had grown up alongside them. Over those years they had taught me over and over what mattered and what didn't really matter.

And that is why that definition became my favorite. The exact correspondence between different things, to me, meant living on the outside in a way that matched what was on the inside. Over my coaching career, sometimes things flowed with ease, and sometimes things were hard. When things were hard, it was easy to think I was messing everything up or look for someone else to blame. A million times that year I had to offer forgiveness to myself for my last season not being my best, but I had remembered, when things got really hard, to look within myself for the answers. And that was my wish for them, as we all readied ourselves to close this chapter together.

I hoped that I had taught them to live a life that matched what was in their hearts. I hoped that I had taught them symmetry.

Chapter 28

P orn played on two huge projection televisions hung on the wall in front of me. We were back at the big club in Philly. I was waiting at the bar for a soda water with lime, and the club was packed. It was New Year's Eve.

I could have maybe pushed my way forward and gotten my drink more quickly, but I was distracted by the porn. Two women were playing with a black silicone dildo. The blonde put the dildo into the vagina of the brunette, in out, in out, repeat. Then the brunette pulled it out insistently and shoved it into her own mouth. I hated this kind of porn. No woman in the world wants to suck a dildo. I love penises, but you will never find me fighting over a fake one to put in my mouth. Eww.

I wanted to look away from the screen, but I was trying to figure out part of the plot. The women were wearing matching sequined tops, and I wanted to know why. Were they doing a choreographed dance duet when a dildo was tossed on stage and the sudden appearance of a phallus caused an urgent and shared compulsion to rip off their matching turquoise bottoms? The bartender handed me my drink, and I turned away, disappointed that I would never solve the mystery.

"Want to take a lap?" I asked Manny. He nodded. We were

back for the first time in half a decade, and we were falling back into our old routine. We were also welcomed by the same old cast of characters.

Old lady in the white garter belt was wearing black for New Year's, and her husband was in a snazzy tuxedo. Instead of assuming her regular position at the dancing pole, she was perched gleefully on a velvet couch, chatting with another couple around their age.

Leon and Liza were thrilled to see us. It had been quite a while since Manny had run into them at the supermarket.

"He always wants to knock on your door when we come to the post office," Liza chided, slapping Leon on the arm, "but, I tell him, 'Leon, we *can't* do that.'" Leon smiled wider than the Cheshire cat.

"You haven't forgotten when we live now, have you?" he teased me.

"How could I?" I asked. "I drive past it almost every day."

We excused ourselves and continued with our walk around. We were there to survey the situation, to see if the environment still held any appeal. There had been years after our most recent visit that we wouldn't even consider it, but we were both in a place of shared and consistent curiosity. We stopped at the pit and looked inside.

The first time we had visited this club, the night we sacrificed the raccoon for a moment of pleasure, I had rested my drink on this half-wall and leaned my arms against it as I looked inside.

Three women were together on a mattress, naked, save for stiletto heels. They knelt, faces meeting in a three-way kiss, hands each cupping a butt cheek from behind. Then one woman laid flat on her back, the second finding her way between her legs, and the third straddling and sitting on her face. I had felt an ache between my legs, the blood vessels beneath my skin dilating to accommodate the rush of blood. I shifted from one leg to another, and when my labia slid past each other my suspicion was confirmed. I was wet. A man stood beside me, a host-couple-in-training who had introduced himself after Leon and Liza had given us the tour.

"Whoa," I said, "I bet this never gets old." I motioned toward the woman-on-woman sexfest in front of us.

"Meh," he shrugged. "It's sort of like live porn now."

Yeah, live porn is fucking hot. What are you talking about, you crazy man? I looked back to the pit and shifted again, foot to foot, to feel my own wetness, assuring myself that he was the one who was crazy, not me.

A half-decade later, I stood in front of that pit, and again there was a similar female sexfest playing out before me. And I yawned. I regretted my decision to not have an afternoon nap. And then I caught myself. I felt a little bored. I shifted back and forth. I wasn't wet, not even a little.

I looked to Manny to see if he was entranced by the action. His eyes were wandering around the room. I guessed he was looking at the ceiling joists.

"Let's check out the back rooms," I motioned toward the corridor leading to the play rooms.

Manny sipped his soda. "Sure," he agreed.

We grasped hands and walked toward the back. The window for the coat check was blacked out, and I caught my reflection as I walked past it. I had recently chopped my hair off inch-by-inch in our master bathroom until it was a full sixteen inches shorter. Before entering, I had shaken my head upside down in the parking lot, loosening the mass of wand curls in my now bobbed hair. Head hanging, I looked at my leopard print stilettos with their metallic gold heels and up my legs to the super short gold sequined dress. I had gained weight, feeling curvier and healthier than I had in a long time. Over my dress I wore a short vegan leather jacket. Catching my reflection, the combination of the leather and gold, with my wild angled bob, I felt incredibly fierce and sexy.

I smiled at my reflection and turned in the direction we were walking. Time slowed down as I focused on a familiar set of eyes. Mid-laugh, mid-sentence, those eyes turned and locked on me. She continued nodding to her friends as her eyes widened, her brain making the rapid connections. It had been five years. We both looked different and the same. Mine, a face she wanted to forget but couldn't. Hers, a reminder of a friend I wished I had but couldn't. It was Jess.

I kept pace with Manny, each step feeling like an eternity, until we turned right into a long hallway.

I pulled Manny close to me as soon as we were around the corner. "Did you see her?" I asked, panicked.

"Who?" he was oblivious.

"Jess, she's here. With a guy with a beard, and I don't know who else. I think there was another couple with them." I paused. "She saw me, too."

Manny looked at me questionably, "Okay?" he said. "And? What do you want to do?"

I had considered what I would do if this night had caused us to run into Brad with a new girlfriend. I knew I would want to turn around and walk out. But, this, this scenario, was not one I considered.

"I just never thought we'd see her here," I whispered to Manny.

He looked confused, "Why not?" he asked.

"I just," I looked for the words, "I guess I just thought she would have learned her lesson."

Manny's eyes widened in surprise, and my own shock of what had just come out of my mouth made mine widen too.

"Let's go," I said.

"Okay." He shrugged and nodded.

The drive home was quiet, both of us in our own thoughts. Manny was probably thinking about the stock market, but I was orchestrating a massive distillation of moral observations.

"Do you know what Jacki told me this week?" I asked Manny.

"I bet you're going to tell me," he teased.

"She told me that whenever I point my finger at someone else," I said, pointing at him. "There is one finger pointing at them," I tapped my index finger and continued, "and three fingers pointing back at me." I turned my hand over and looked at the three fingers curled on my palm.

"Do you remember what I said about Jess? That I thought she would have learned her lesson?"

"Yeah, I remember." He nodded and kept listening.

"I can't believe I said that. I can't believe that I still thought that we made out better because we didn't get divorced." I looked out the window at the Philly skyline. "Like, you know, I'm super glad we didn't get divorced."

"Why, thank you." He smiled.

"But I can't actually say that Jess made out better or worse than us. Really, maybe divorcing Brad was the best thing that ever happened to her. I mean, she's with a guy who can grow a beard now." I smiled and leaned back.

"No, but really," I continued, "the reason that our marriage actually got better was because I let go of the idea that staying married was the best outcome. That is when things actually started to change."

"It was," Manny agreed.

"Sex clubs were never the problem." I looked back out the window. "But, they are not a solution."

"I agree there," Manny nodded.

"It was an intensifier. It was like we were forced to look at our marriage through a microscope while also having an aerial view. That was hard." I turned to him. "But I wouldn't change any of it."

He reached for my hand and kissed it. "Me, either," he said.

We were home before midnight and toasted with champagne on our couch. Then we had fabulous sex in front of the full-length mirror we had recently purchased.

"Can you believe we went all this time without a mirror in

our bedroom?" I often asked him. We had taken the things we loved about the lifestyle and left the rest.

Manny stopped taking the boys to church on holidays, but we still attended the Greek church if we were invited to an event. Luke, ever organized, was planning out his weekend schedule in his head when he asked what time we would be back from the baptism we were attending. He stumbled over the word, pronouncing it, "b-boptism."

I laughed, thinking of the scene in *My Big Fat Greek Wedding* when Aunt Toula is telling the groom's parents about the lump she had on the back of her neck.

The doctors did the b-bop, b-bop, the b-bopsy ...

"We will be at the b-boptism all day, and I know what we are watching tonight for family movie night." My eyes gleamed, and Luke's twinkled in anticipation. "Remember my first date with Daddy?" I asked.

"*My Big Fat Greek Wedding*?" Luke asked. Our boys never forget the details of a good story.

"Yup." I smiled wide, the anticipation growing under my chest like an inflating balloon.

Later that night, the boys sprawled out on the couch, all calling their favorite spots. Manny and I joined them, ready to share with them the movie that neither of us had re-watched since our first date, nearly eighteen years before.

The boys laughed until they nearly cried, understanding even the subtle jokes. All three even fell off the couch when the American man thought he was being told the Greek words to welcome everyone inside and was instead tricked into announcing, "Hey, everyone. I have three testicles!"

Near the end I looked down and saw that Manny and I were holding hands. I don't know at what point in the night we had reached for each other. There had been no clumsiness. With his arm against mine, his body felt like an extension of my own. I leaned onto his shoulder and looked at our boys, eyes shining, mid-laugh, stretched out beside us under a sea of throw blankets. The dog lay at Manny's feet.

Jack said, "Dad, you told Mom your family was nothing like that?"

Manny smiled, nodding.

"Dad, they are exactly like that."

"That means you are like that, too," Manny replied, and Jack's eyes shone with pride.

I'd learned that very few of the choices we made had the power to save or destroy us, but the fear of them did have the power to keep us each in a tiny little box. A box that was not a natural and joyous fit for many of us, if it really fit anyone at all. And that fear did have the power to keep me small, and scared and half alive, and spending all my time curating my facades for all the different people who I thought needed me to be different things for them.

The thing that I learned about the facades I had built up for other people is that all the work and stress was in the maintenance of them. And as I dropped them, one by one, I realized there was no effort in letting each fall. It was like trying to maintain a sandcastle, trying to keep it looking perfect from all sides, as the waves and the wind tried to sweep it away. I thought about the power of the waves. I had always thought that in order for water to be useful it had to be shaped, cooled, and made rigid. But the real potential, the extraordinary power of water was in its rushing, flowing state.

What started as a journey for excitement and connection uncovered that we had what we needed all along. We just had to allow it and uncover it. The work of maintaining all the sides of me I thought people wanted to see had been exhausting. But all the effort had been in keeping the facades standing—and I figured out why. All of life was working to bring them down, intent on completing the demolition. I incessantly scrambled to maintain the sandcastle, fearful I would have to search and scavenge and pillage to pull together pieces to rebuild myself if I let the facades fall. But I didn't need to have that fear.

Because underneath, I found my real self, like a bronze statue, already complete, already strong. An exquisite statue that I had been covering with sand all that time. It was more beautiful and resilient and true than any sand facade. I had tricked myself into believing that I needed to maintain all the facades for the different people in my life, the different roles that I played. The upkeep was intense, but I feared letting them fall and having to rebuild would be even harder. But it was not. The secret was that I just needed to stop building them up. I needed to just let go. And the facades fell away, like a sandcastle being touched by the waves and the wind. And underneath, I found my core self, solid, complete, and fully human.

Manny and I were working to avoid the compulsion to build sandcastles around ourselves and the people we loved by trying to control their decisions or shield them from hurt. We needed to allow them to feel fully human.

I saw how the quality of the relationships I had with others always mirrored the relationship I have with my true self. In order to truly commit to loving and being loved by the people in my life, I had to be tenderly intimate and fiercely loyal to the deepest parts of myself. I needed to uncover what I was hiding and drop the facades I had created to mask my true self.

I needed to bare myself to myself.

I needed to get a little naked.

ACKNOWLEDGMENTS

To these people, I express my gratitude.

To Rebekah, for offering me a friendship that changed the way I see myself.

To Sheila, for being the best listener I have ever met.

To Demetria, for being my personal Greek Goddess of protection.

To Kati, for being there in a thousand different ways on a thousand different days.

To Tina, for helping me see clearly.

To Katie, for always believing in my magic.

To Stephanie, for being my yes friend.

To Bridget, for always going into the cave with me.

To Mike, for early reads and constant encouragement.

To Maryann, my story doula, for arriving exactly when I needed you.

To Allison, for offering me a partnership that changed everything.

To Jamie, for lending me a hand and your very smart brain.

To Geena, for being exactly you.

To Jacki, for responding to every bat signal.

To my siblings and siblings in-law, thank you for loving me in spite of telling this story, loving me for telling this story, and everything in between.

To my father-in-law, for always translating the funny parts.

To my mother-in-law, for seeing how alike we are.

To my dad, for trusting me.

To my mom—any courage I have came from you.

To Jack, for teaching me what I should ignore.

To Luke, for teaching me when I should pay closer attention

To Niko, for teaching me how to enjoy it all.

To Manny, I hope we have a hundred lifetimes together to dig deeper, but in case this is our one shot, let's never stop stopping.

Please help other readers discover *Swing* by leaving a review at the sites below.

goodreads

BARNES
&NOBLE

ABOUT THE AUTHOR

Through her candid presence on social media, Ashleigh Renard has built a committed mass-following who tune in daily for her fresh, no-fuss advice on everything from keeping monogamy hot, to renego- tiating a marriage, to getting kids to clean the house (because nothing makes her prouder than child labor). With savvy and  plenty of humor, her down-to-earth voice tackles topics that are relatable to anyone struggling with the awkwardness of living in a meat suit at Earth School. She resides in Bucks County, Penn- sylvania with her husband, their three children, a cat, and a dog. As a child she thought Pennsylvania the most unfortunately named state, too similar to Transylvania. To her delight, it has ample sunlight and a remarkably low population of vampires. Laugh with her daily on Instagram.

instagram.com/ashleighrenard

CPSIA information can be obtained
at www.ICGtesting.com
Printed in the USA
BVHW072152170521
607551BV00005BA/341

9 781736 596883